BLACK & BLUE

A (th)ink ANTHOLOGY

Dedicated to the man whose loins whence I came, my father, Mr. Keith Knight Sr.

Thanks to Jennifer & Jason for their skills and support; to Ken Gibbs and the Africana.com staff for asking me to come up with the strip in the first place; to all my faithful readers; to my family; Mr. Rall for the neat quote; and, most of all, thanks to my lovely wife, Kerstin Konietzka-Knight, the only K.K.K. I'll ever love...

☆ ☆ ☆ ☆ ☆ ☆ ☆ ☆

Also by Keith Knight: *Dances With Sheep; Fear of a Black Marker; What A Long Strange Strip It's Been.*

ISBN 0-916397-88-2

It is your patriotic duty to send correspondence to Keith Knight, P.O. Box 591794, San Francisco, CA 94159-1794. keef@kchronicles.com www.kchronicles.com

Design by Jason Chandler at Favorite Studios, Inc. with help from Elizabeth Schneider.

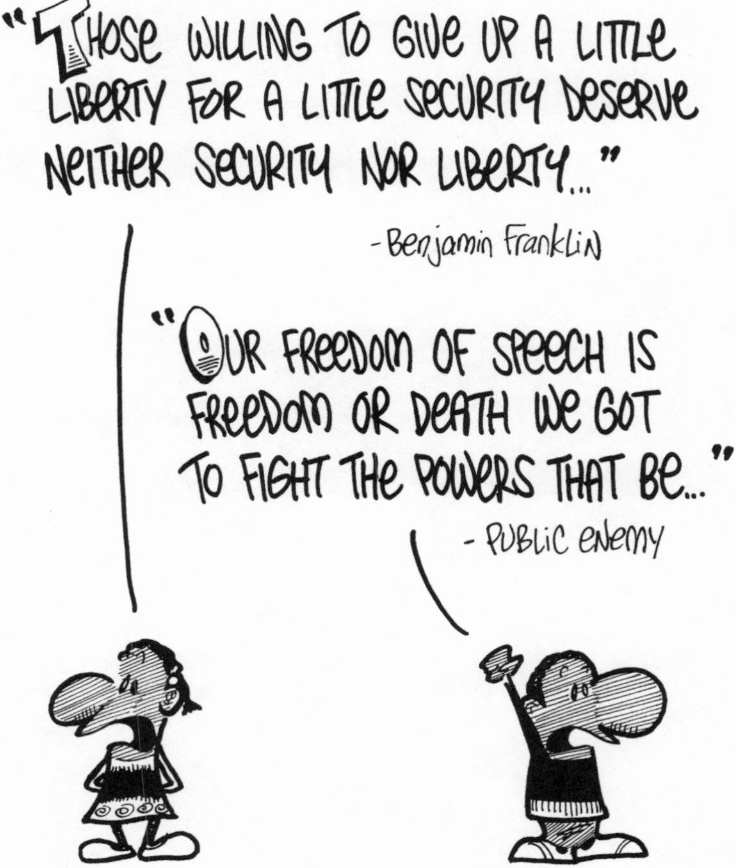
"Those willing to give up a little liberty for a little security deserve neither security nor liberty..."
-Benjamin Franklin
"Our freedom of speech is freedom or death we got to fight the powers that be..."
- Public Enemy

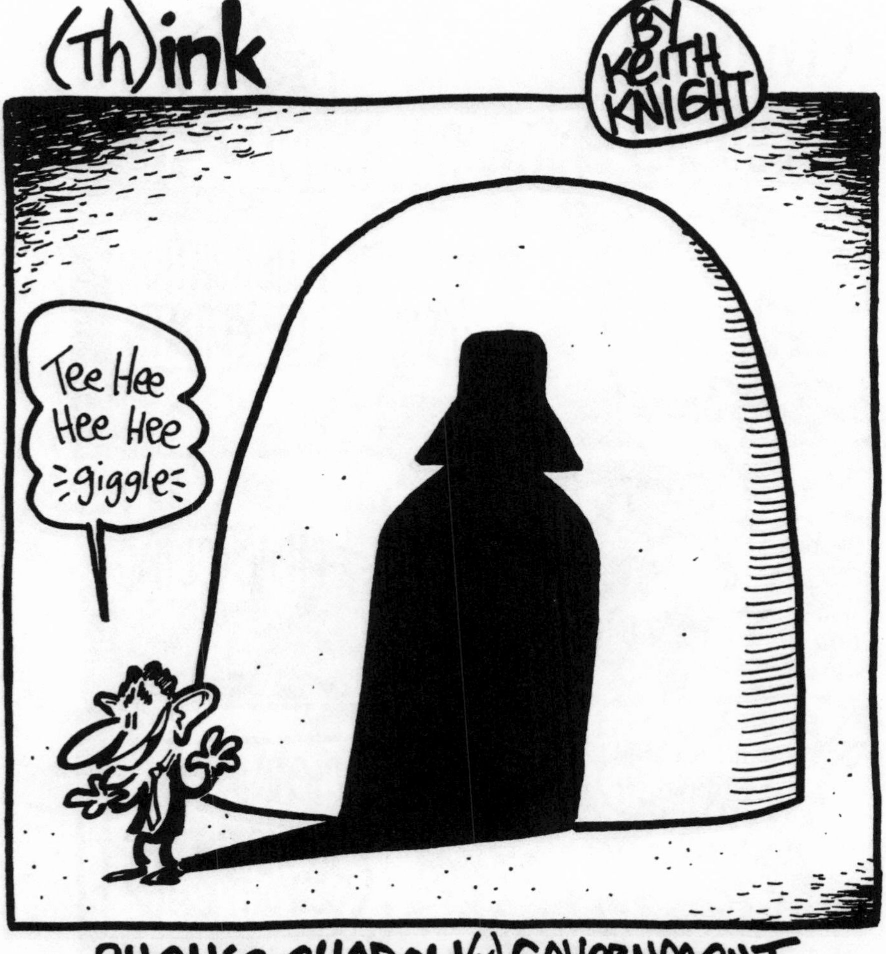
(Th)ink
BY KEITH KNIGHT
Tee Hee
Hee Hee
giggle
BUSH'S SHADOW(Y) GOVERNMENT

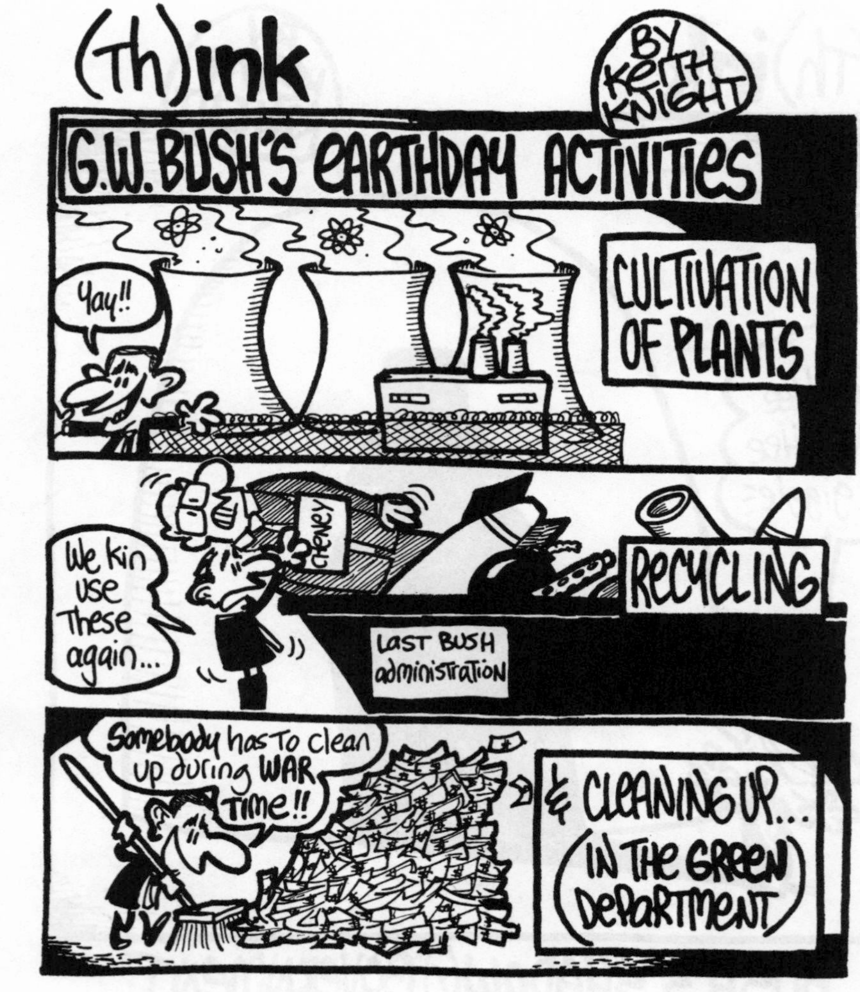
(Th)ink
BY KEITH KNIGHT
G.W. BUSH'S EARTHDAY ACTIVITIES
Yay!!
CULTIVATION OF PLANTS
CHENEY
We kin use These again...
RECYCLING
LAST BUSH administration
Somebody has To clean up during WAR TIME!!
& CLEANING UP...
(IN THE GREEN DEPARTMENT)

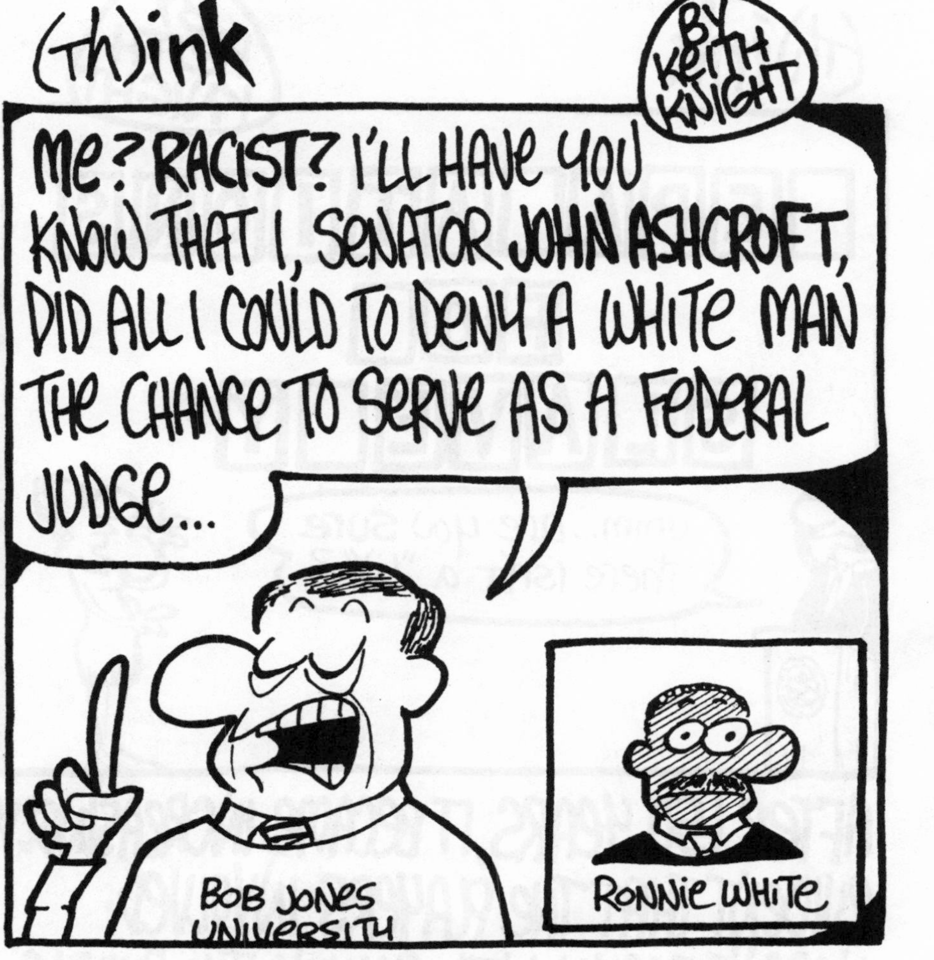
(TH)ink
BY KEITH KNIGHT
ME? RACIST? I'LL HAVE YOU KNOW THAT I, SENATOR JOHN ASHCROFT, DID ALL I COULD TO DENY A WHITE MAN THE CHANCE TO SERVE AS A FEDERAL JUDGE...
BOB JONES UNIVERSITY
RONNIE WHITE

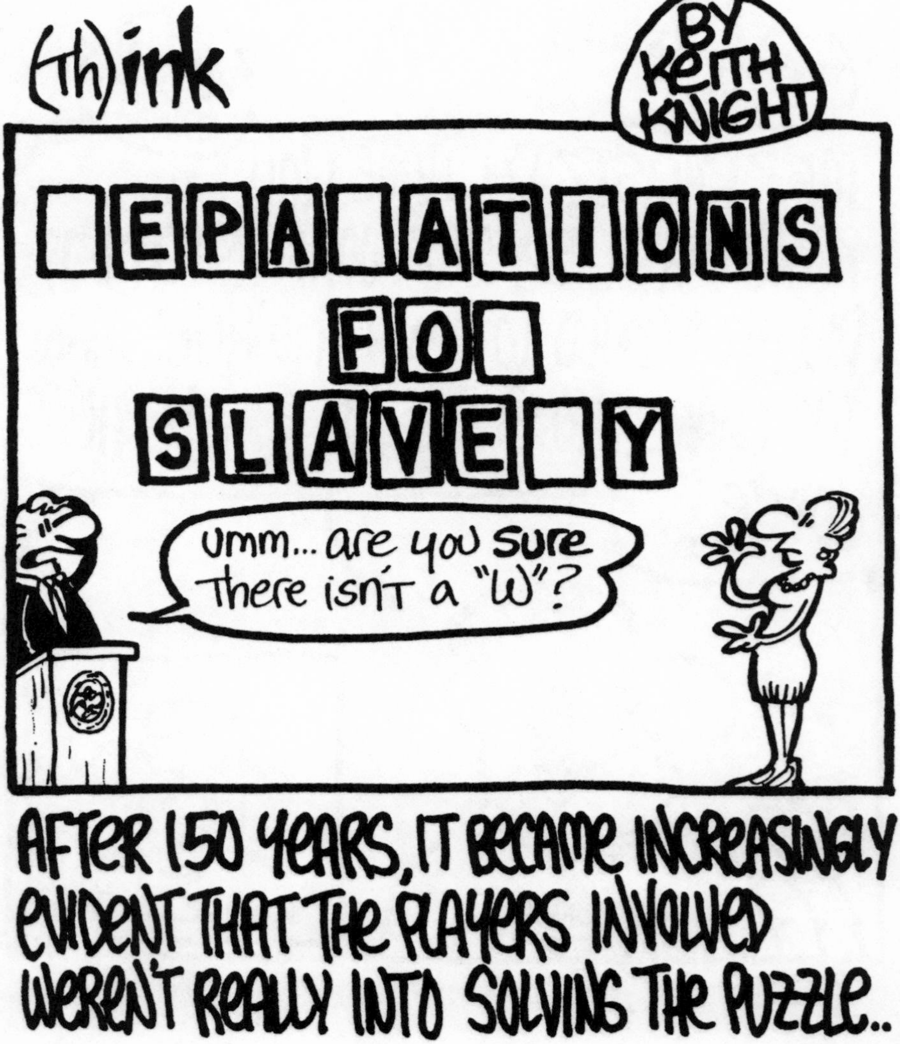
(th)ink
BY KEITH KNIGHT
EPA ATIONS
FO
SLAVE Y
umm... are you sure there isn't a "W"?
AFTER 150 YEARS, IT BECAME INCREASINGLY EVIDENT THAT THE PLAYERS INVOLVED WEREN'T REALLY INTO SOLVING THE PUZZLE..

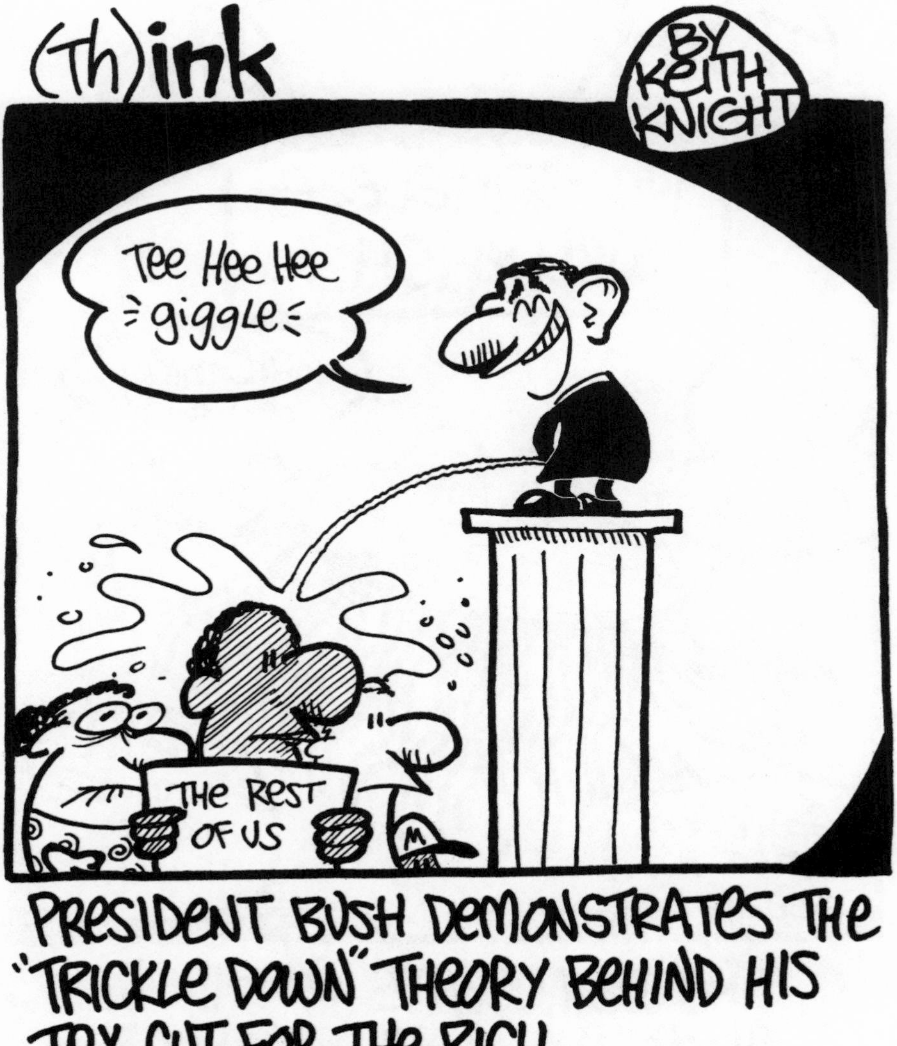
(Th)ink
BY KEITH KNIGHT
Tee Hee Hee
giggle
THE REST OF US
PRESIDENT BUSH DEMONSTRATES THE "TRICKLE DOWN" THEORY BEHIND HIS TAX CUT FOR THE RICH....

(Th)ink
BY KEITH KNIGHT
THE SPINELESS JELLYFISH
DUH... Yes, George...
Anything you say, George...
God bless America, George...
See How Patriotic we are, George?

THE DEMOCRATS CONSIDER ADOPTING A NEW MASCOT

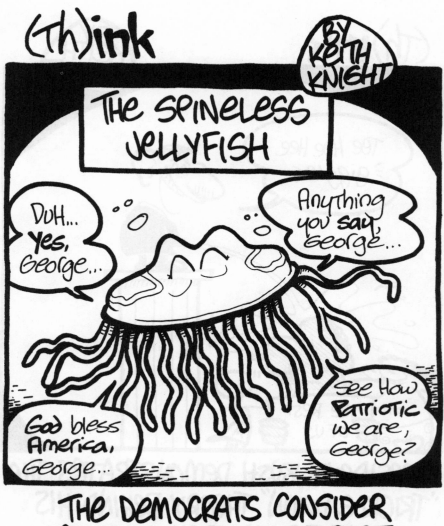

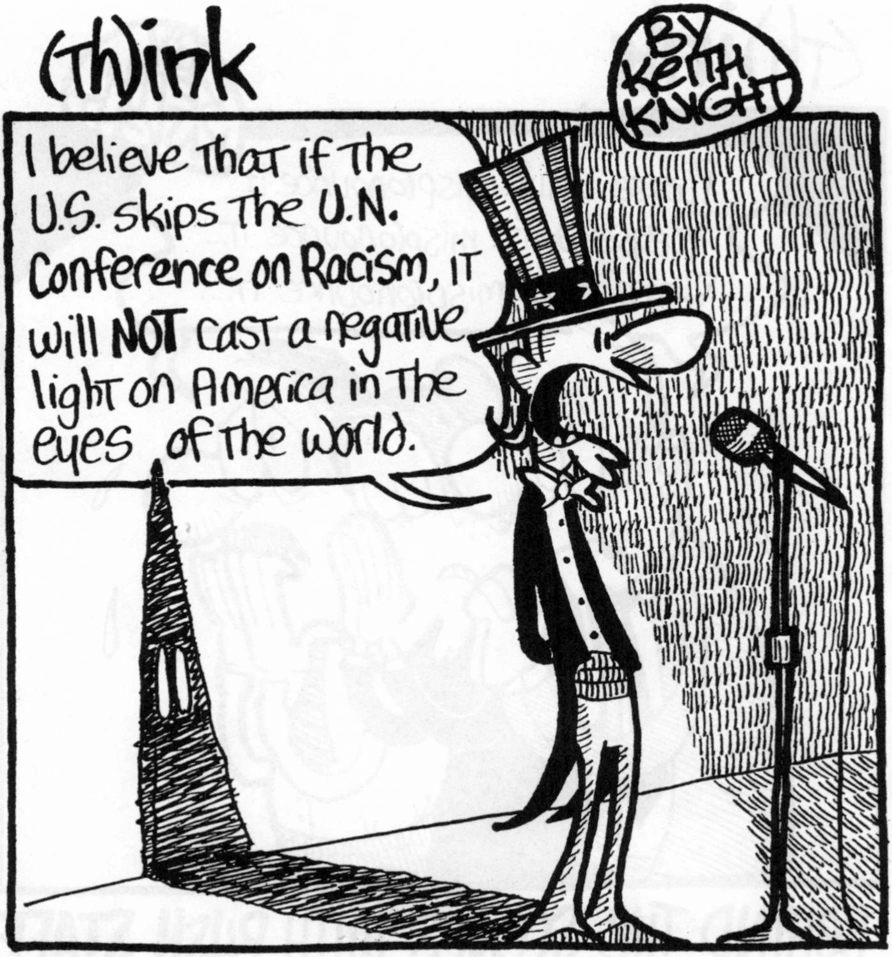
(th)ink
BY KEITH KNIGHT
I believe that if the U.S. skips the U.N. Conference on Racism, it will **NOT** cast a negative light on America in the eyes of the world.

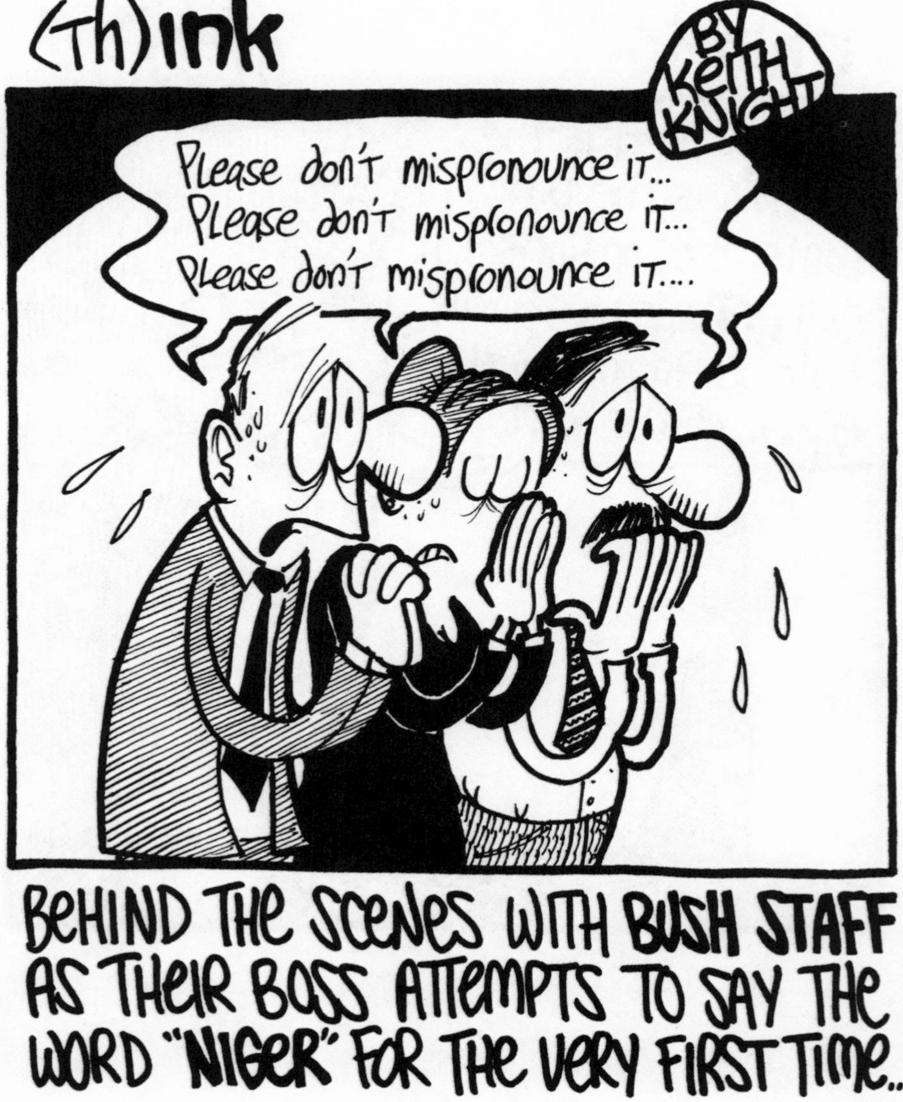
(Th)ink
BY KEITH KNIGHT
Please don't mispronounce it...
Please don't mispronounce it...
Please don't mispronounce it....
BEHIND THE SCENES WITH BUSH STAFF AS THEIR BOSS ATTEMPTS TO SAY THE WORD "NIGER" FOR THE VERY FIRST TIME...

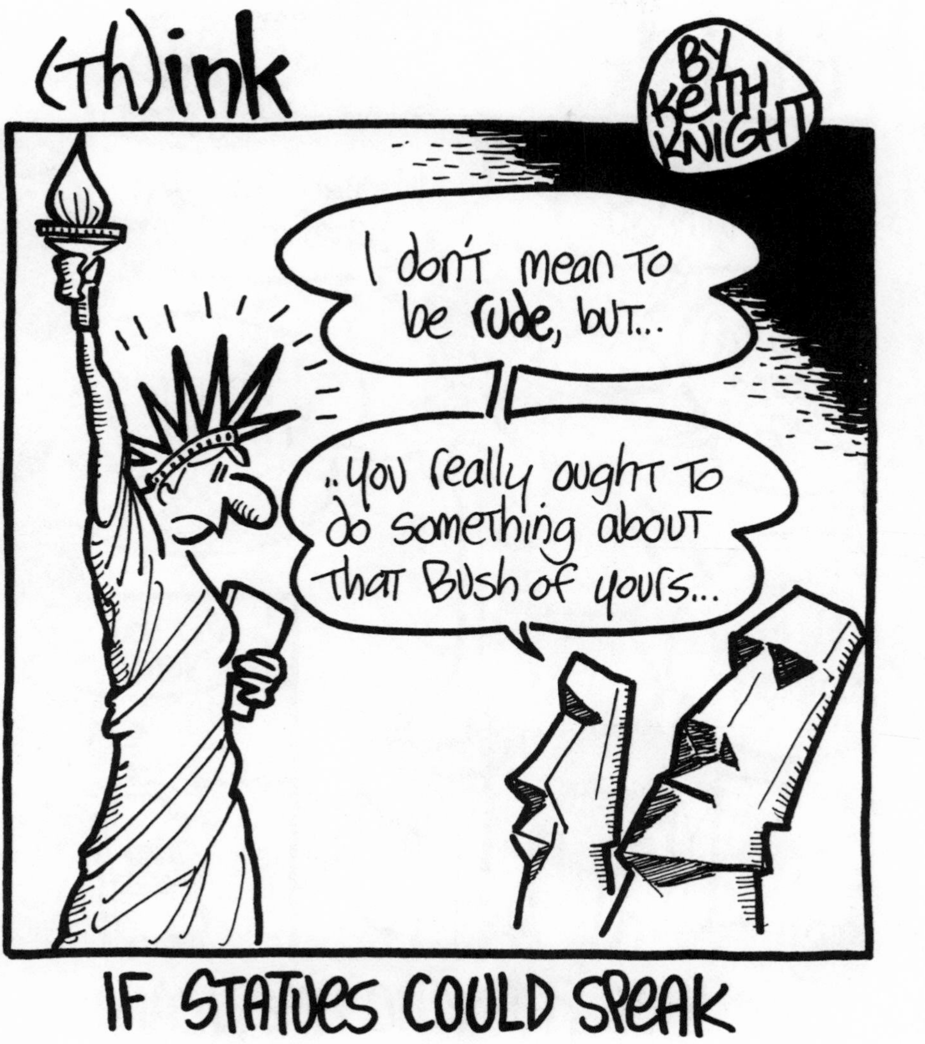
(th)ink
BY KEITH KNIGHT
I don't mean to be rude, but...
..you really ought to do something about that Bush of yours...

IF STATUES COULD SPEAK

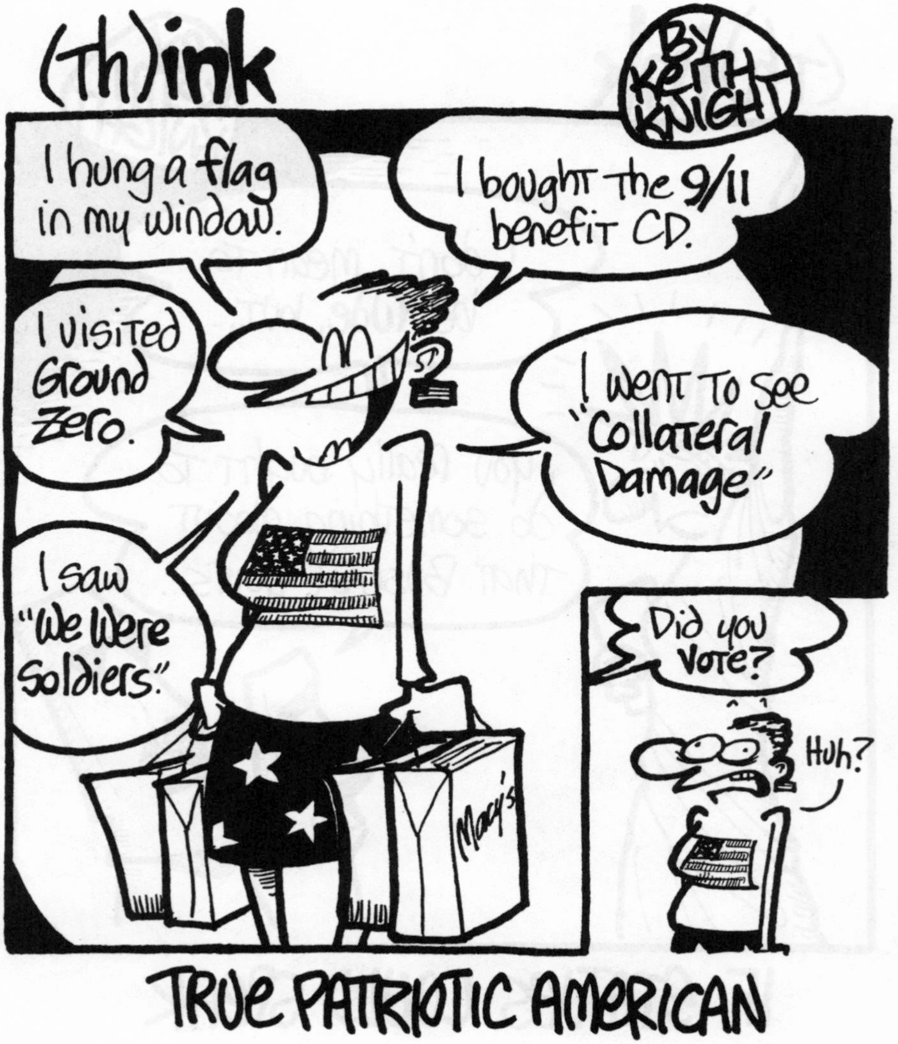
(Th)ink
BY KEITH KNIGHT
I hung a flag in my window.
I bought the 9/11 benefit CD.
I visited Ground Zero.
I went to see "Collateral Damage"
I saw "We Were Soldiers."
Did you vote?
Huh?
Macy's
TRUE PATRIOTIC AMERICAN

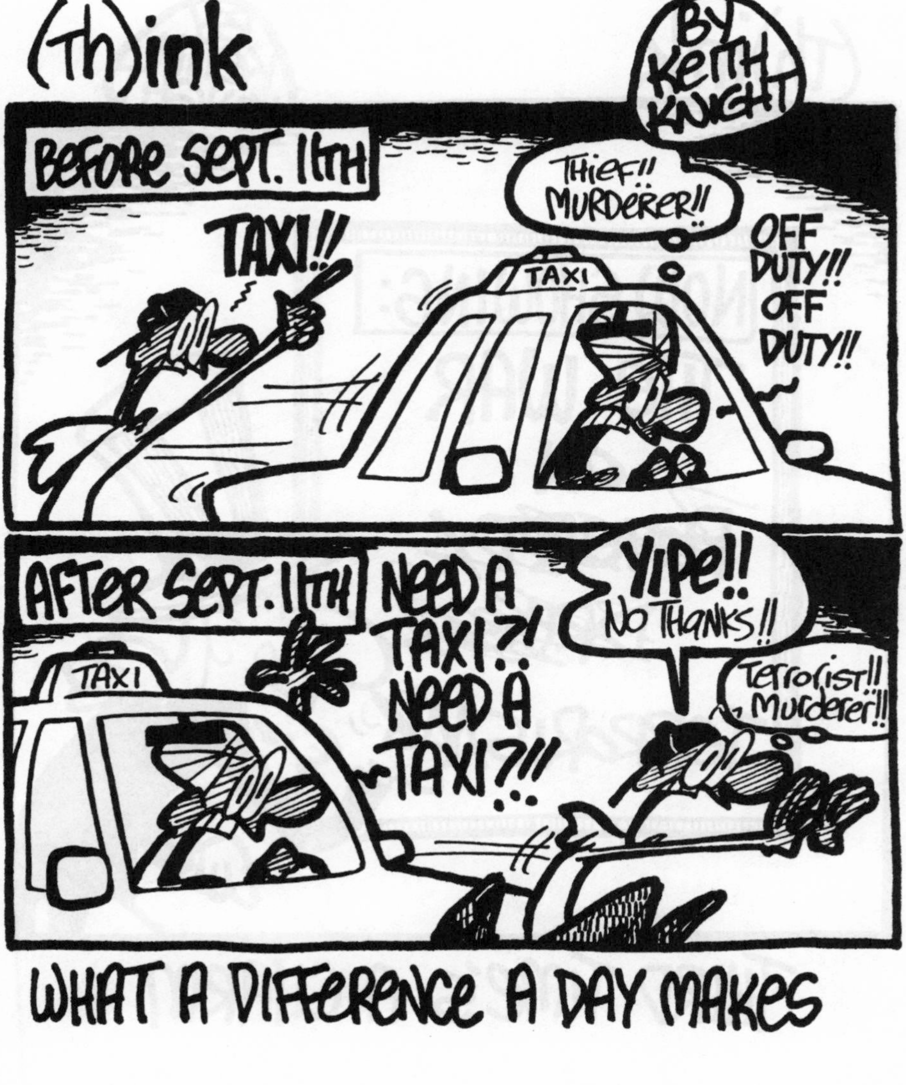
(Th)ink
By Keith Knight
Before Sept. 11th
TAXI!!
Thief!! Murderer!!
TAXI
OFF DUTY!! OFF DUTY!!
After Sept. 11th
Need a Taxi?! Need a Taxi?!!
TAXI
Yipe!! No Thanks!!
Terrorist!! Murderer!!
What a difference a day makes

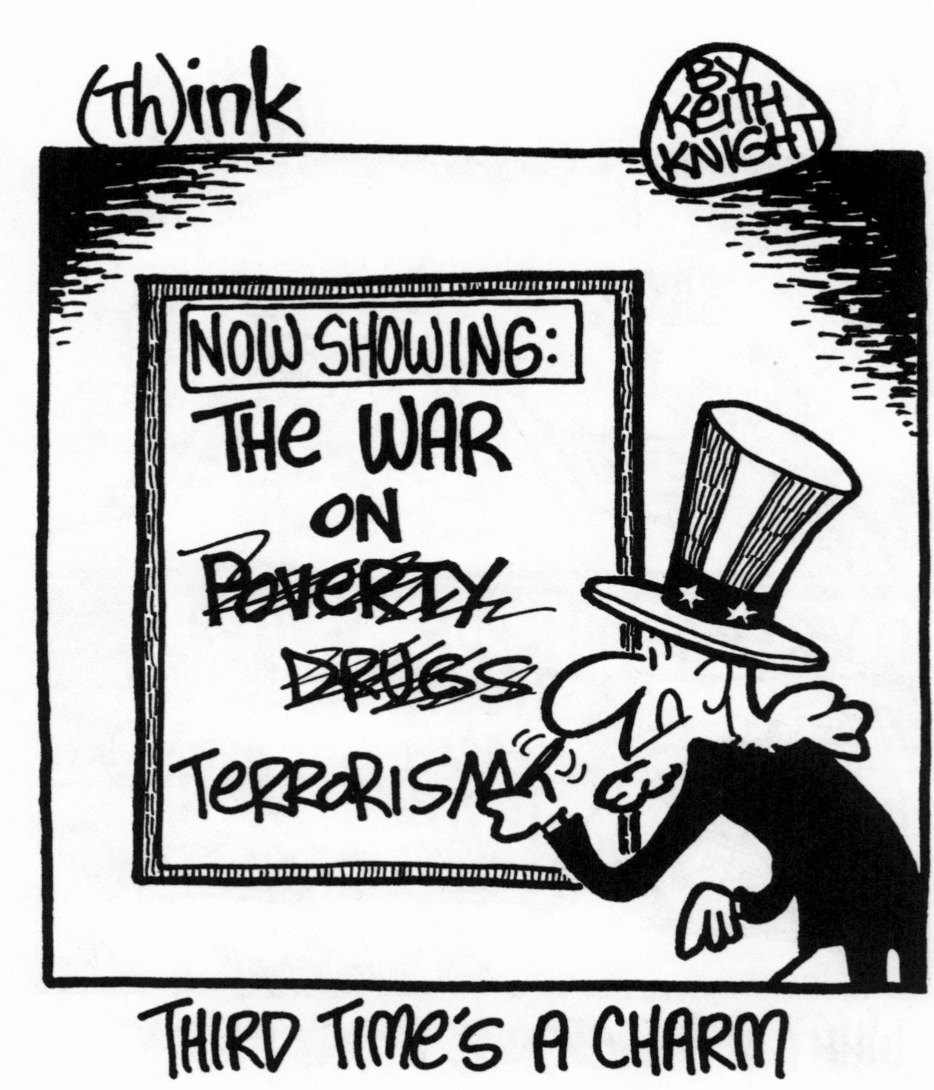
(th)ink
BY KEITH KNIGHT
NOW SHOWING:
THE WAR
ON
~~POVERTY~~
~~DRUGS~~
TERRORISM

THIRD TIME'S A CHARM

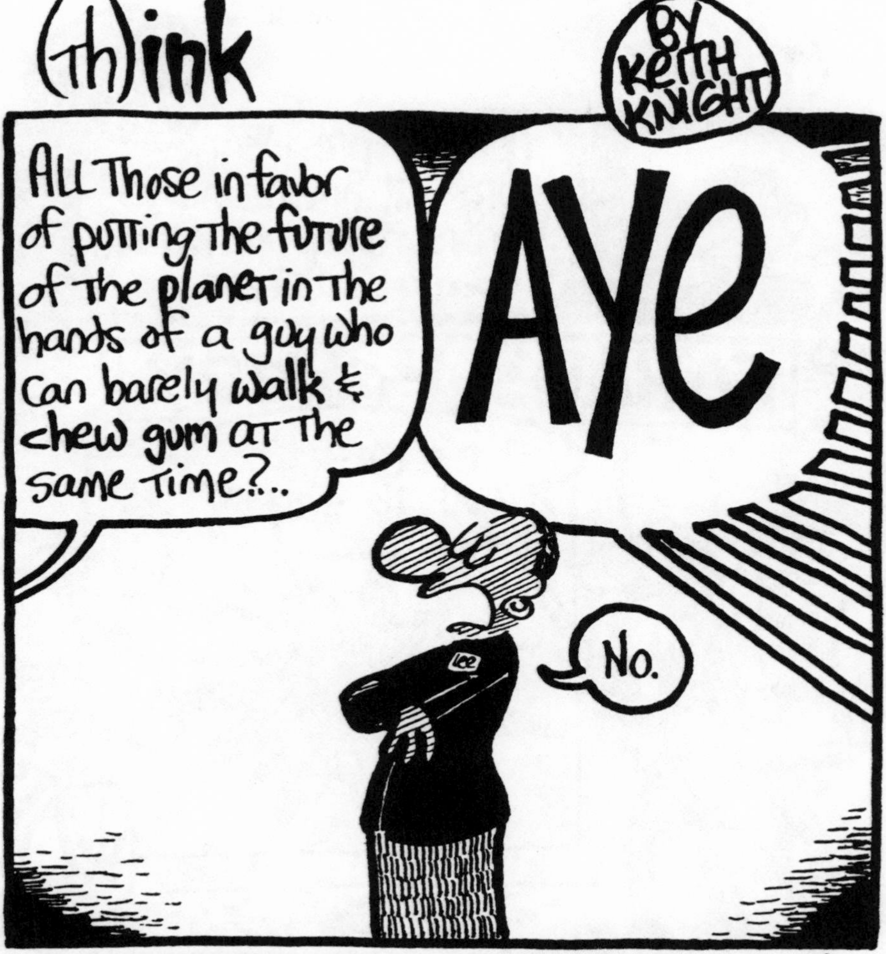
(th)ink
By Keith Knight
All Those in favor of putting the future of the planet in the hands of a guy who can barely walk & chew gum at the same Time?...
Aye
No.
Lee
"Nobody Does It Like Barbara Lee"

(Th)ink

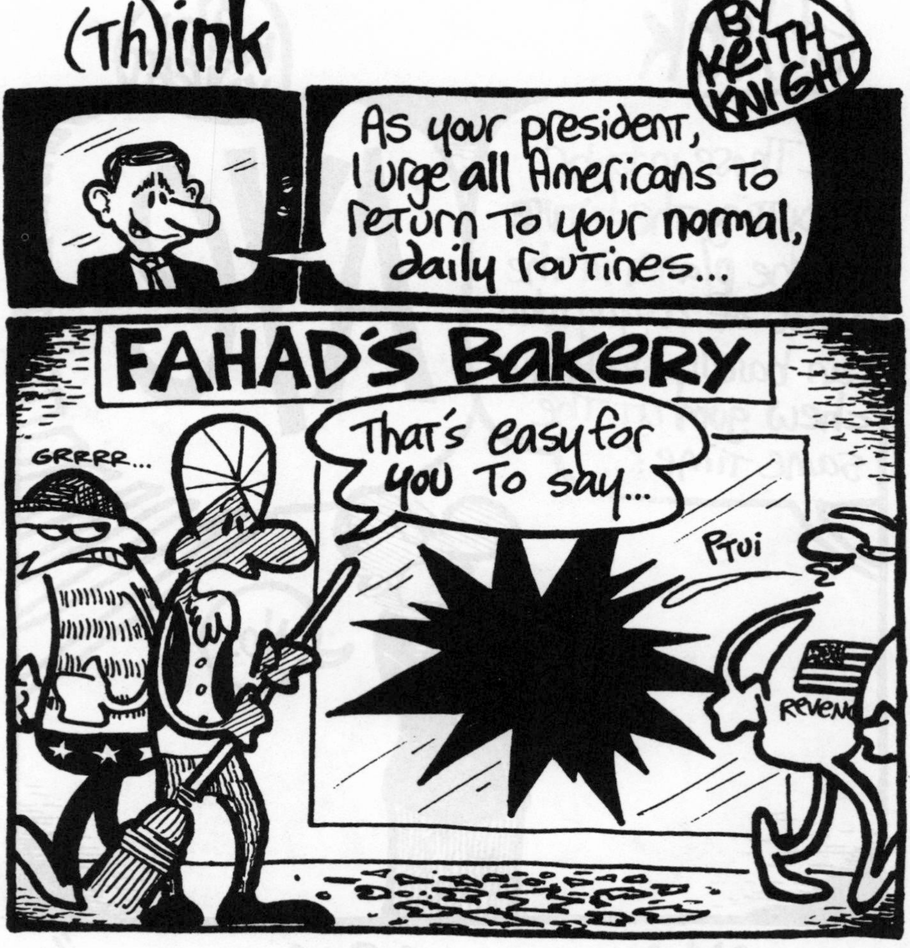
BY KEITH KNIGHT
As your president, I urge all Americans to return to your normal, daily routines...
FAHAD'S BAKERY
GRRRR...
That's easy for you to say...
PTUI
REVEN

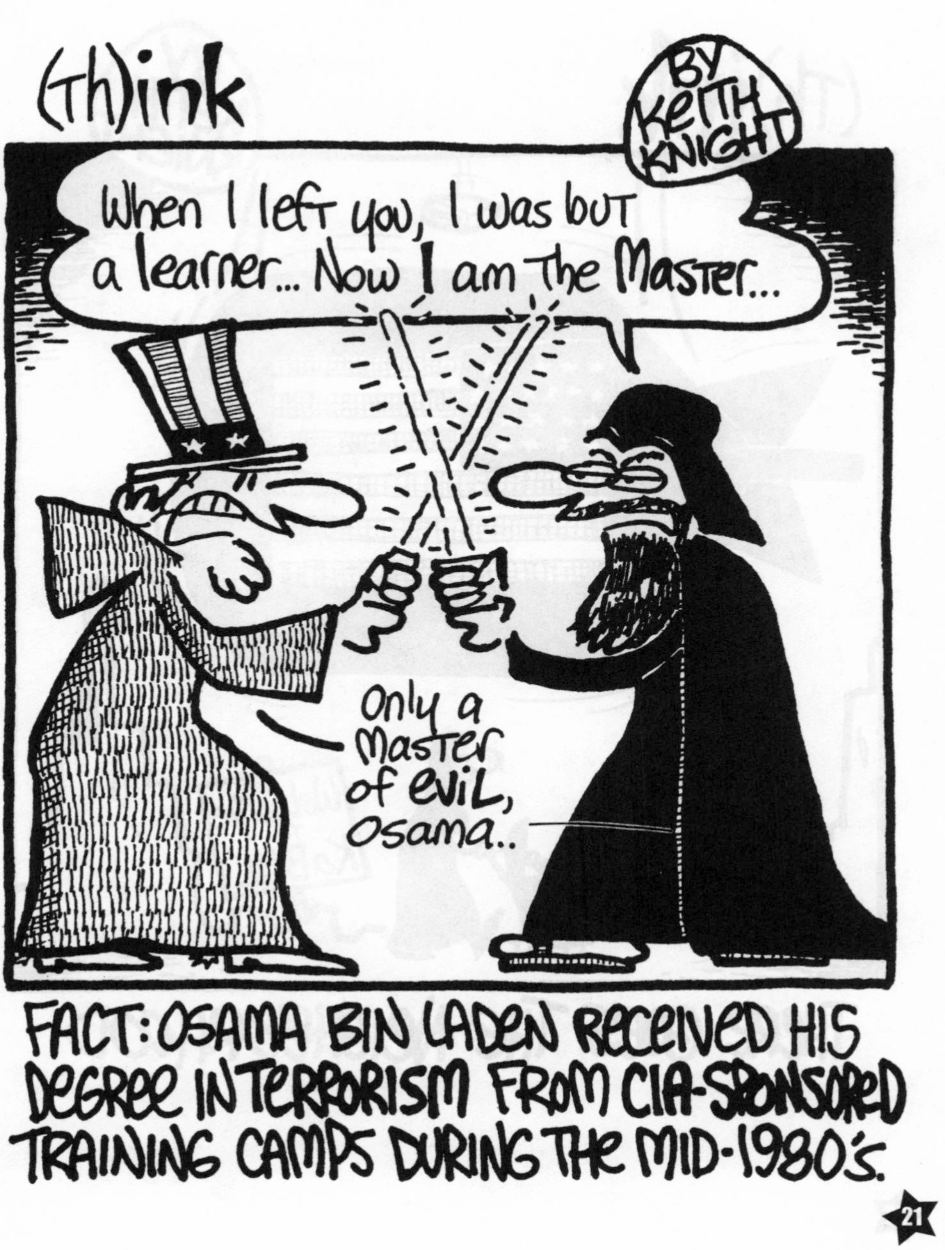
(th)ink
BY KEITH KNIGHT
When I left you, I was but a learner... Now I am the Master...
Only a Master of evil, Osama..

FACT: OSAMA BIN LADEN RECEIVED HIS DEGREE IN TERRORISM FROM CIA-SPONSORED TRAINING CAMPS DURING THE MID-1980'S.

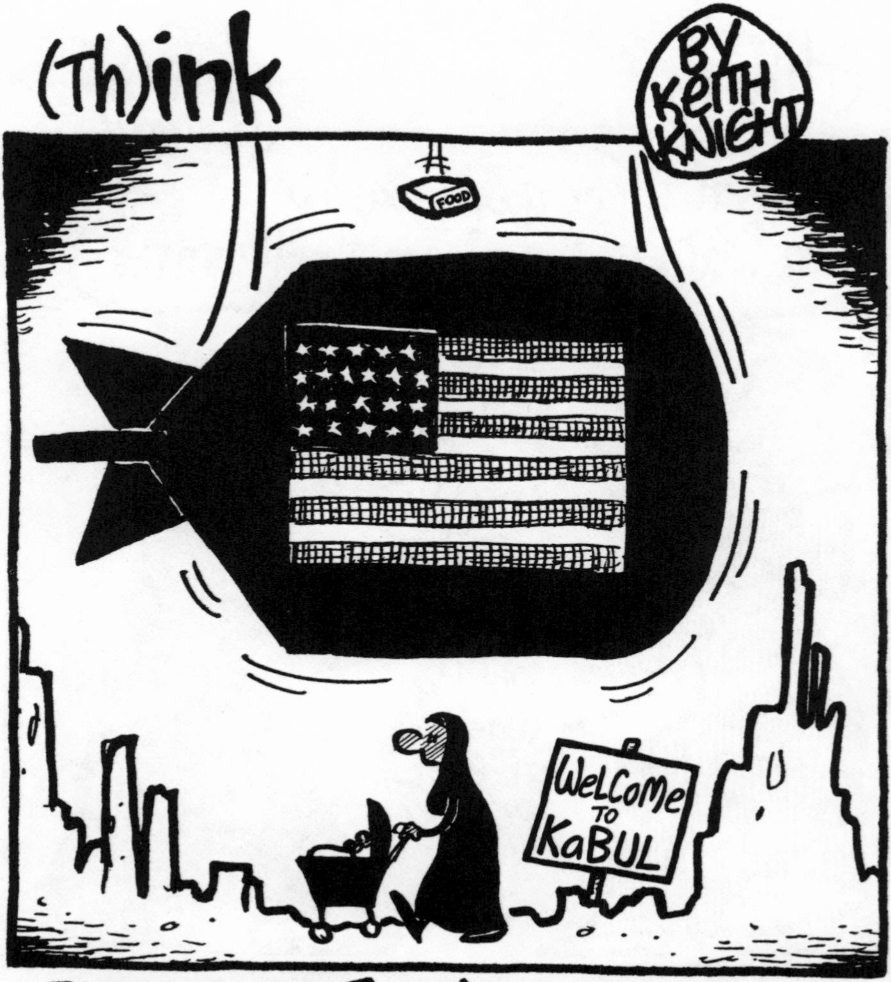
(Th)ink
BY KEITH KNIGHT
FOOD
WELCOME TO KaBUL
THERE GOES THE NEIGHBORHOOD

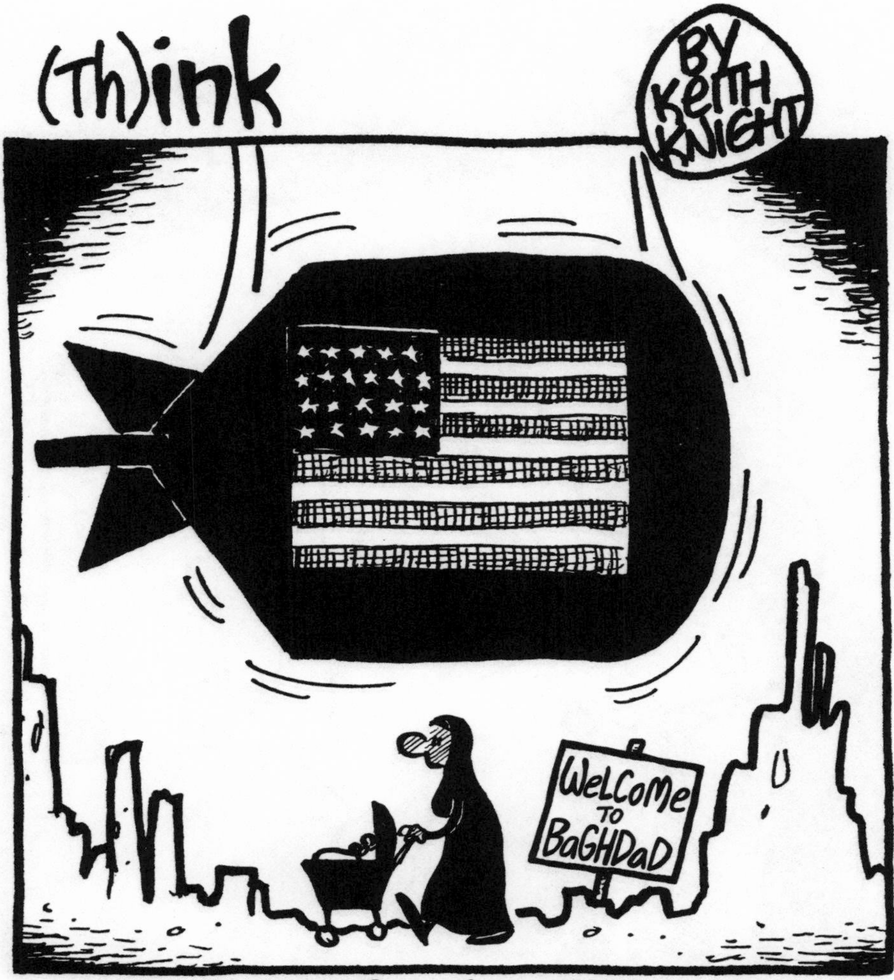
(Th)ink
BY KEITH KNIGHT
WELCOME TO BAGHDAD
THERE GOES THE NEIGHBORHOOD

(th)ink BY KEITH KNIGHT

AL-QaeDa
AL-JaZeeRa
AL-GoRe
AL B.SuRe

CONNECTING THE DOTS WITH
ATTORNEY GENERAL JOHN ASHCROFT

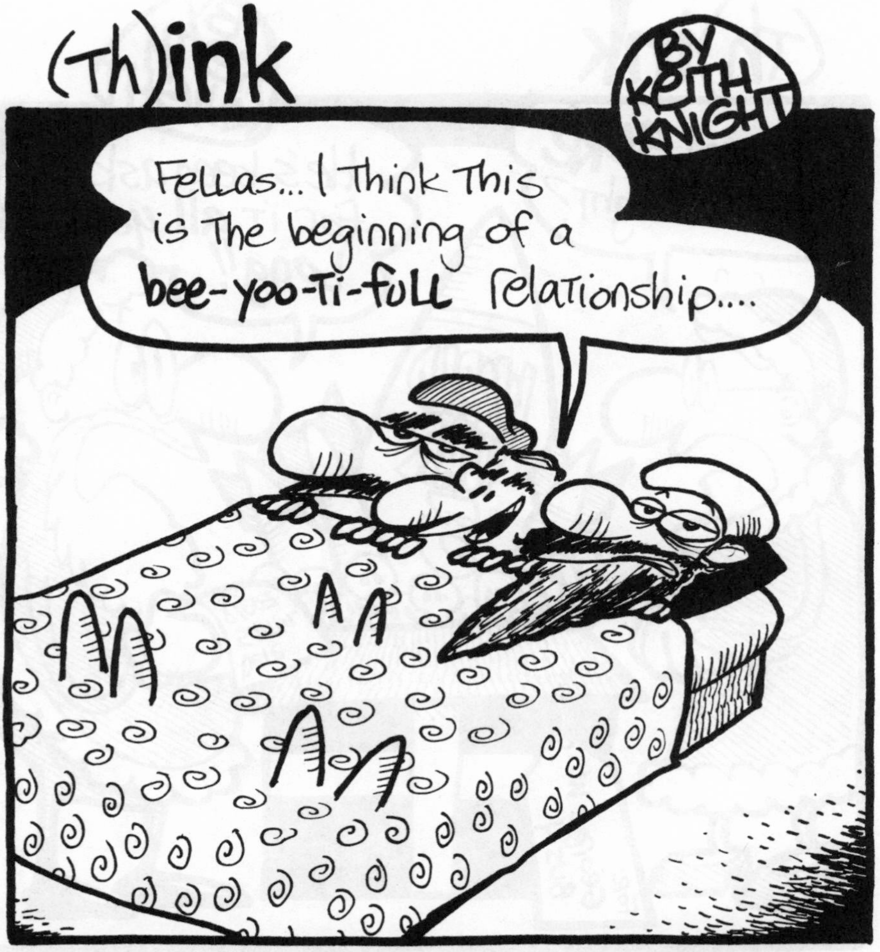
(Th)ink
BY KEITH KNIGHT
Fellas... I think this is the beginning of a **bee-yoo-ti-full** relationship....

POLLS REVEAL THAT AS LONG AS THEY ARE **FEARFUL**, VOTERS TEND TO VOTE **REPUBLICAN**

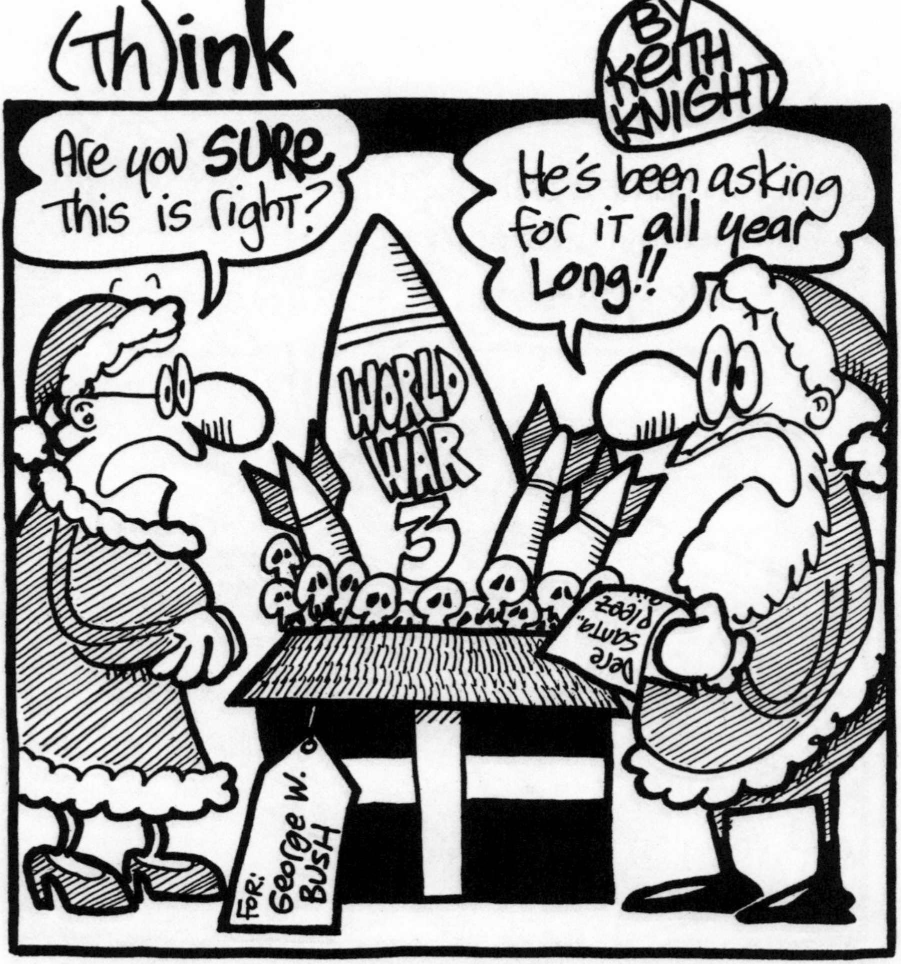
(Th)ink
By Keith Knight
Are you SURE this is right?
He's been asking for it all year Long!!
World War 3
Dere Santa, Pleez
For: George W. Bush

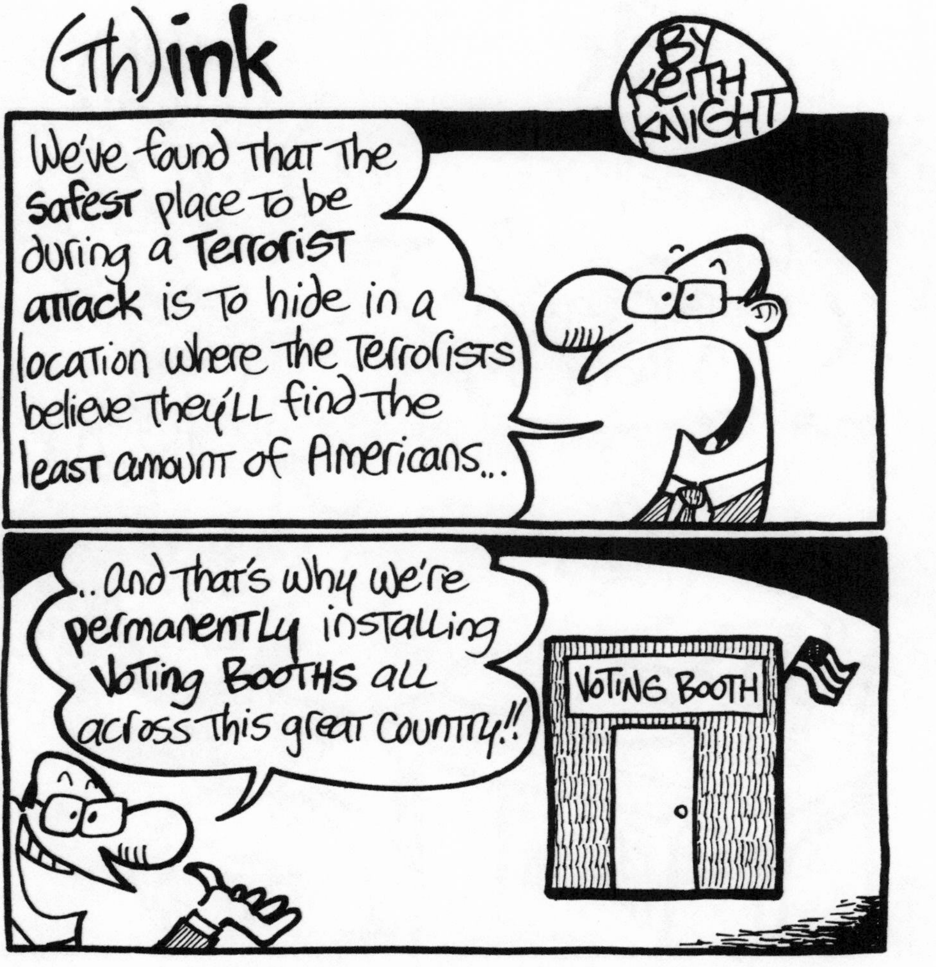
(Th)ink
BY KEITH KNIGHT
We've found that the safest place to be during a terrorist attack is to hide in a location where the terrorists believe they'll find the least amount of Americans...
...and that's why we're permanently installing voting booths all across this great country!!
VOTING BOOTH

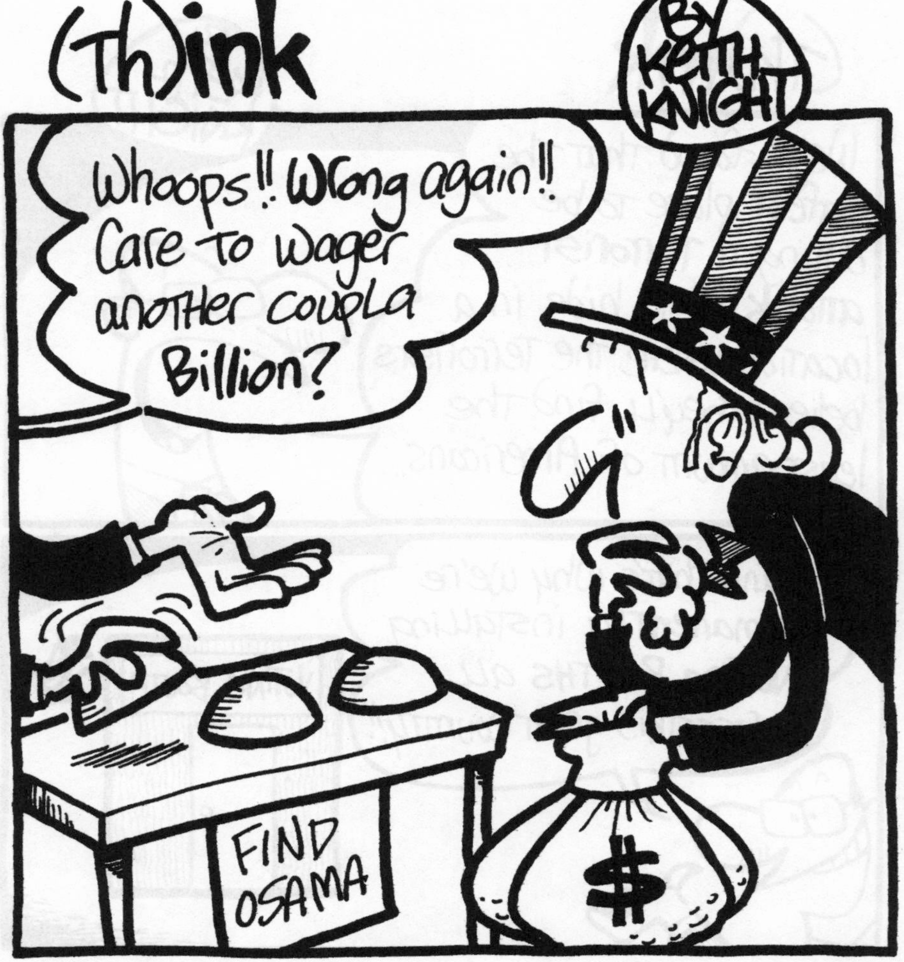
(Th)ink
By Keith Knight
Whoops!! Wrong again!! Care to wager another coupla Billion?
FIND OSAMA
$

(th)ink

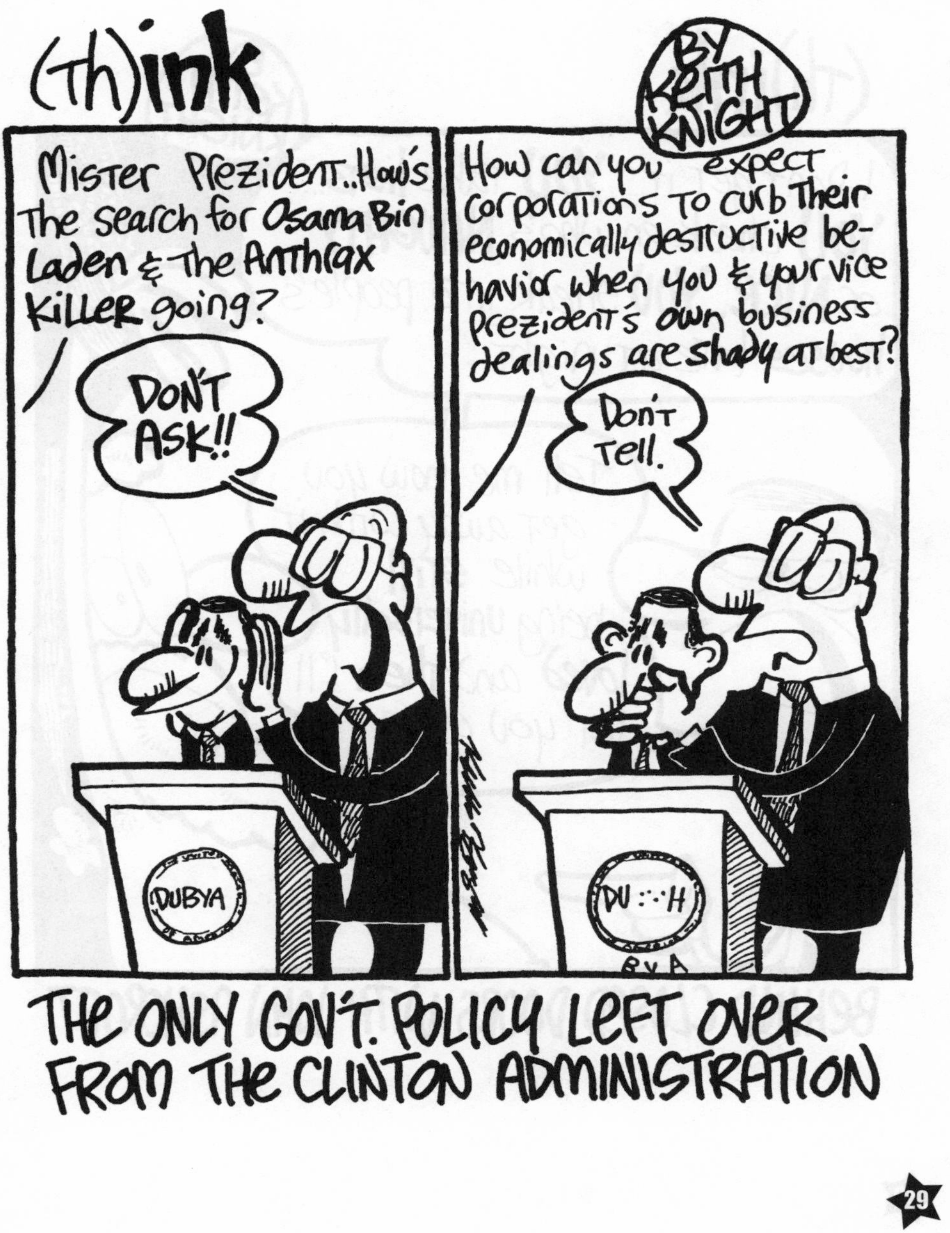
By Keith Knight
Mister Prezident..How's the search for Osama Bin Laden & the Anthrax Killer going?
DON'T ASK!!
How can you expect corporations to curb their economically destructive behavior when you & your vice prezident's own business dealings are shady at best?
Don't Tell.
DUBYA

THE ONLY GOV'T. POLICY LEFT OVER FROM THE CLINTON ADMINISTRATION

(Th)ink

By Keith Knight

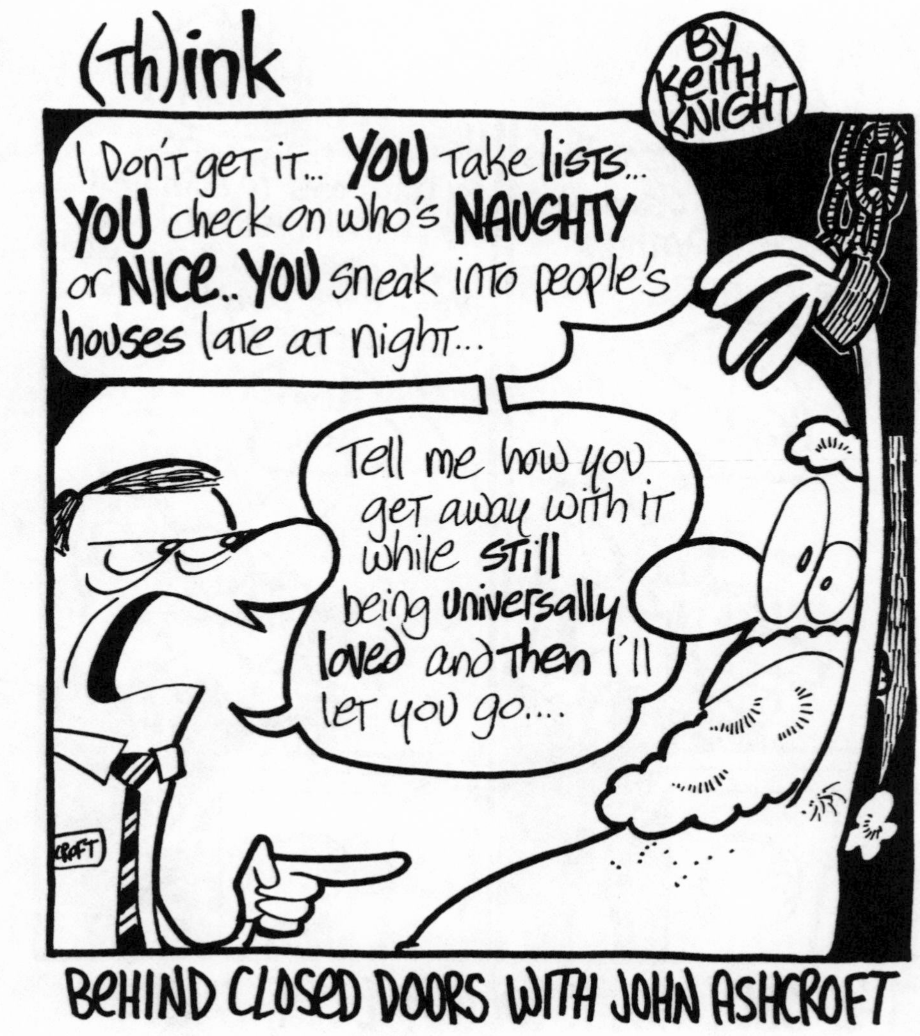
I Don't get it... YOU take lists... YOU check on who's NAUGHTY or NICE.. YOU sneak into people's houses late at night...
Tell me how you get away with it while still being universally loved and then I'll let you go....
CROFT

BEHIND CLOSED DOORS WITH JOHN ASHCROFT

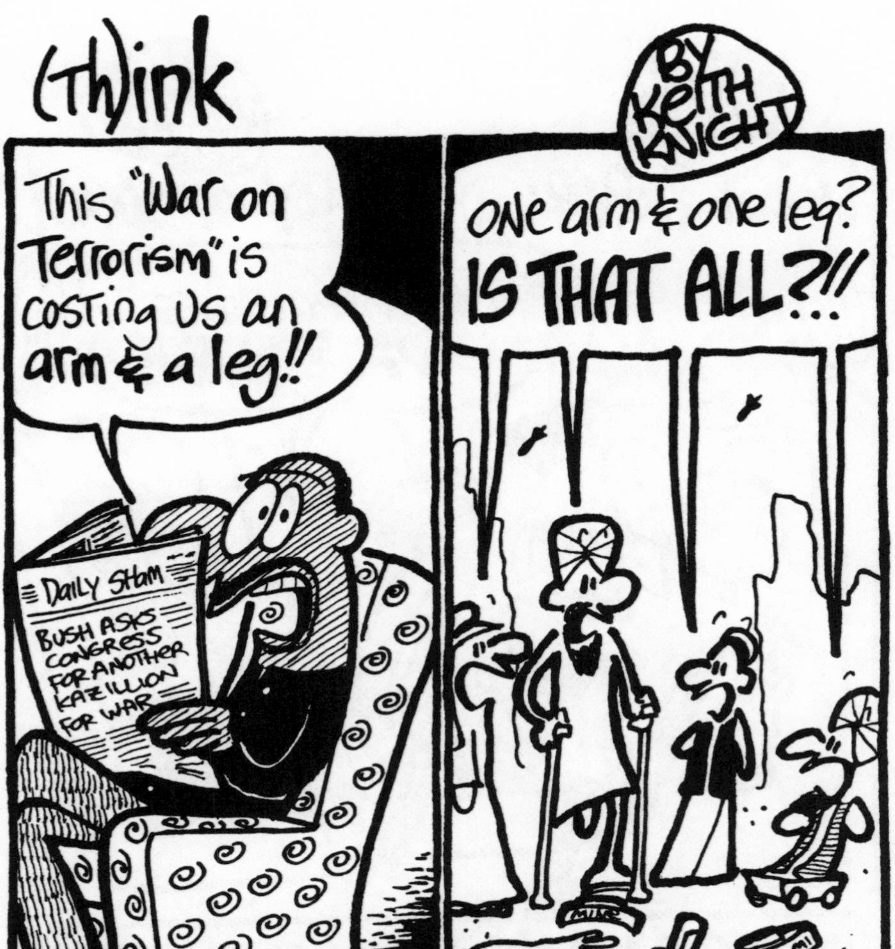
(th)ink
BY KEITH KNIGHT
This "War on Terrorism" is costing us an arm & a leg!!
DAILY SHAM
BUSH ASKS CONGRESS FOR ANOTHER KAZILLION FOR WAR
ONE arm & one leg? IS THAT ALL?!!...

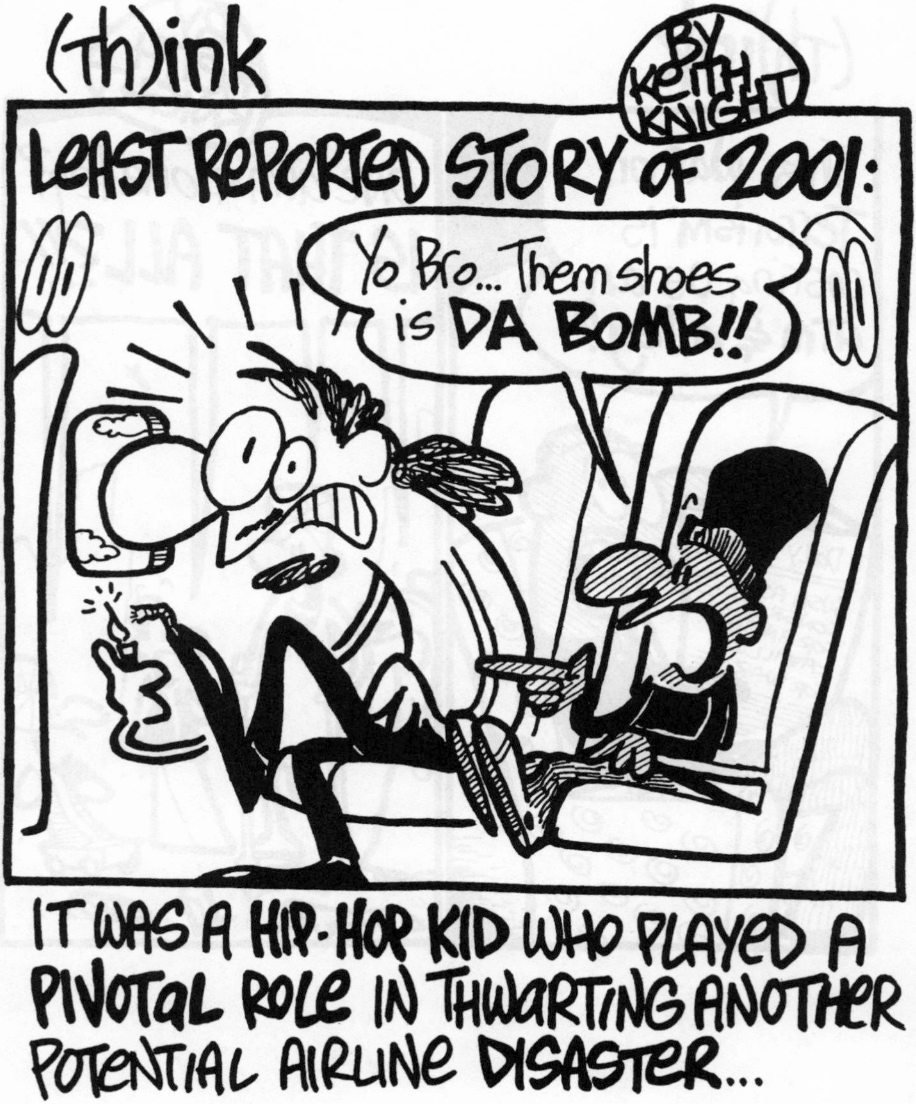
(th)ink
BY KEITH KNIGHT
LEAST REPORTED STORY OF 2001:
Yo Bro... Them shoes is DA BOMB!!
IT WAS A HIP-HOP KID WHO PLAYED A PIVOTAL ROLE IN THWARTING ANOTHER POTENTIAL AIRLINE DISASTER...

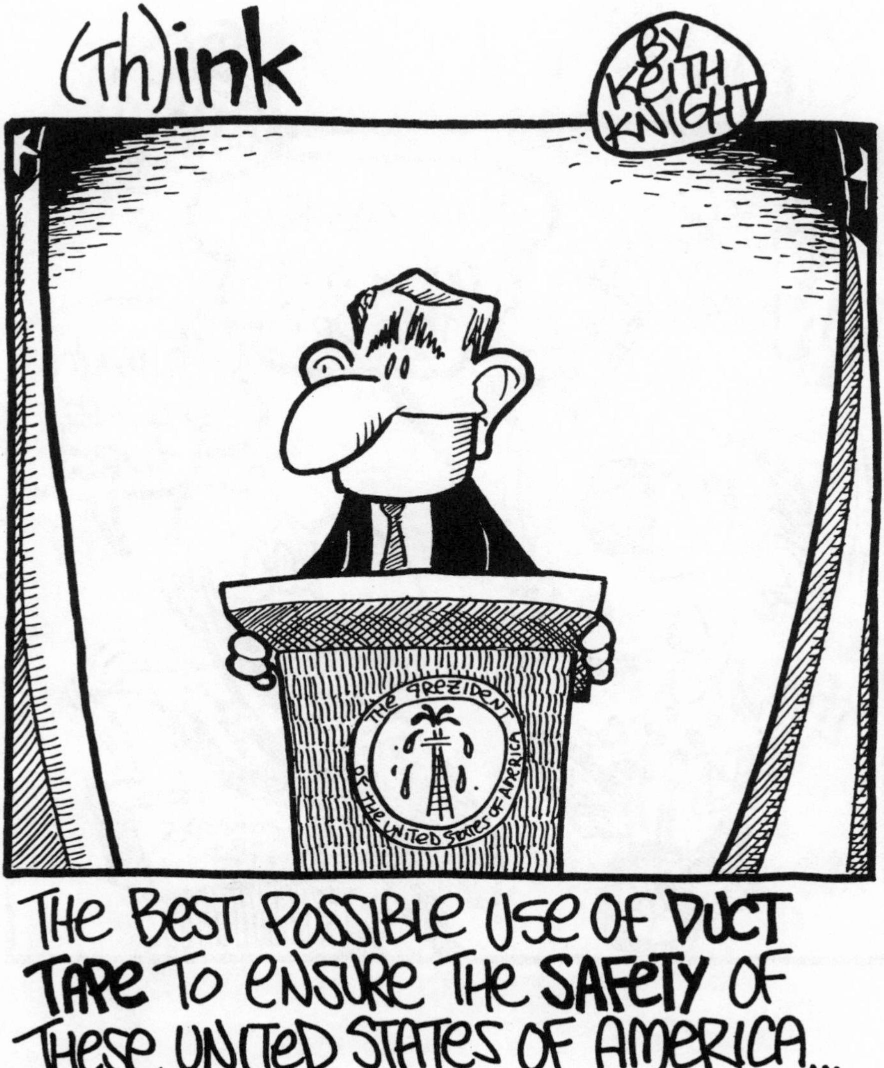
(Th)ink
BY KEITH KNIGHT
THE PREZIDENT OF THE UNITED STATES OF AMERICA
THE BEST POSSIBLE USE OF DUCT TAPE TO ENSURE THE SAFETY OF THESE UNITED STATES OF AMERICA...

(Th)ink

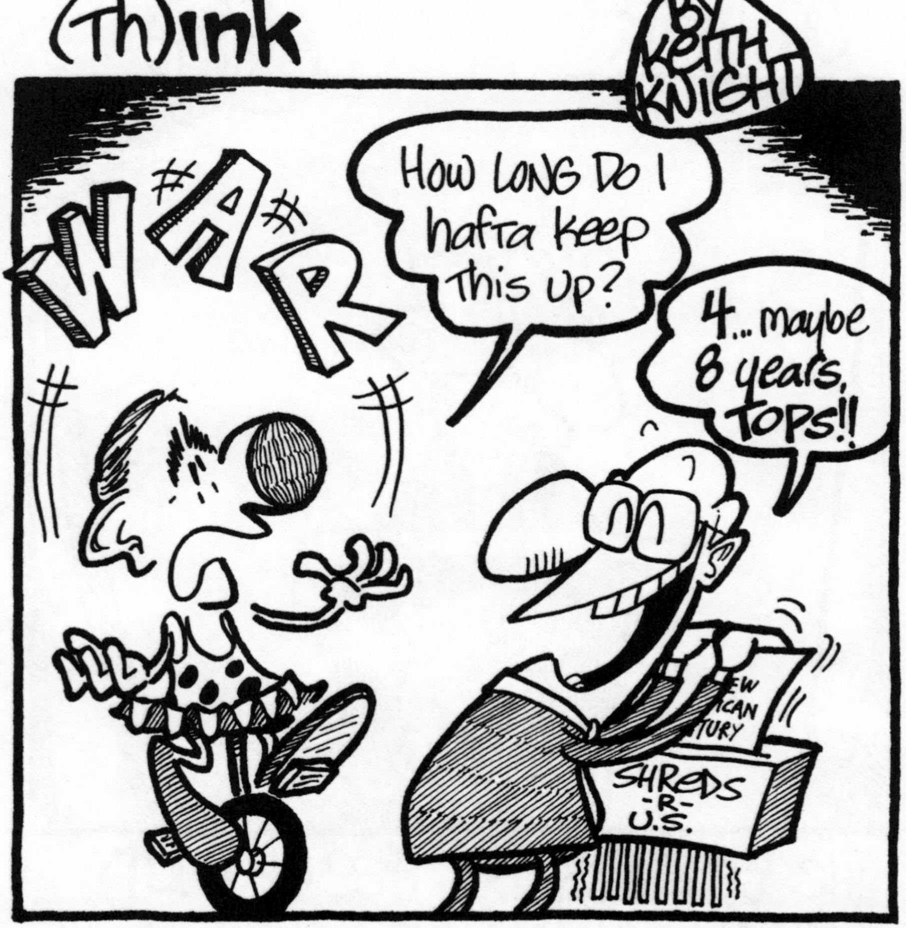
BY KEITH KNIGHT
WAR
HOW LONG DO I hafta keep this up?
4... maybe 8 years, TOPS!!
SHREDS -R- U.S.

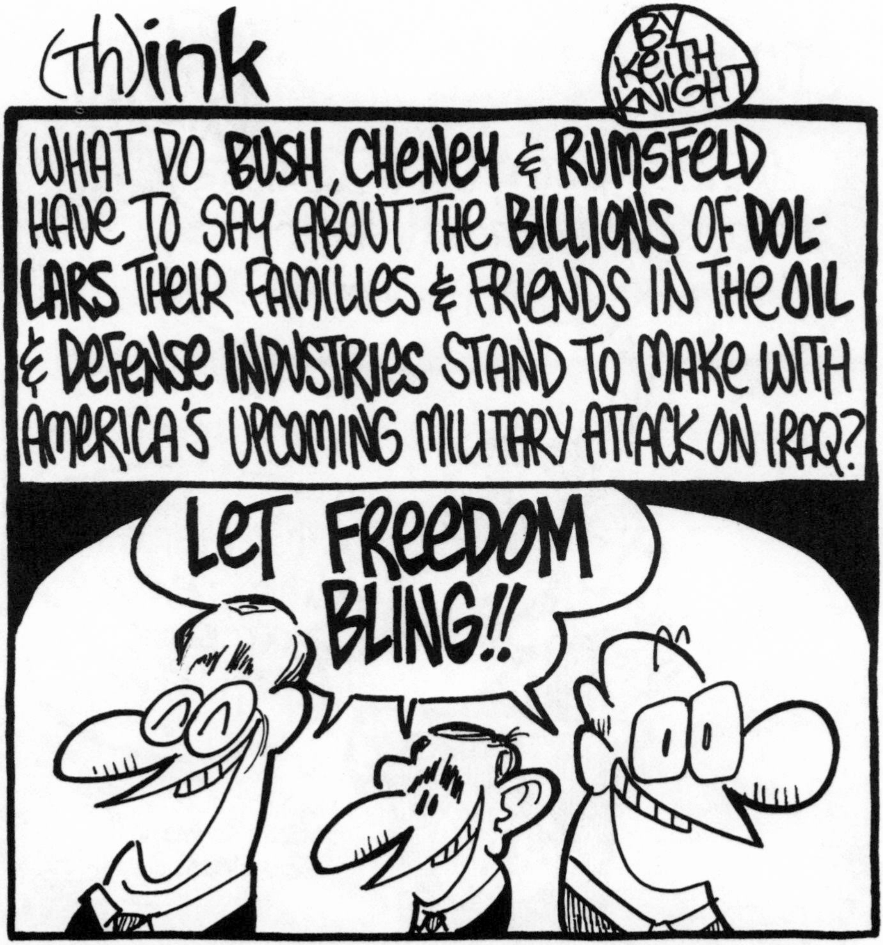
(TH)INK
BY KEITH KNIGHT
WHAT DO BUSH, CHENEY & RUMSFELD HAVE TO SAY ABOUT THE BILLIONS OF DOLLARS THEIR FAMILIES & FRIENDS IN THE OIL & DEFENSE INDUSTRIES STAND TO MAKE WITH AMERICA'S UPCOMING MILITARY ATTACK ON IRAQ?
LET FREEDOM BLING!!

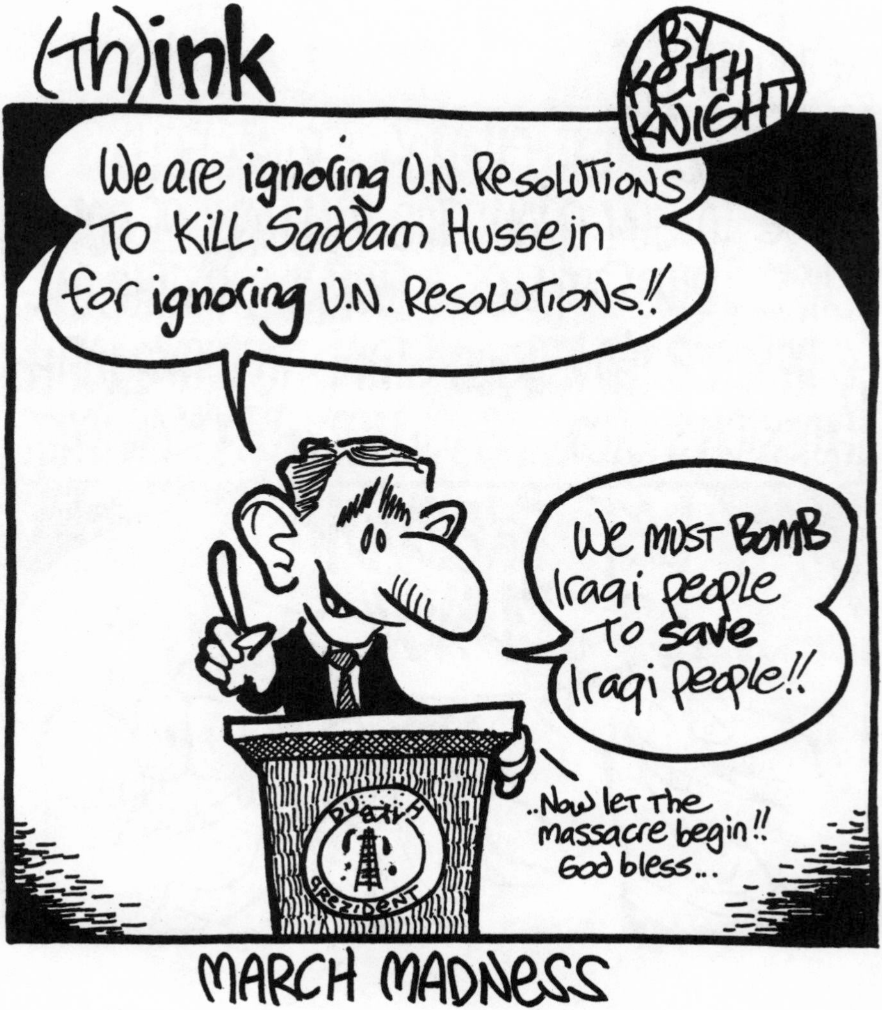
(th)ink
BY KEITH KNIGHT
We are ignoring U.N. RESOLUTIONS TO KILL Saddam Hussein for ignoring U.N. RESOLUTIONS!!
We MUST BOMB Iraqi people To save Iraqi people!!
..Now let the massacre begin!! God bless...
GREZIDENT
MARCH MADNESS

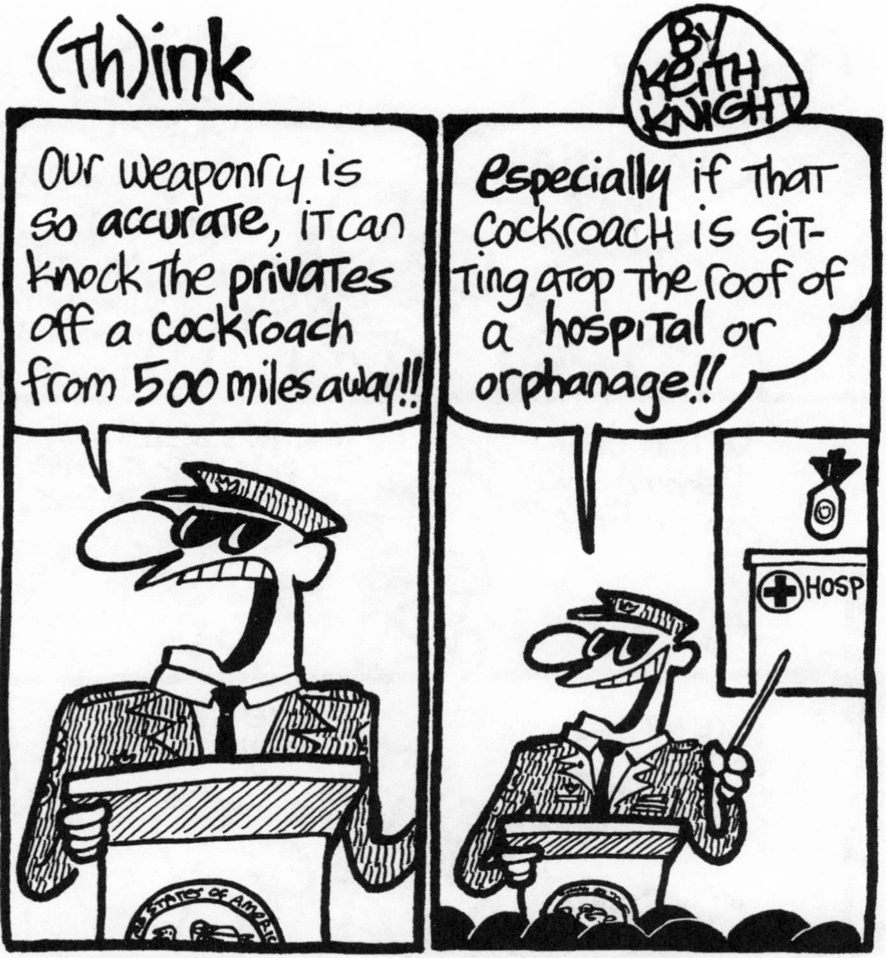
(Th)ink
By Keith Knight
Our weaponry is so accurate, it can knock the privates off a cockroach from 500 miles away!!
especially if that cockroach is sitting atop the roof of a hospital or orphanage!!
HOSP

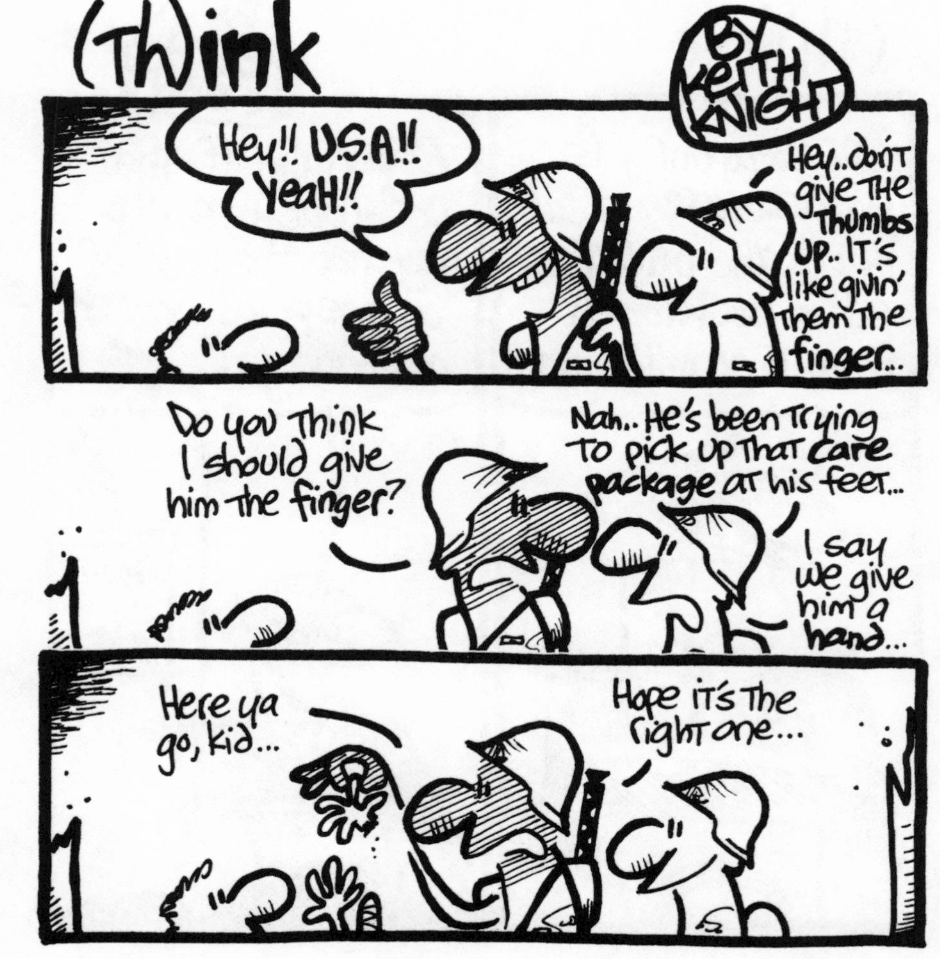
(Th)ink
By Keith Knight
Hey!! U.S.A!! Yeah!!
Hey.. don't give the Thumbs up.. It's like givin' them the finger...
Do you think I should give him the finger?
Nah.. He's been trying to pick up that care package at his feet...
I say we give him a hand...
Here ya go, kid...
Hope it's the right one...

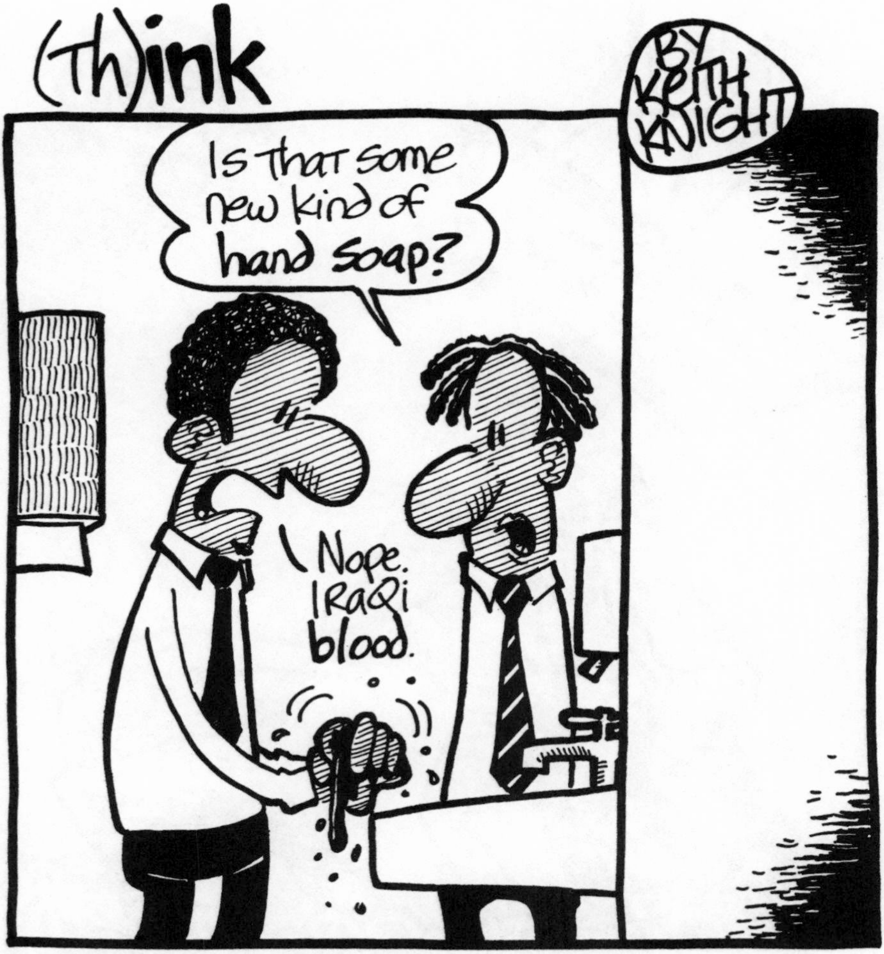
(th)ink
BY KEITH KNIGHT
Is that some new kind of hand soap?
Nope. Iraqi blood.

(th)ink

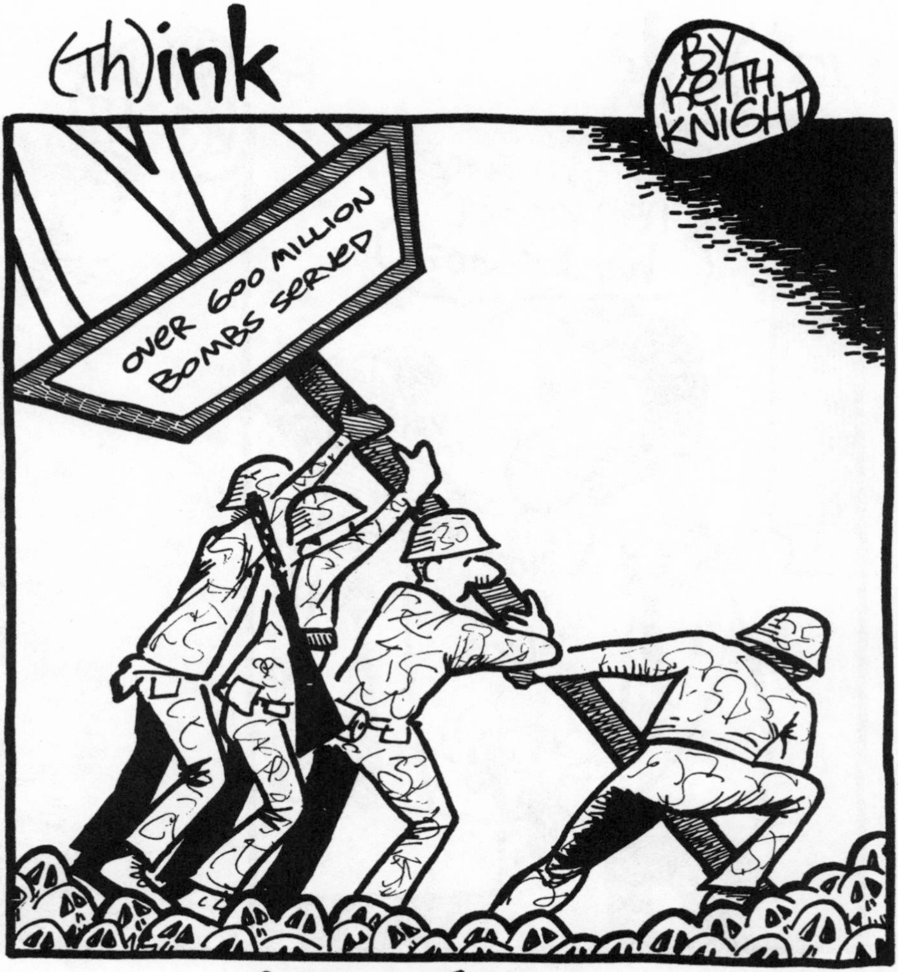
BY KEITH KNIGHT
OVER 600 MILLION BOMBS SERVED

ALMOST THERE

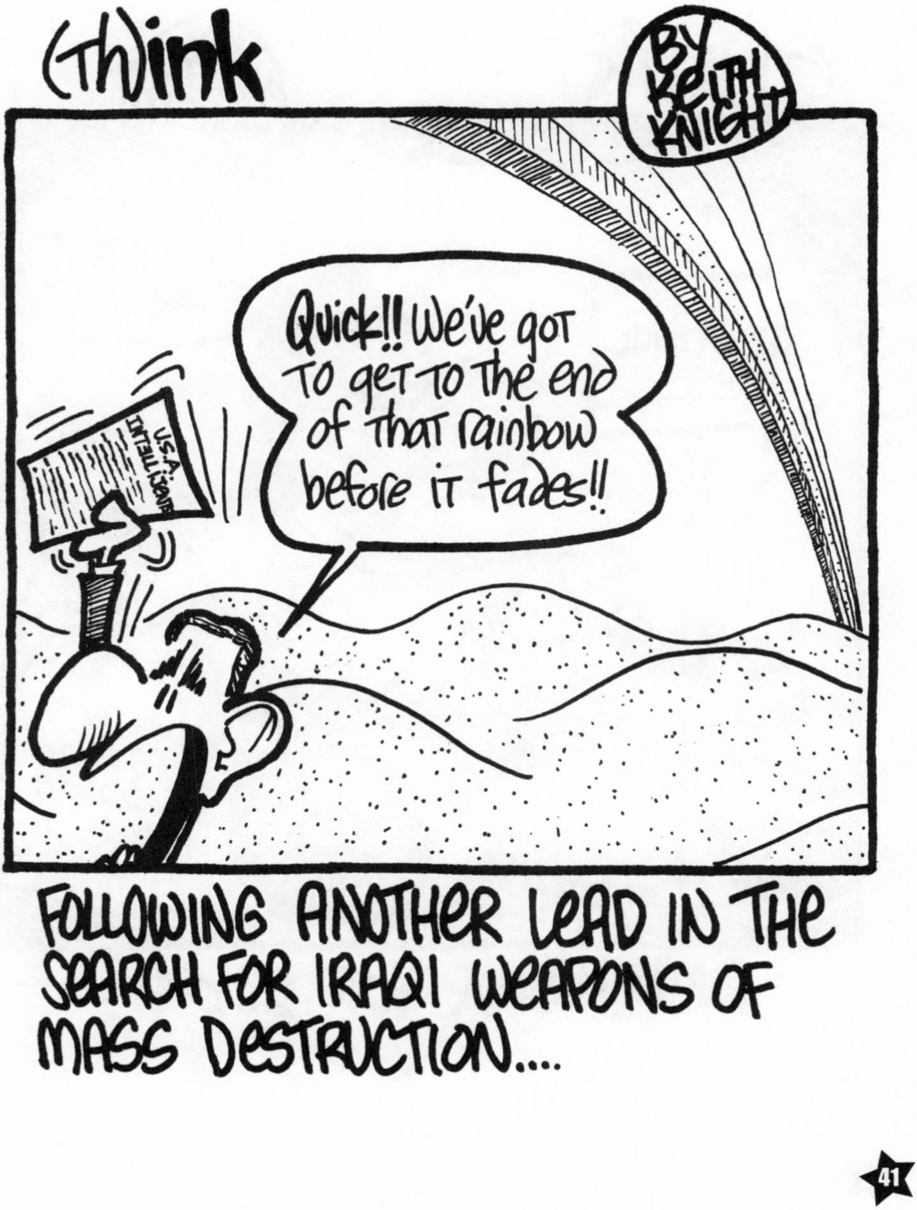
(TH)ink
BY KEITH KNIGHT
Quick!! We've got to get to the end of that rainbow before it fades!!
U.S.A.

FOLLOWING ANOTHER LEAD IN THE SEARCH FOR IRAQI WEAPONS OF MASS DESTRUCTION....

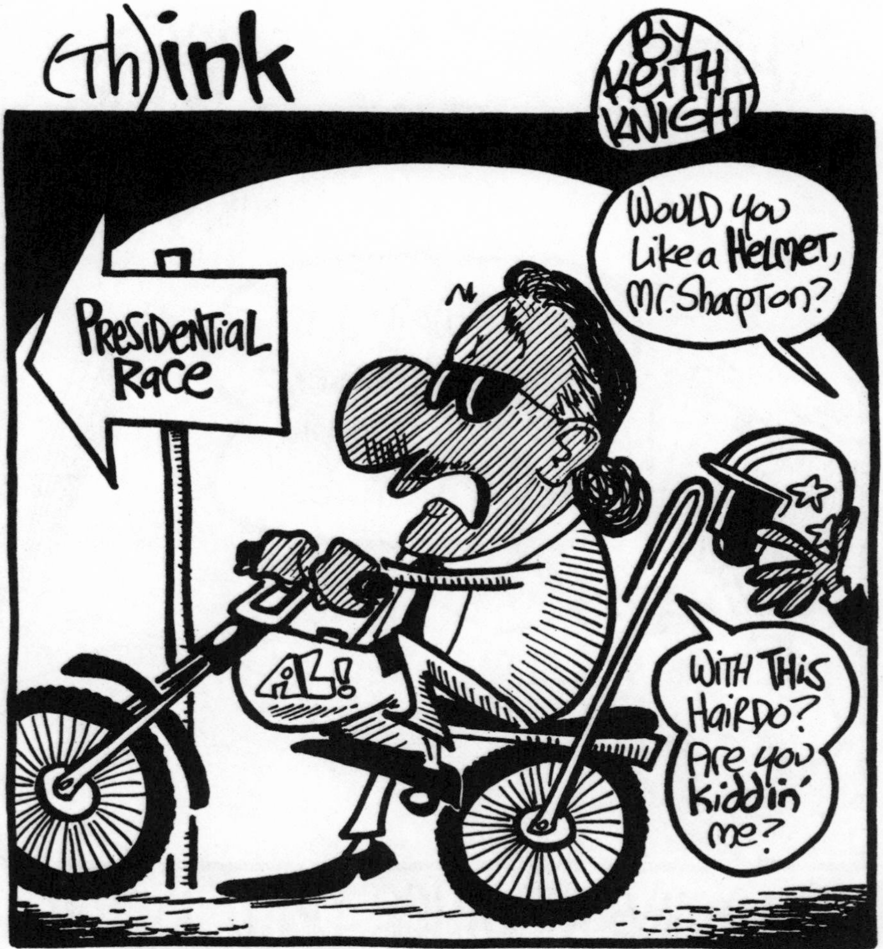
(Th)ink
BY KEITH KNIGHT
PRESIDENTIAL RACE
WOULD YOU LIKE A HELMET, MR. SHARPTON?
AL!
WITH THIS HAIRDO? ARE YOU KIDDIN' ME?

REV-VIN' UP FOR 2004

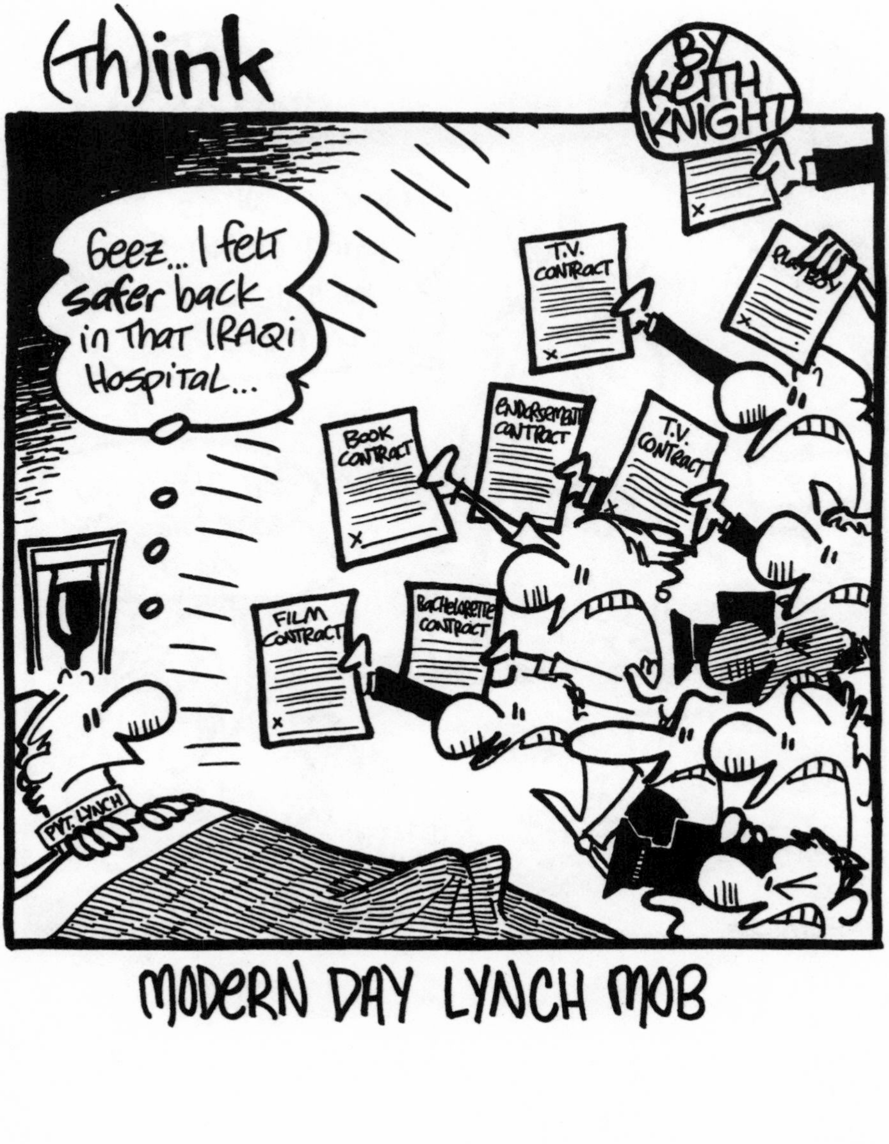
(th)ink
BY KEITH KNIGHT
Geez... I felt safer back in That IRAQi Hospital...
T.V. CONTRACT
PLAYBOY
ENDORSEMENT CONTRACT
BOOK CONTRACT
T.V. CONTRACT
FILM CONTRACT
BACHELORETTE CONTRACT
PVT. LYNCH

MODERN DAY LYNCH MOB

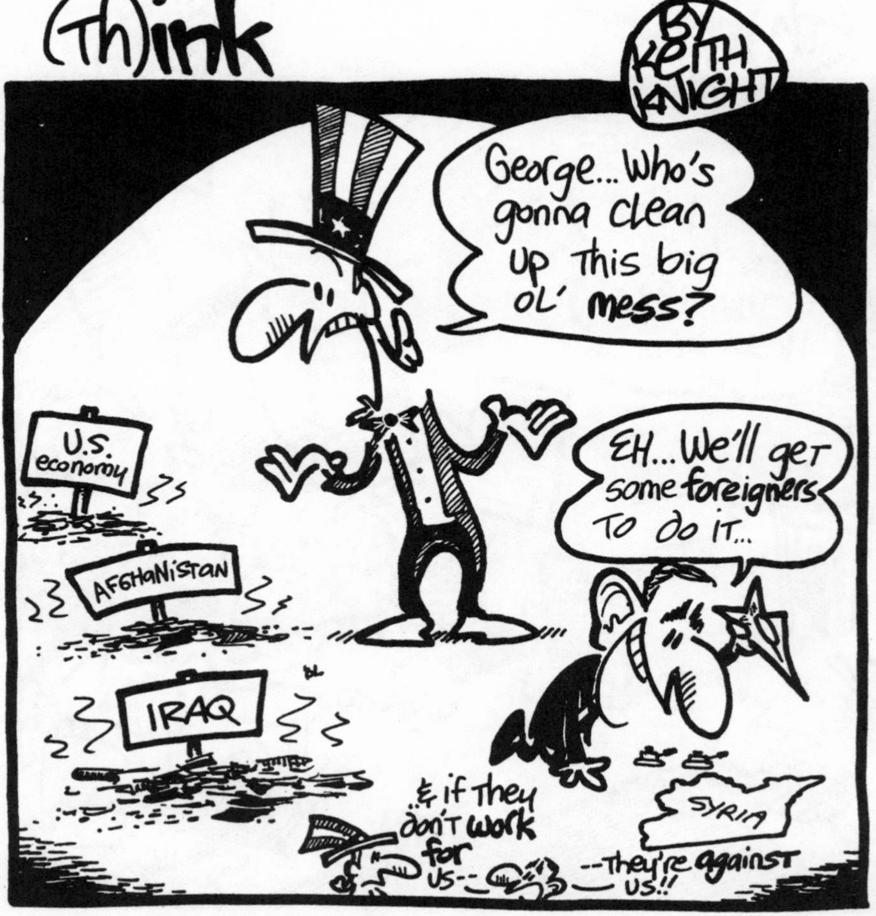
(Th)ink
BY KEITH KNIGHT
George... Who's gonna clean up this big ol' mess?
EH... We'll get some foreigners to do it...
U.S. economy
AFGHANISTAN
IRAQ
SYRIA
...& if they don't work for us--
--They're against us!!

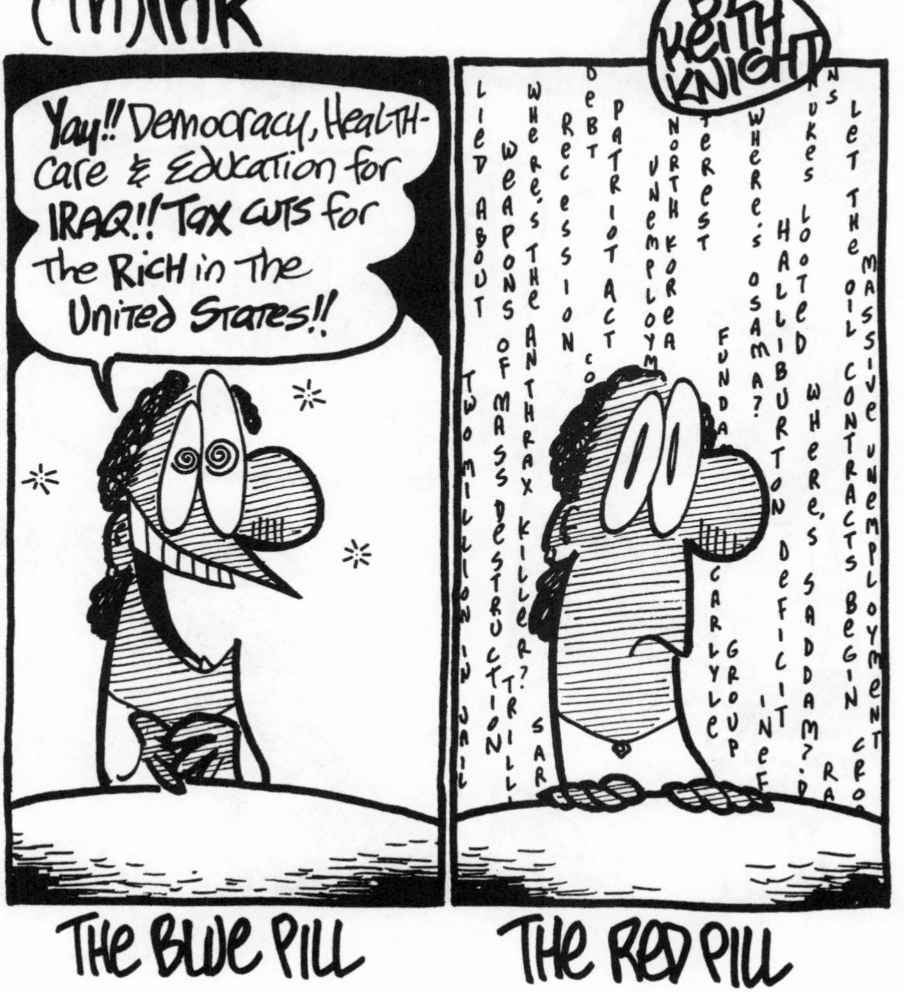
(TH)INK
BY KEITH KNIGHT
Yay!! Democracy, Health-care & Education for IRAQ!! Tax cuts for the Rich in the United States!!
THE BLUE PILL
LIED ABOUT
TWO MILLION IN JAIL
WEAPONS OF MASS DESTRUCTION
WHERE'S THE ANTHRAX KILLER?
RECESSION
DEBT
PATRIOT ACT
NORTH KOREA
WHERE'S OSAMA?
HALLIBURTON DEFICIT
NUKES LOOTED
WHERE'S SADDAM?
LET THE OIL CONTRACTS BEGIN
MASSIVE UNEMPLOYMENT
CARLYLE GROUP
THE RED PILL

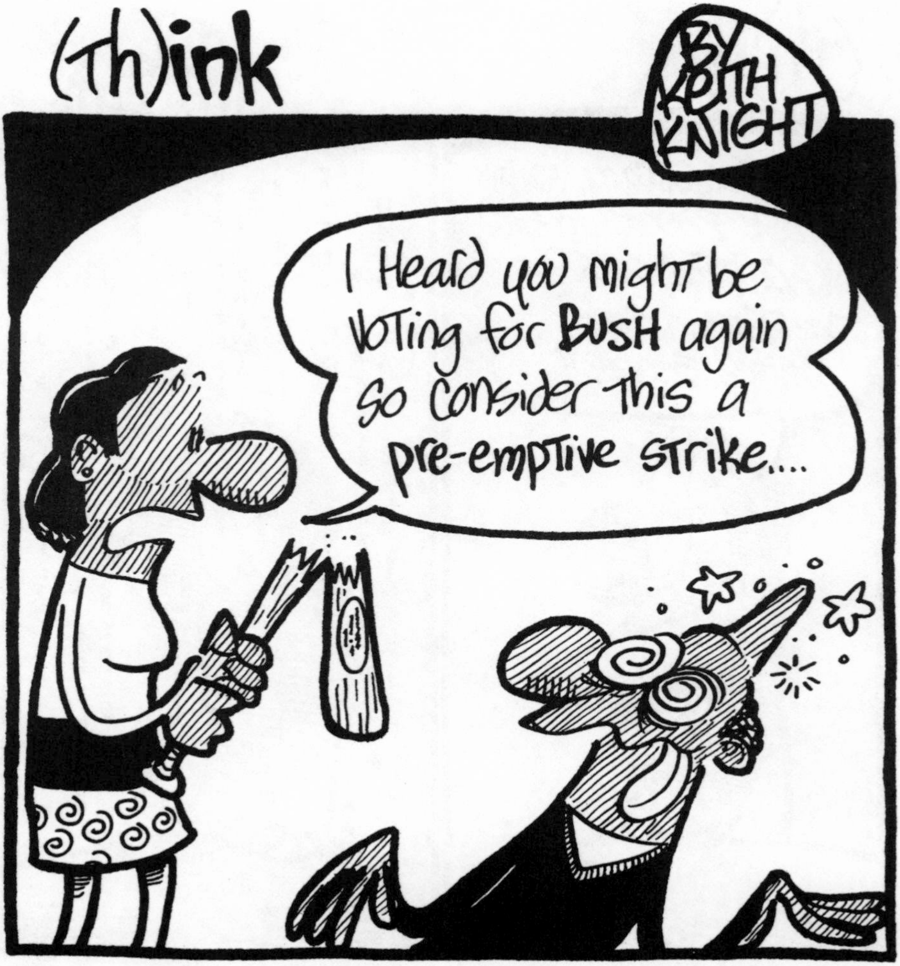
(th)ink
BY KEITH KNIGHT
I Heard you might be voting for BUSH again so consider this a pre-emptive strike....

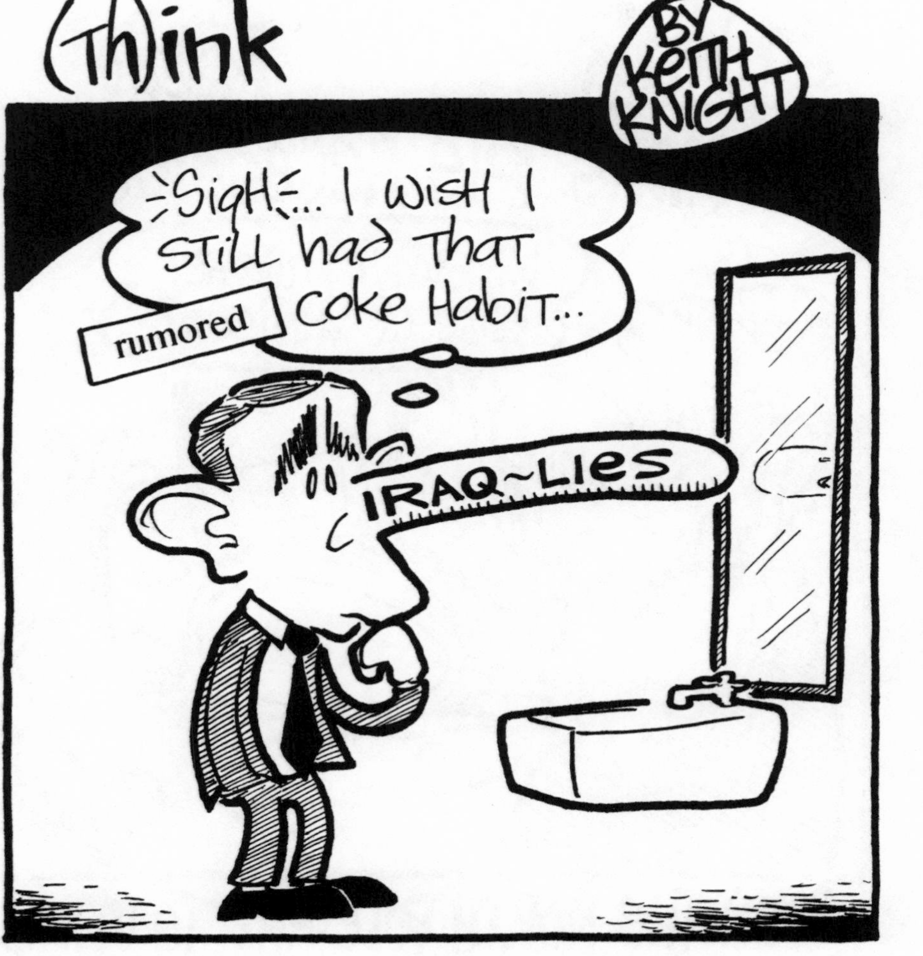
(Th)ink
BY KEITH KNIGHT
SIGH... I WISH I STILL HAD THAT rumored COKE HABIT...
IRAQ~LIES

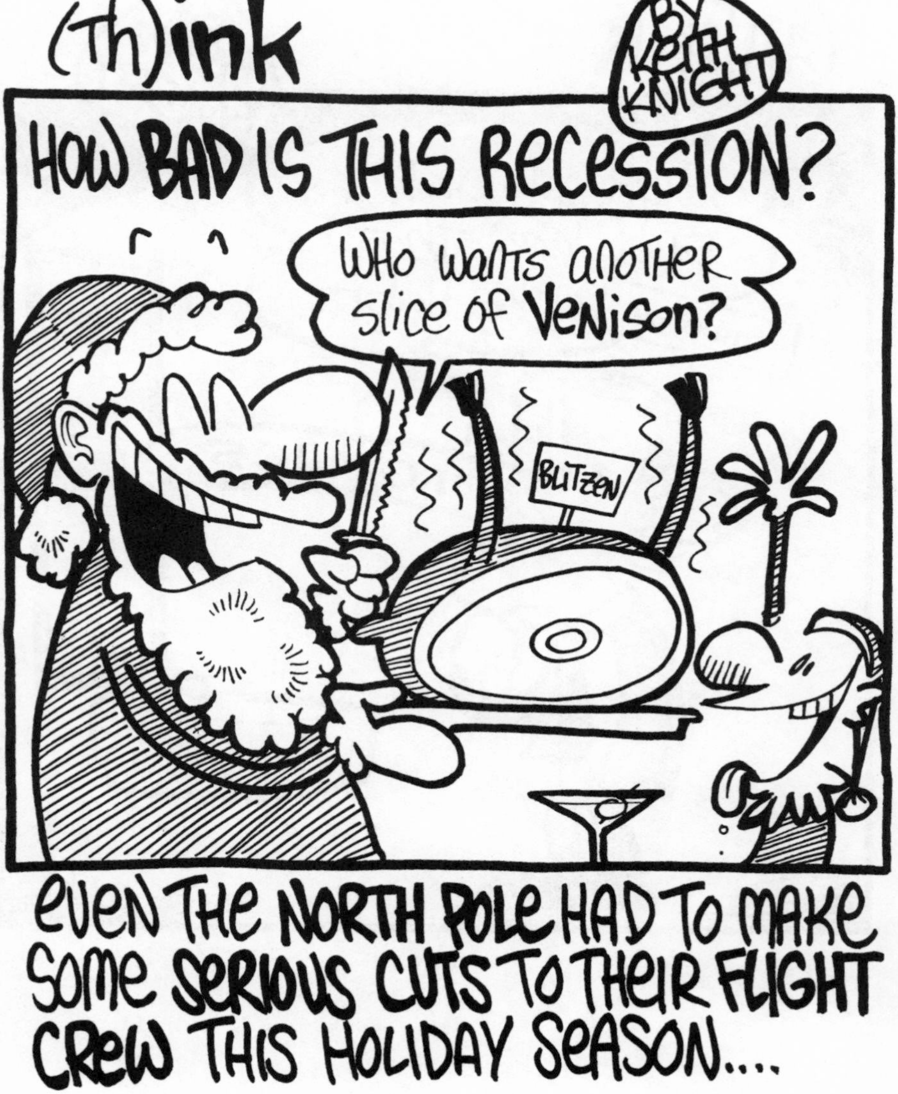
(Th)ink
BY KEITH KNIGHT
HOW BAD IS THIS RECESSION?
WHO WANTS ANOTHER slice of VENISON?
BLITZEN
EVEN THE NORTH POLE HAD TO MAKE SOME SERIOUS CUTS TO THEIR FLIGHT CREW THIS HOLIDAY SEASON....

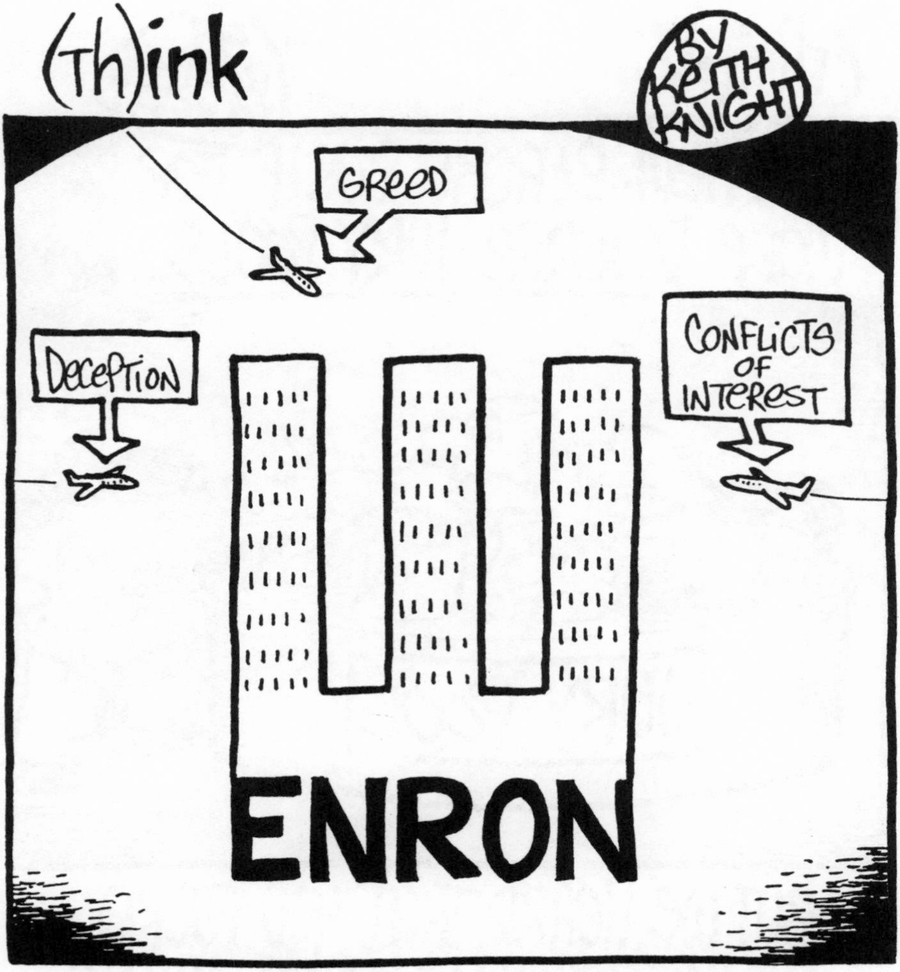
(TH)ink
BY KEITH KNIGHT
GREED
DECEPTION
CONFLICTS OF INTEREST
ENRON

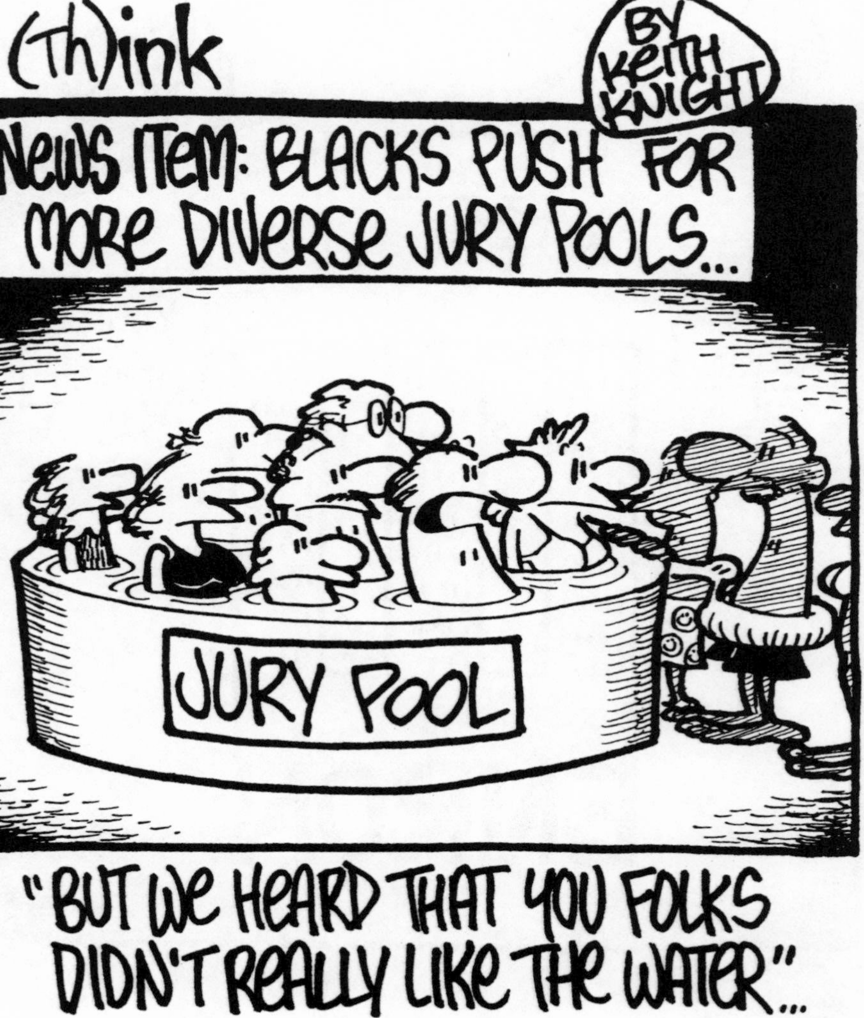
(Th)ink
BY KEITH KNIGHT
NEWS ITEM: BLACKS PUSH FOR MORE DIVERSE JURY POOLS...
JURY POOL
"BUT WE HEARD THAT YOU FOLKS DIDN'T REALLY LIKE THE WATER"...

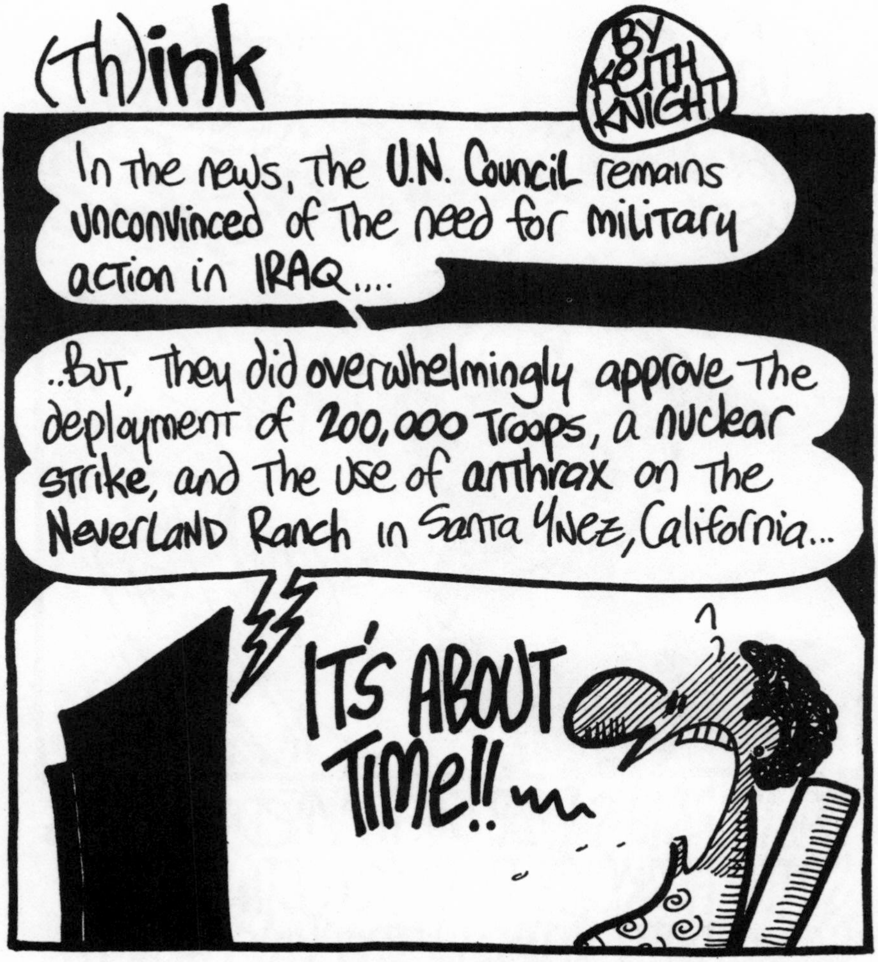
(Th)ink
By Keith Knight
In the news, the U.N. Council remains unconvinced of the need for military action in IRAQ....
..But, they did overwhelmingly approve the deployment of 200,000 troops, a nuclear strike, and the use of anthrax on the Neverland Ranch in Santa Ynez, California...
IT'S ABOUT TIME!!

(Th)ink

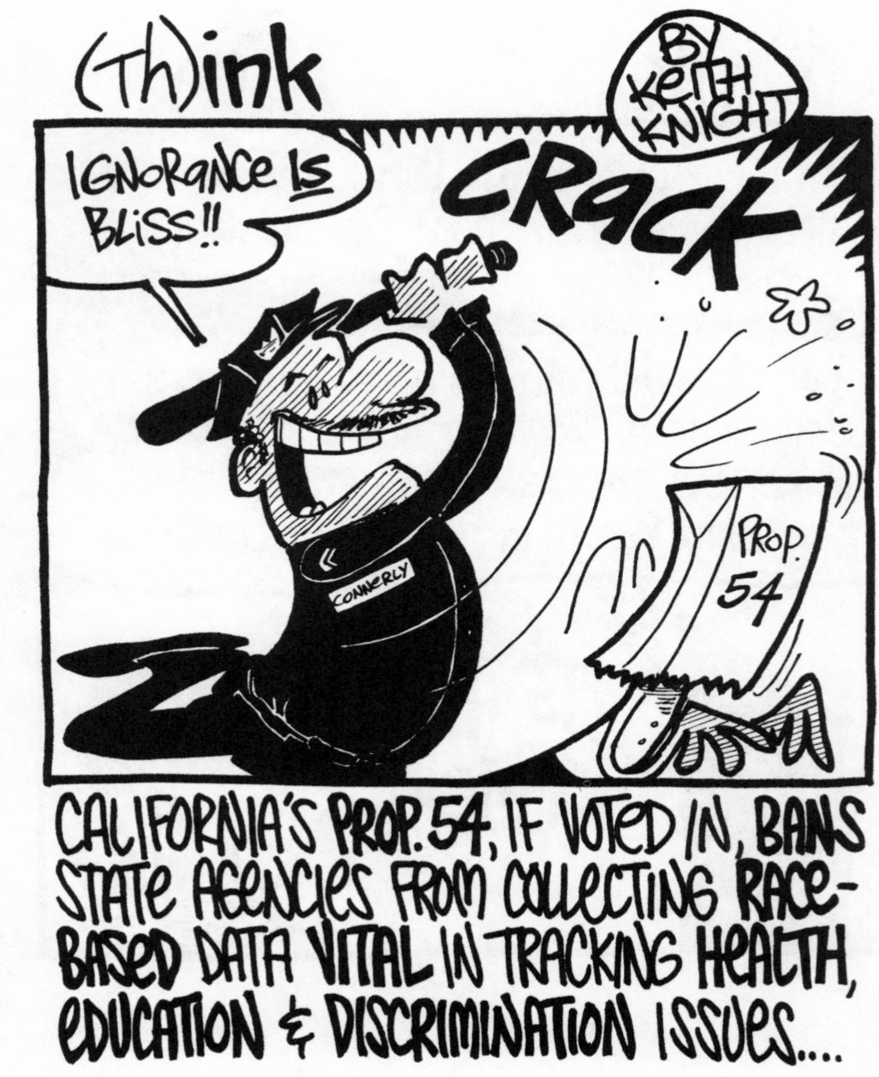
BY KEITH KNIGHT
IGNORANCE IS BLISS!!
CRACK
CONNERLY
PROP. 54

CALIFORNIA'S **PROP. 54**, IF VOTED IN, **BANS** STATE AGENCIES FROM COLLECTING **RACE-BASED** DATA **VITAL** IN TRACKING **HEALTH**, **EDUCATION** & **DISCRIMINATION** ISSUES....

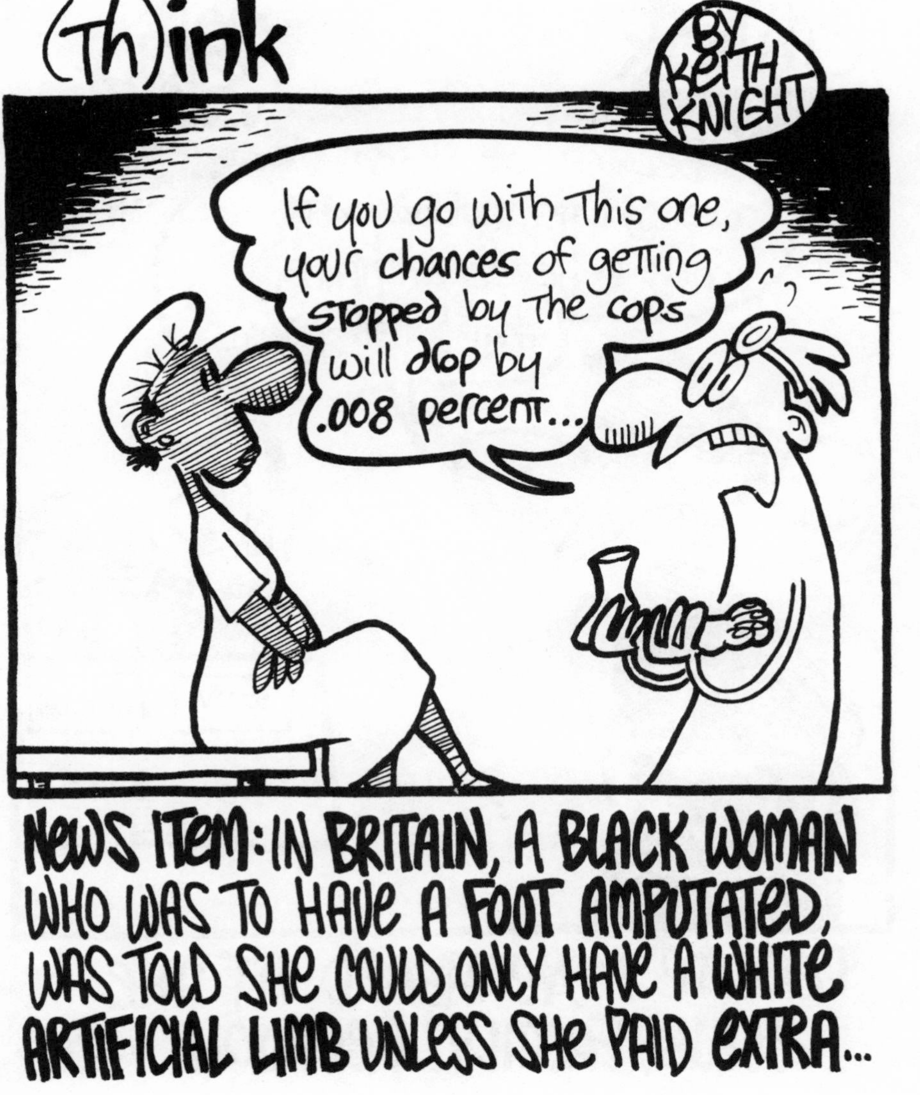
(Th)ink
By Keith Knight
If you go with This one, your chances of getting stopped by The cops will drop by .008 percent...
NEWS ITEM: IN BRITAIN, A BLACK WOMAN WHO WAS TO HAVE A FOOT AMPUTATED, WAS TOLD SHE COULD ONLY HAVE A WHITE ARTIFICIAL LIMB UNLESS SHE PAID EXTRA...

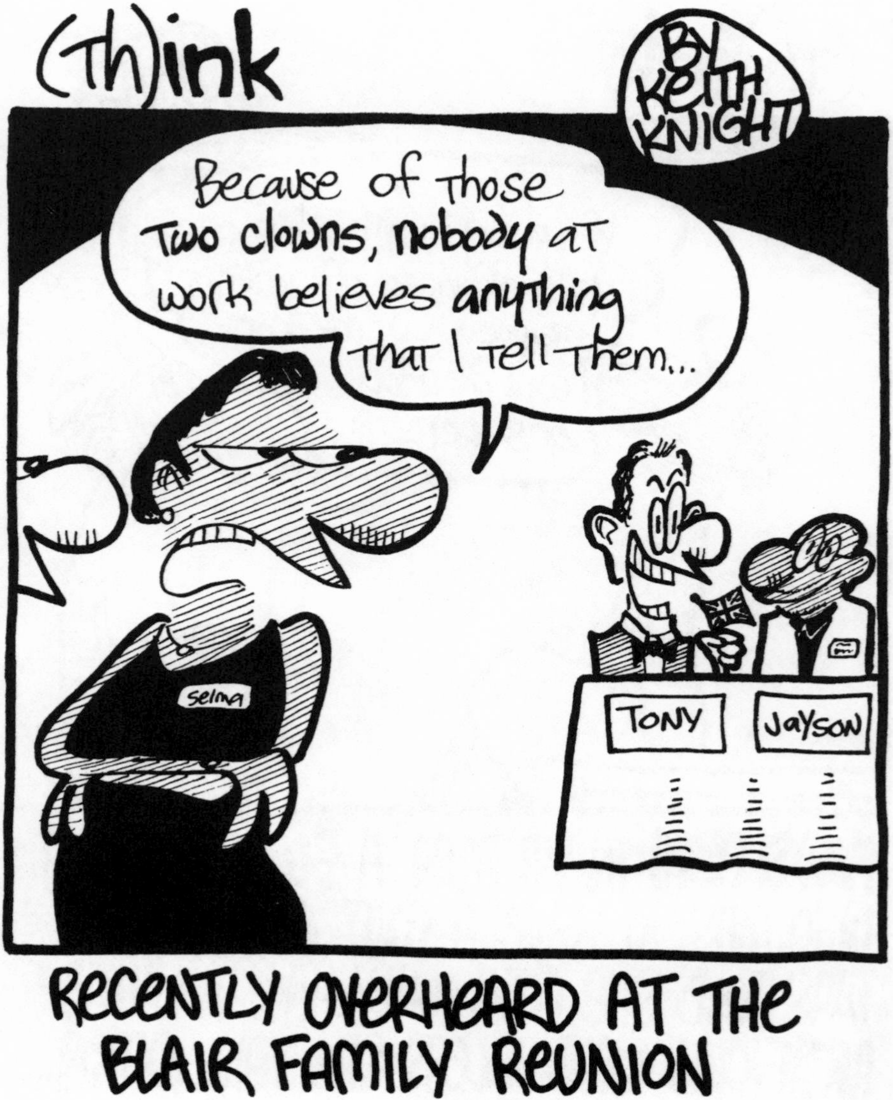
(Th)ink
BY KEITH KNIGHT
Because of those Two clowns, nobody at work believes anything that I tell Them...
selma
TONY
JAYSON

RECENTLY OVERHEARD AT THE BLAIR FAMILY REUNION

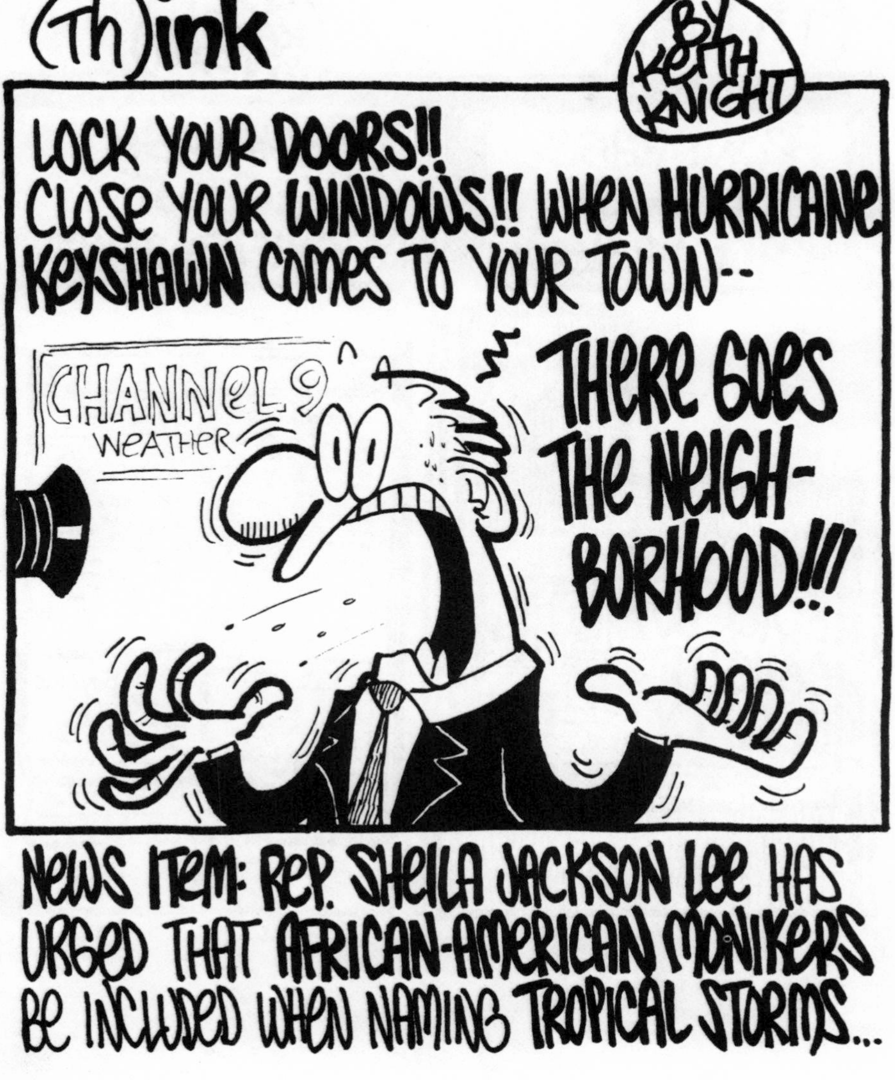
(Th)ink
BY KEITH KNIGHT
LOCK YOUR DOORS!! CLOSE YOUR WINDOWS!! WHEN HURRICANE KEYSHAWN COMES TO YOUR TOWN--
CHANNEL 9 WEATHER
THERE GOES THE NEIGH-BORHOOD!!!
NEWS ITEM: REP. SHEILA JACKSON LEE HAS URGED THAT AFRICAN-AMERICAN MONIKERS BE INCLUDED WHEN NAMING TROPICAL STORMS...

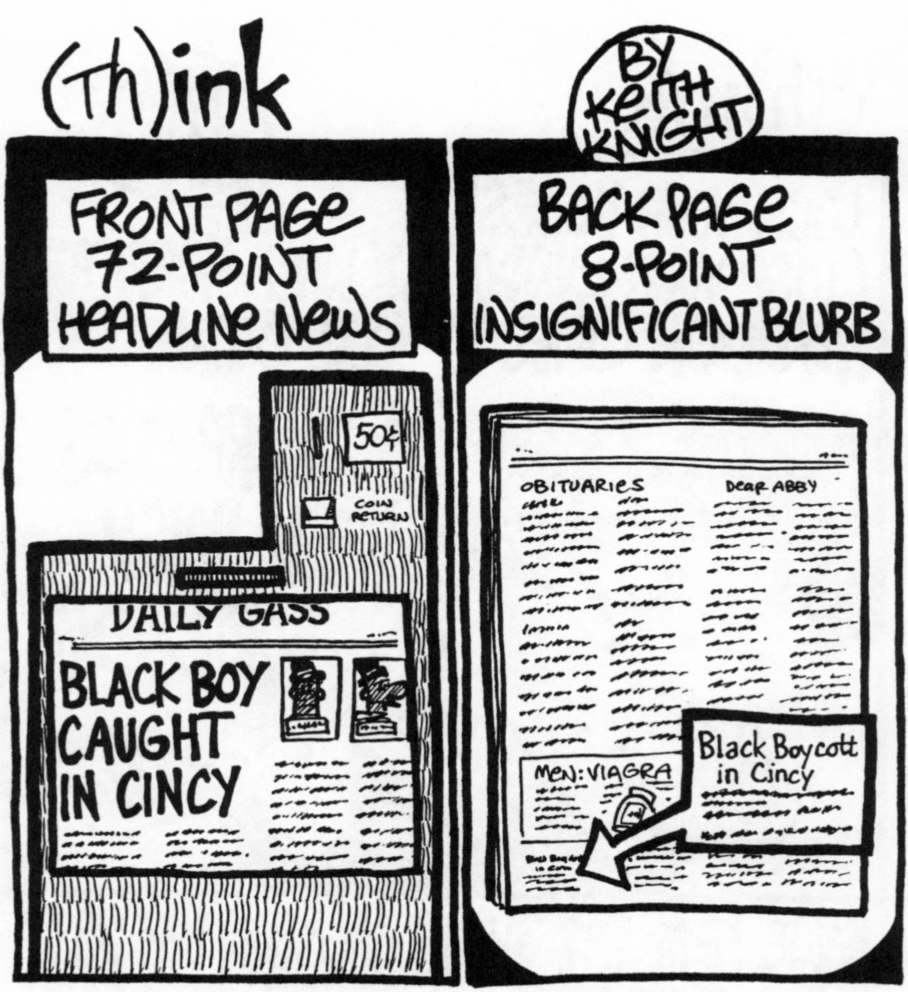
(Th)ink
BY Keith KNIGHT
FRONT PAGE 72-POINT HEADLINE NEWS
50¢
COIN RETURN
DAILY GASS
BLACK BOY CAUGHT IN CINCY
BACK PAGE 8-POINT INSIGNIFICANT BLURB
OBITUARIES
Dear ABBY
MEN: VIAGRA
Black Boycott in Cincy

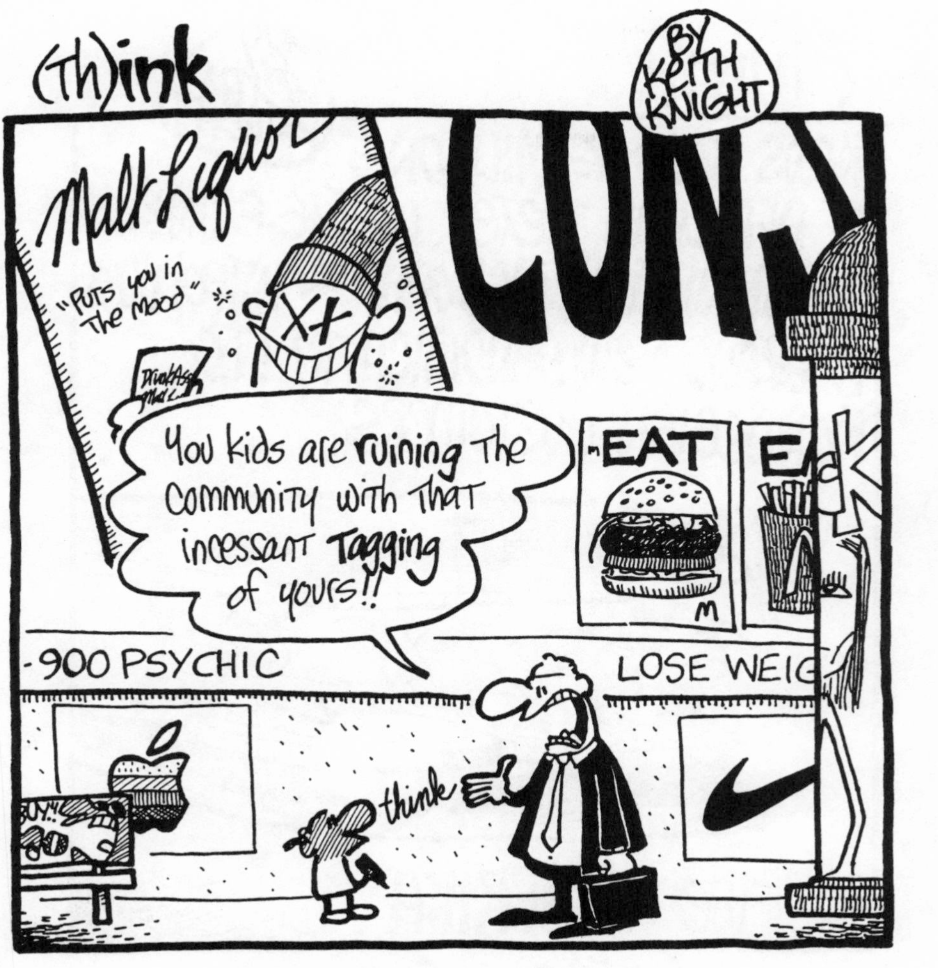

(Th)ink
BY KEITH KNIGHT
Malt Liquor
"PUTS you in The mood"
CON
You kids are ruining The community with That incessant Tagging of yours!!
EAT
-900 PSYCHIC
LOSE WEIG
think

(th)ink
BY KEITH KNIGHT
NEWS ITEM: AS MILLIONS OF AFRICANS TEETER ON THE BRINK OF STARVATION, McDONALDS INTRODUCES A BRAND NEW SANDWICH TO ITS NORWEGIAN CUSTOMERS....
THE McAFRIKA
McTASTELESS™

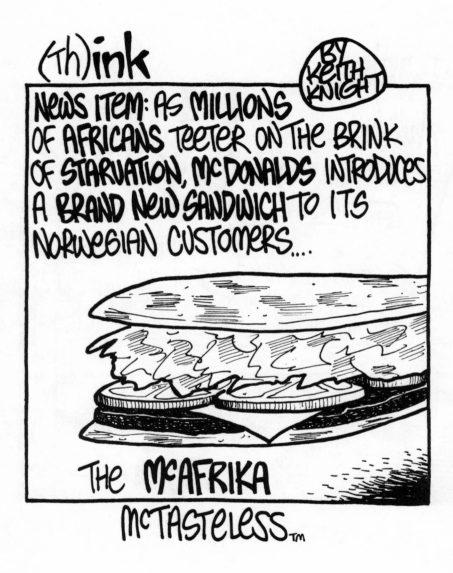

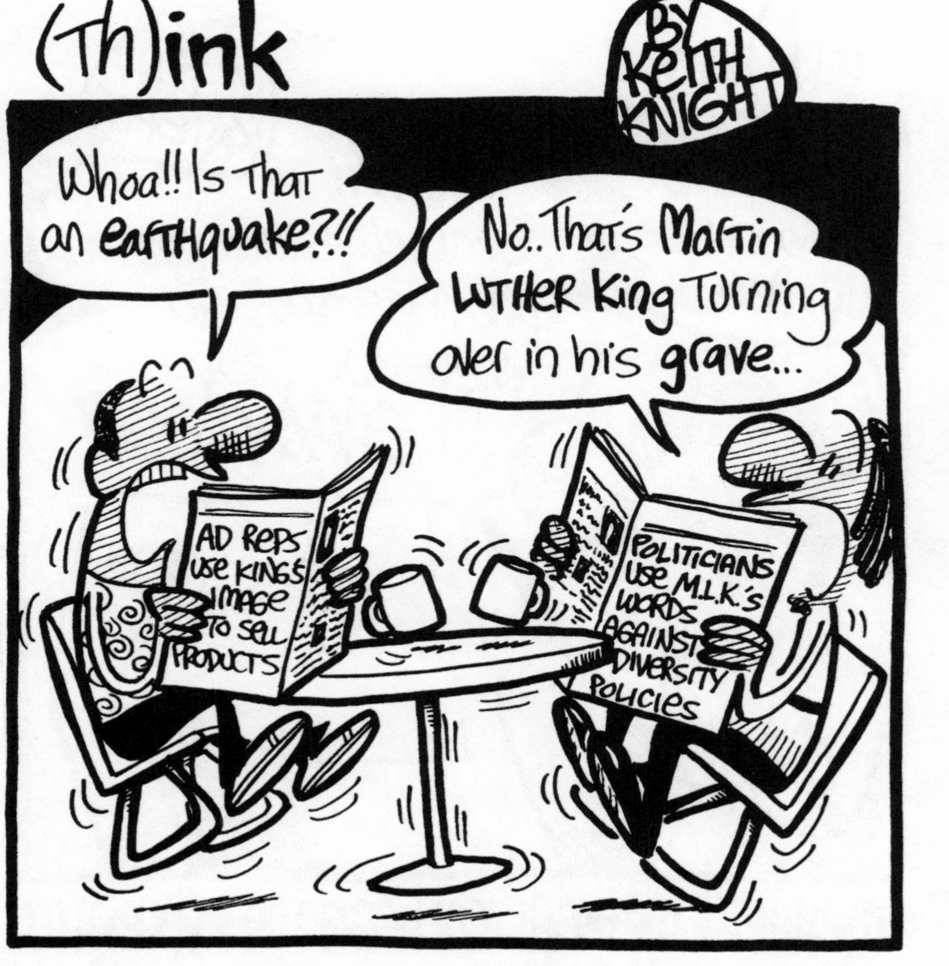
(Th)ink
BY KEITH KNIGHT
Whoa!! Is That an earthquake?!!
No.. That's Martin Luther King Turning over in his grave...
AD REPS USE KING'S IMAGE TO SELL PRODUCTS
POLITICIANS USE M.L.K.'S WORDS AGAINST DIVERSITY POLICIES

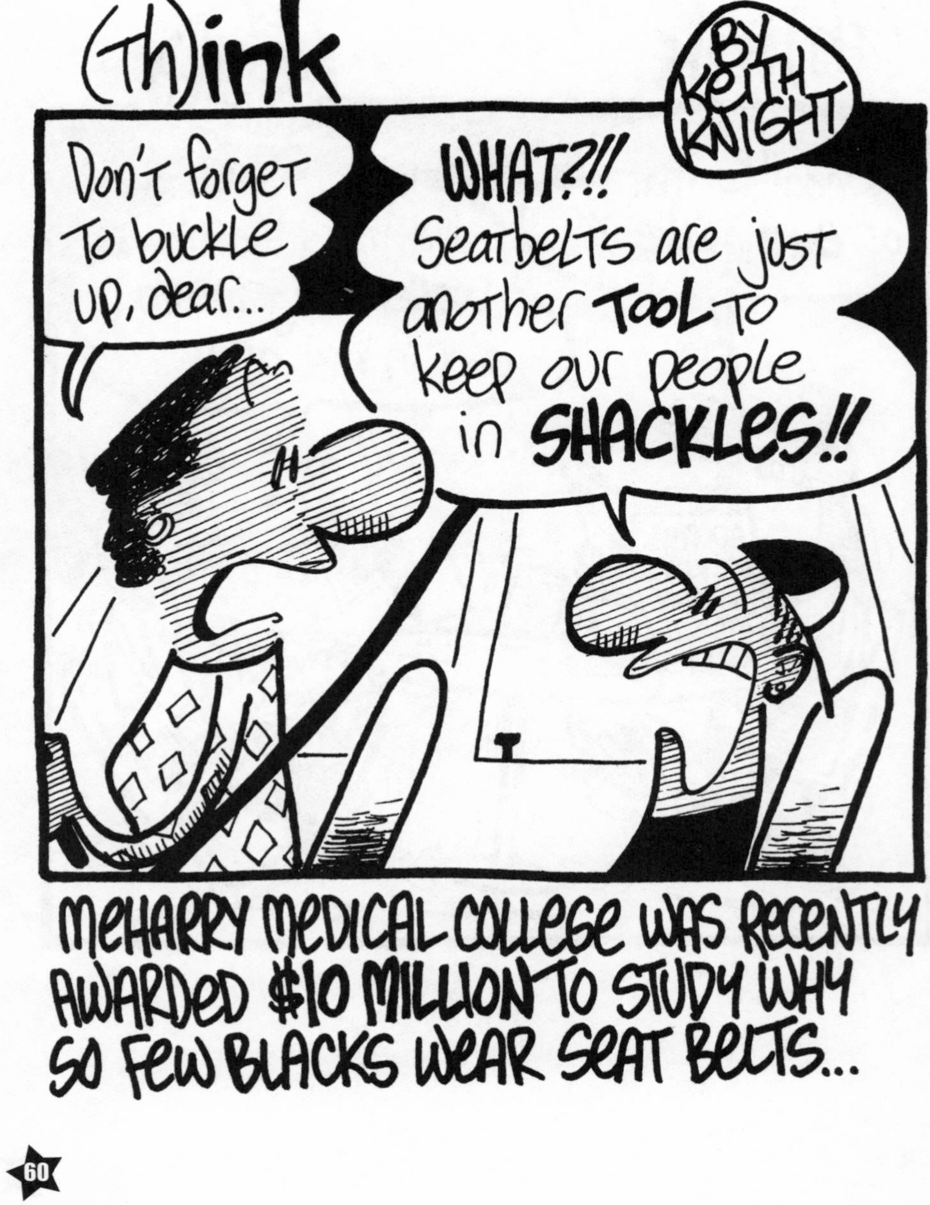
(th)ink
BY KEITH KNIGHT
Don't forget to buckle up, dear...
WHAT?!! Seatbelts are just another TOOL to keep our people in SHACKLES!!

MEHARRY MEDICAL COLLEGE WAS RECENTLY AWARDED $10 MILLION TO STUDY WHY SO FEW BLACKS WEAR SEAT BELTS...

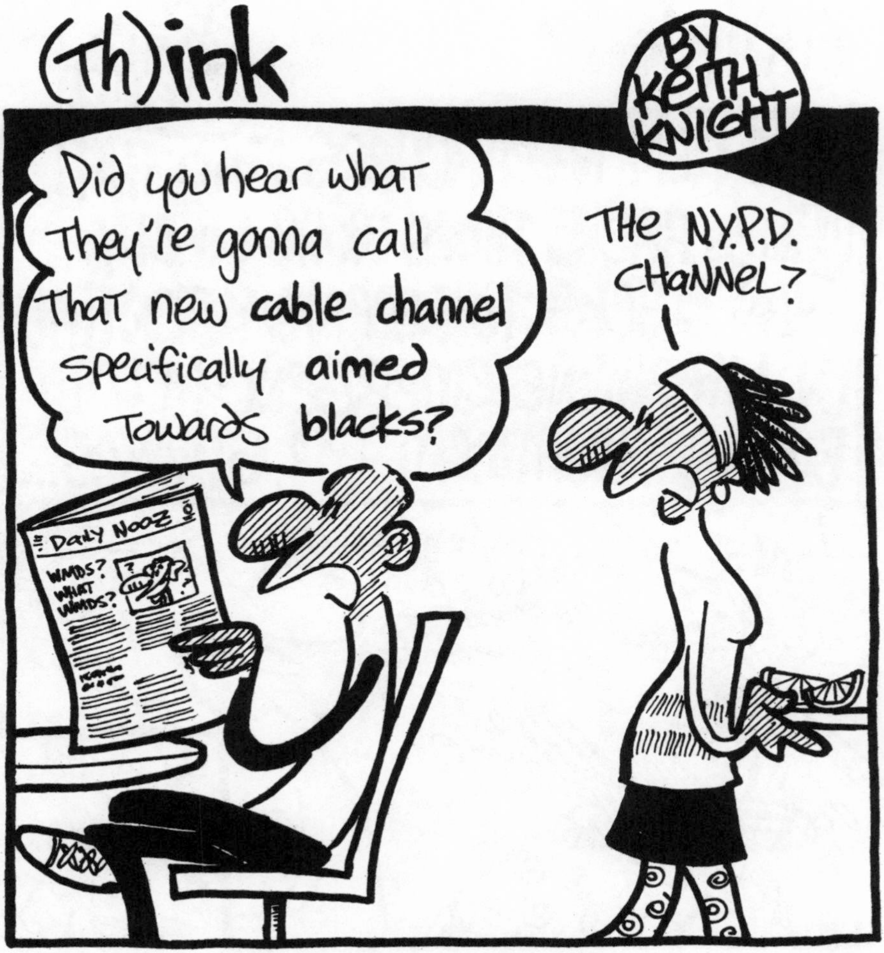
(Th)ink
BY KEITH KNIGHT
Did you hear what they're gonna call that new cable channel specifically aimed towards blacks?
THE N.Y.P.D. CHANNEL?
Daily Nooz
WMDS? WHAT WMDS?

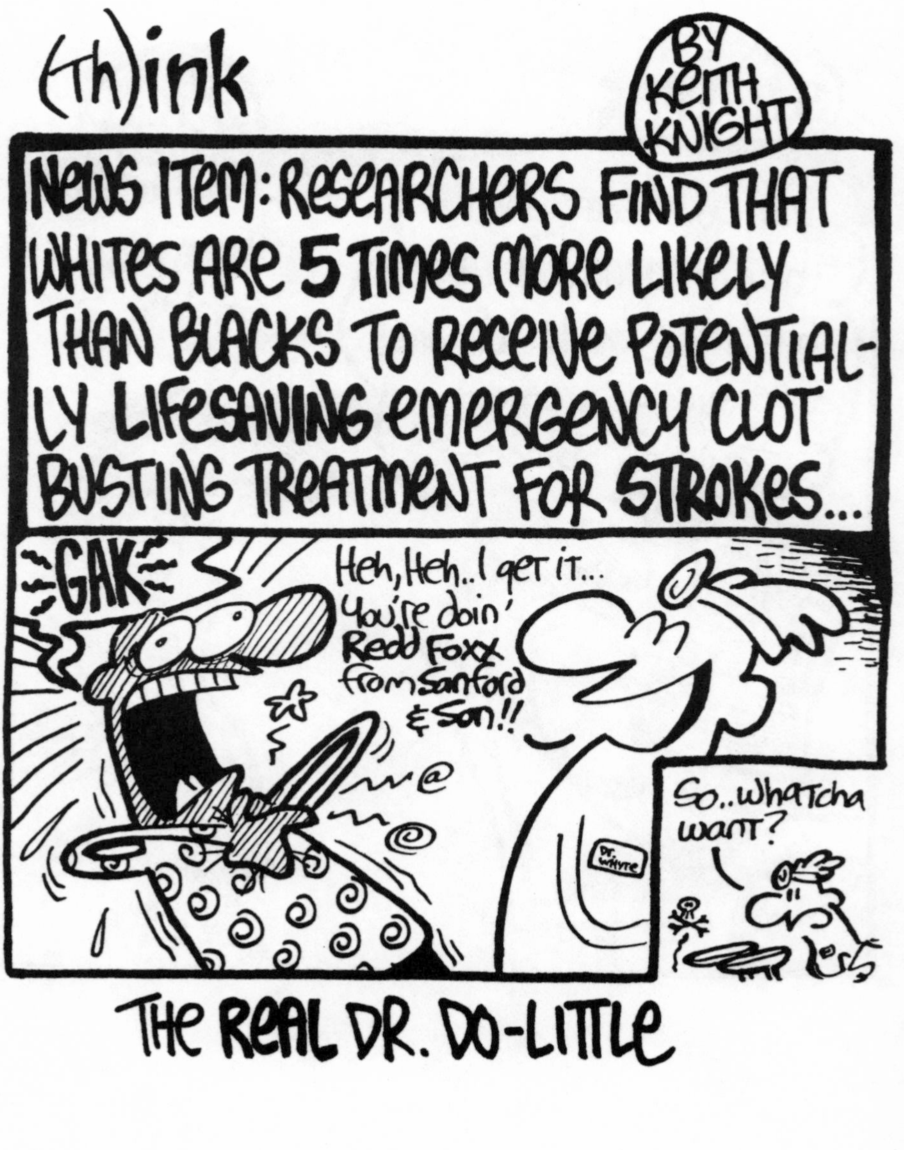
(th)ink
BY KEITH KNIGHT
NEWS ITEM: RESEARCHERS FIND THAT WHITES ARE 5 TIMES MORE LIKELY THAN BLACKS TO RECEIVE POTENTIAL-LY LIFESAVING EMERGENCY CLOT BUSTING TREATMENT FOR STROKES...
GAK
Heh, Heh.. I get it... You're doin' Redd Foxx from Sanford & Son!!
DR. WHYTE
So.. whatcha want?
THE REAL DR. DO-LITTLE

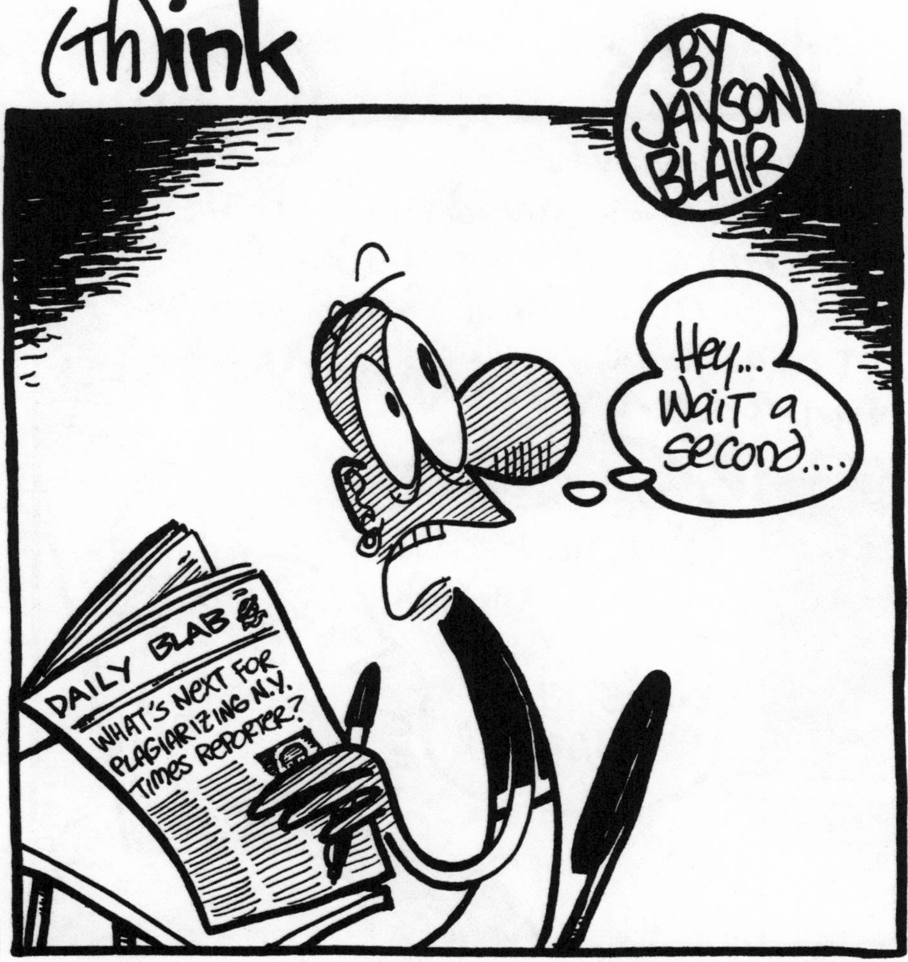
(Th)ink
BY JAYSON BLAIR
Hey... Wait a second....
DAILY BLAB
WHAT'S NEXT FOR PLAGIARIZING N.Y. TIMES REPORTER?

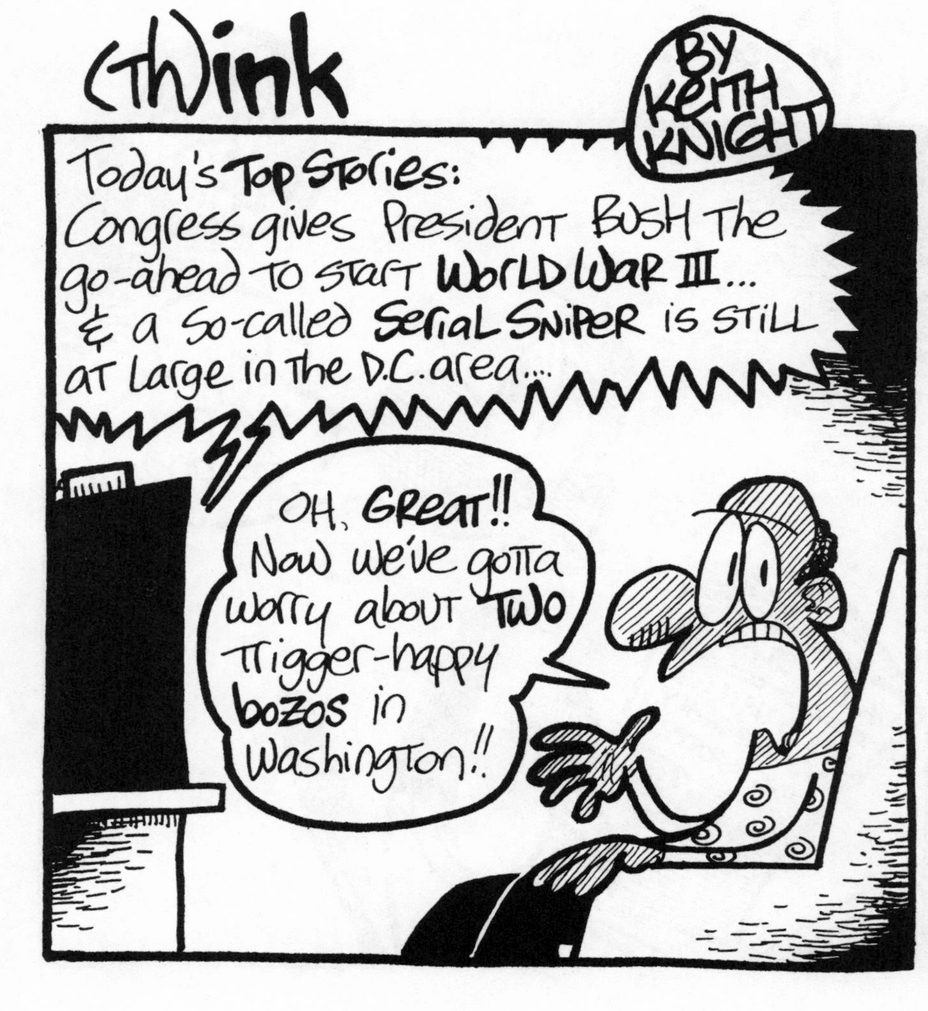
(TH)ink
BY KEITH KNIGHT
Today's TOP STORIES:
Congress gives President BUSH the go-ahead to start WORLD WAR III...
& a so-called SERIAL SNIPER is still at large in the D.C. area....
OH, GREAT!! Now we've gotta worry about TWO trigger-happy bozos in Washington!!

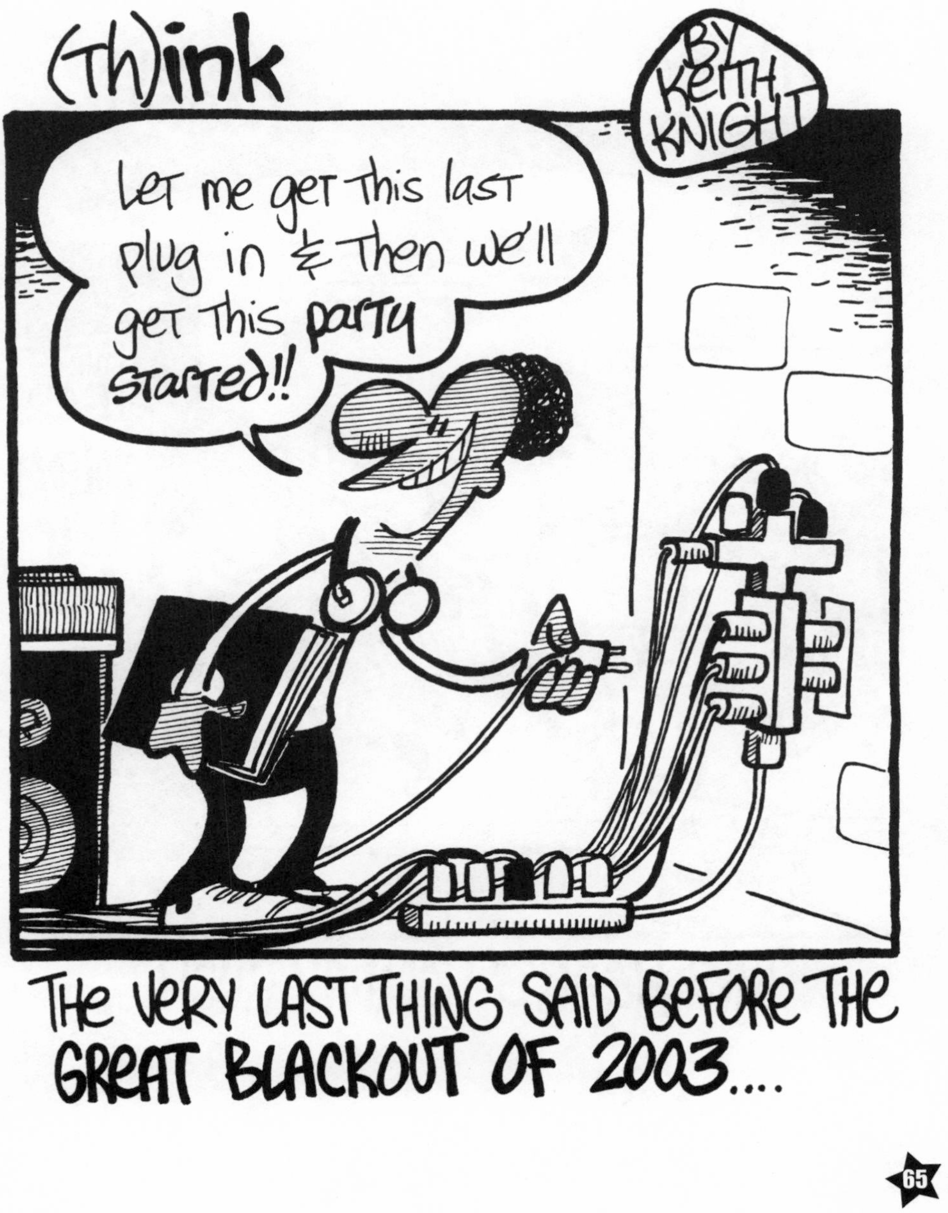
(Th)ink
By Keith Knight
Let me get This last plug in & Then we'll get This party started!!

THE VERY LAST THING SAID BEFORE THE GREAT BLACKOUT OF 2003....

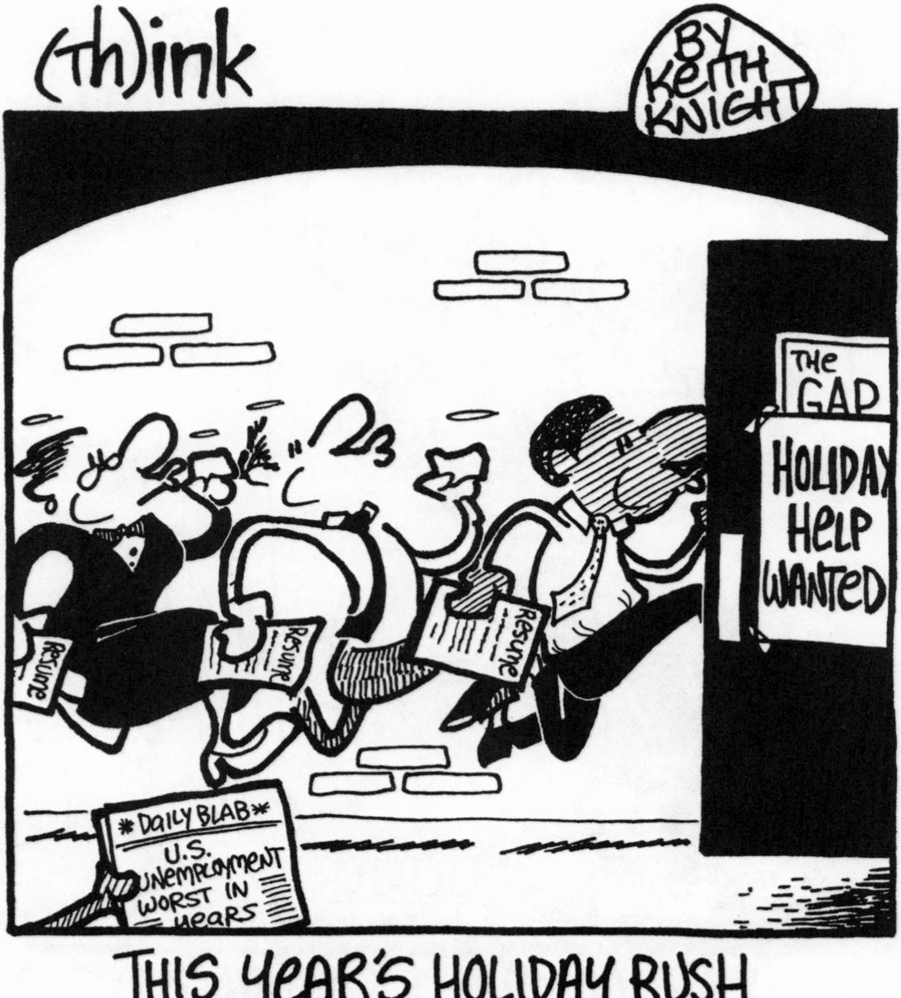
(th)ink
BY KEITH KNIGHT
THE GAP
HOLIDAY HELP WANTED
RESUME
RESUME
RESUME
* DAILY BLAB *
U.S. UNEMPLOYMENT WORST IN YEARS

THIS YEAR'S HOLIDAY RUSH

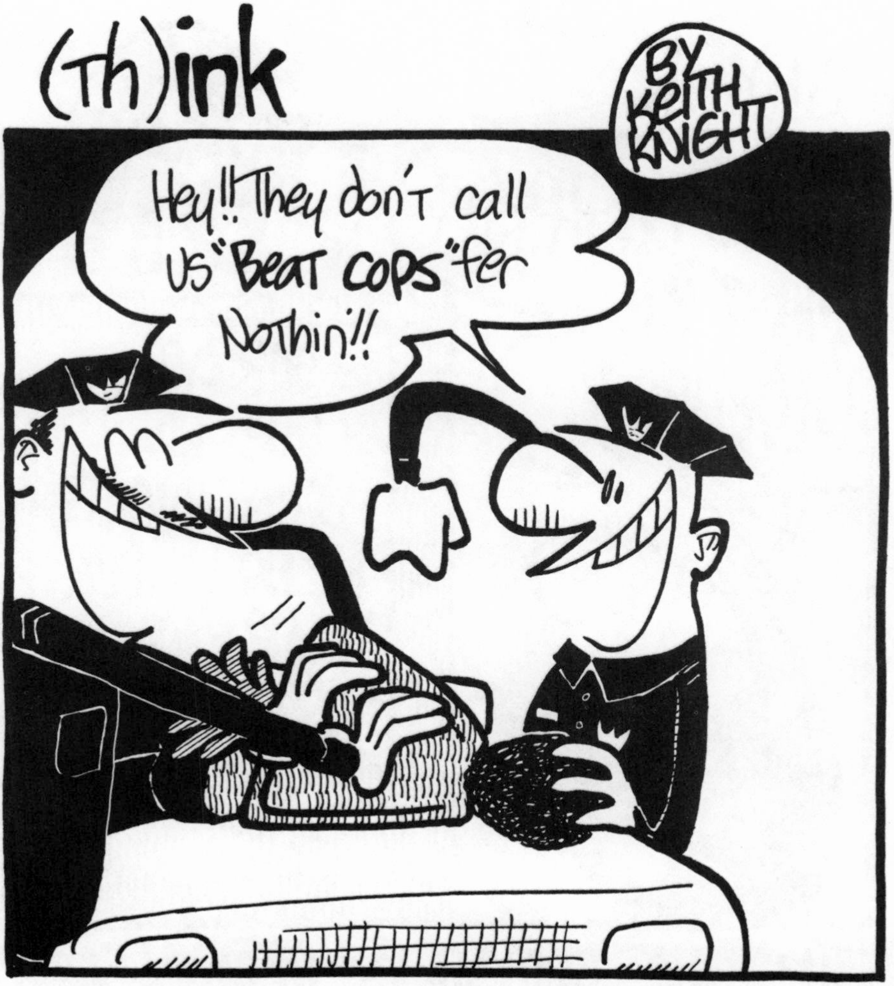
(Th)ink
By Keith Knight
Hey!! They don't call us "Beat cops" fer Nothin'!!

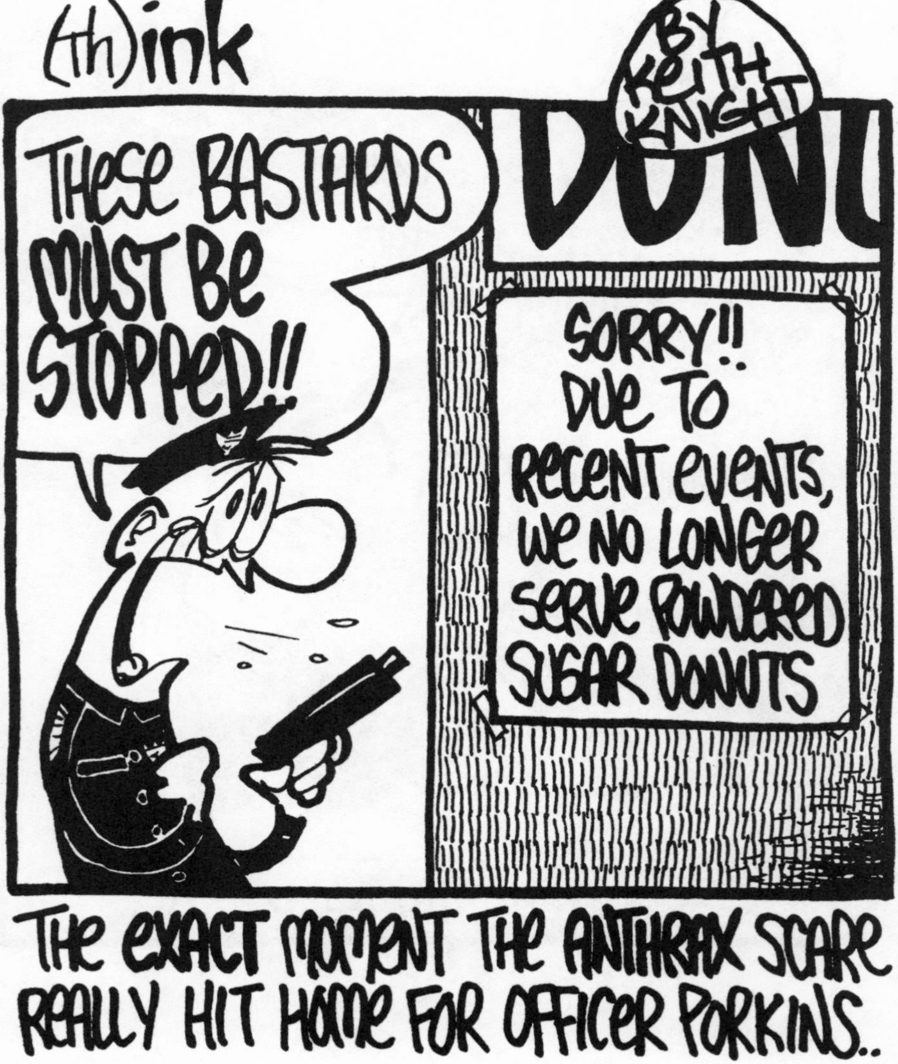
(th)ink
BY KEITH KNIGHT
THESE BASTARDS MUST BE STOPPED!!
DONU
SORRY!! DUE TO RECENT EVENTS, WE NO LONGER SERVE POWDERED SUGAR DONUTS
THE EXACT MOMENT THE ANTHRAX SCARE REALLY HIT HOME FOR OFFICER PORKINS..

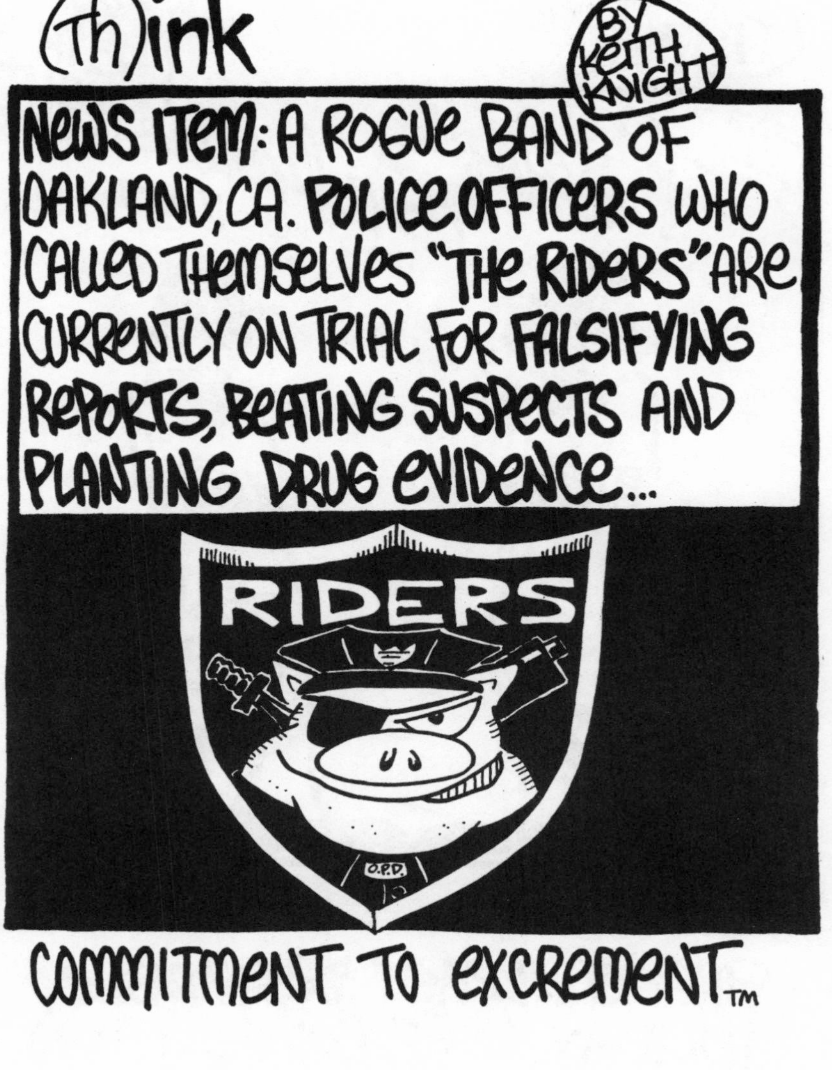
(th)ink
BY KEITH KNIGHT
NEWS ITEM: A ROGUE BAND OF OAKLAND, CA. POLICE OFFICERS WHO CALLED THEMSELVES "THE RIDERS" ARE CURRENTLY ON TRIAL FOR FALSIFYING REPORTS, BEATING SUSPECTS AND PLANTING DRUG EVIDENCE...
RIDERS
O.P.D.
COMMITMENT TO EXCREMENT™

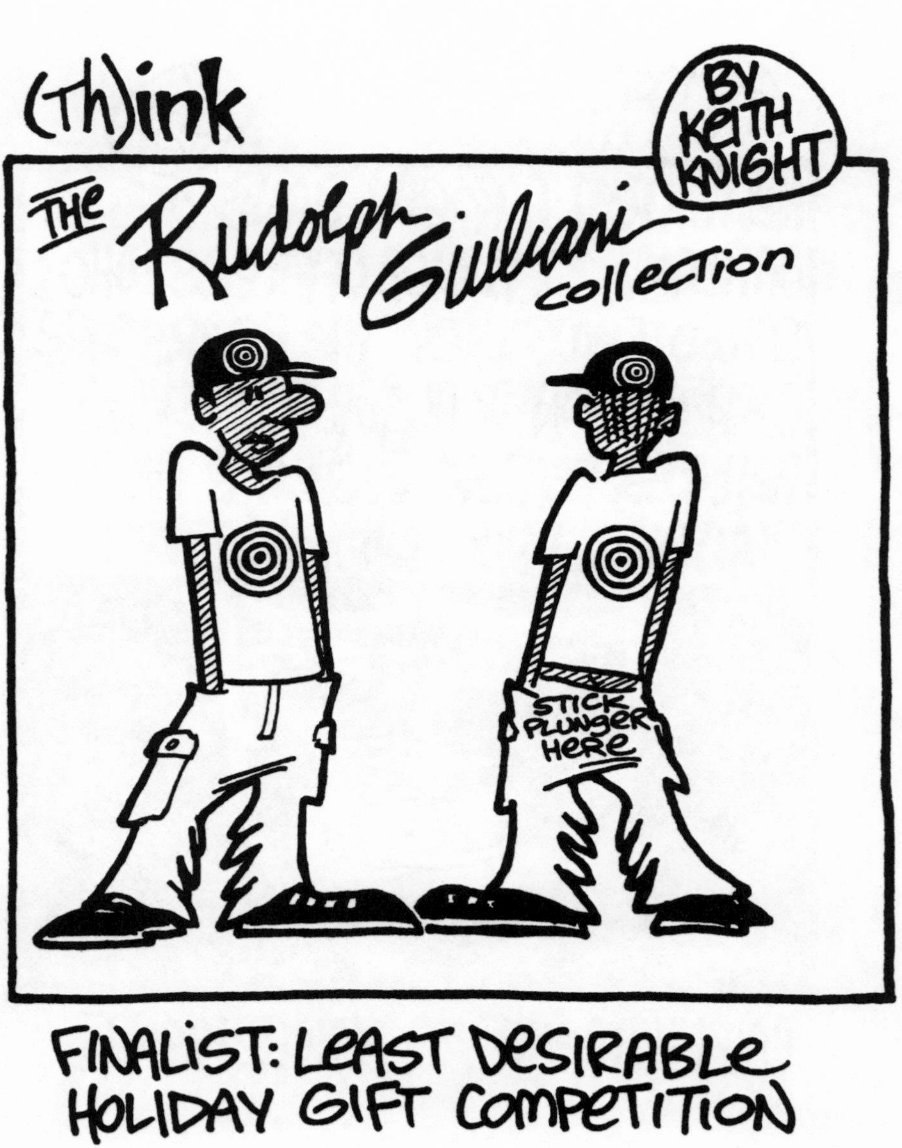
(Th)ink
BY KEITH KNIGHT
THE Rudolph Giuliani collection
STICK PLUNGER HERE
FINALIST: LEAST DESIRABLE HOLIDAY GIFT COMPETITION

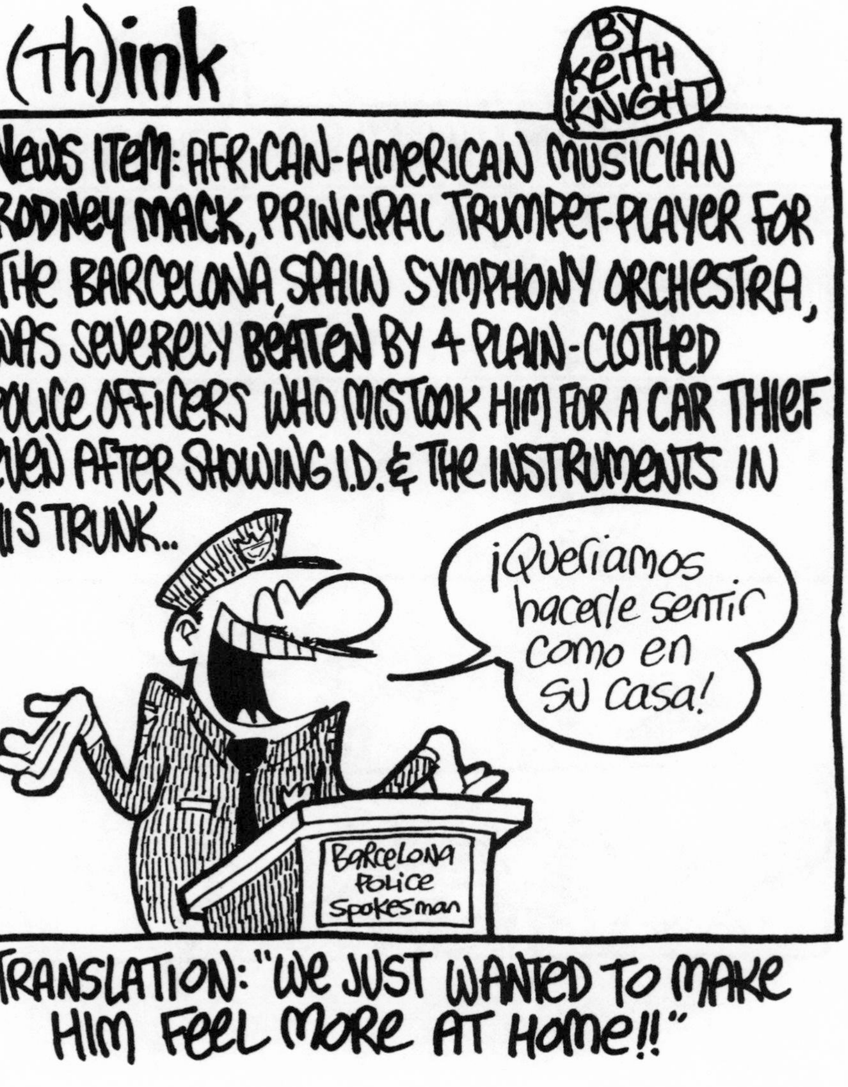
(Th)ink
By Keith Knight
News Item: African-American musician Rodney Mack, principal trumpet-player for the Barcelona, Spain symphony orchestra, was severely beaten by 4 plain-clothed police officers who mistook him for a car thief even after showing I.D. & the instruments in his trunk...
¡Queriamos hacerle sentir como en su casa!
Barcelona Police Spokesman
Translation: "We just wanted to make him feel more at home!!"

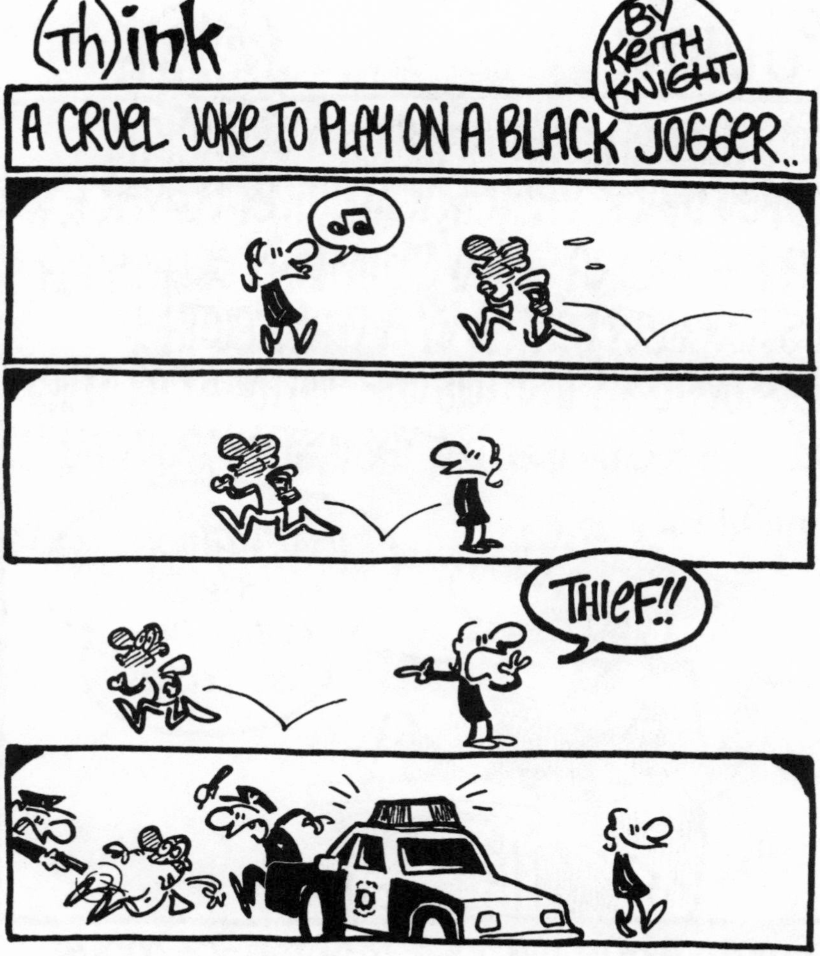
(th)ink
BY KEITH KNIGHT
A CRUEL JOKE TO PLAY ON A BLACK JOGGER..
THIEF!!

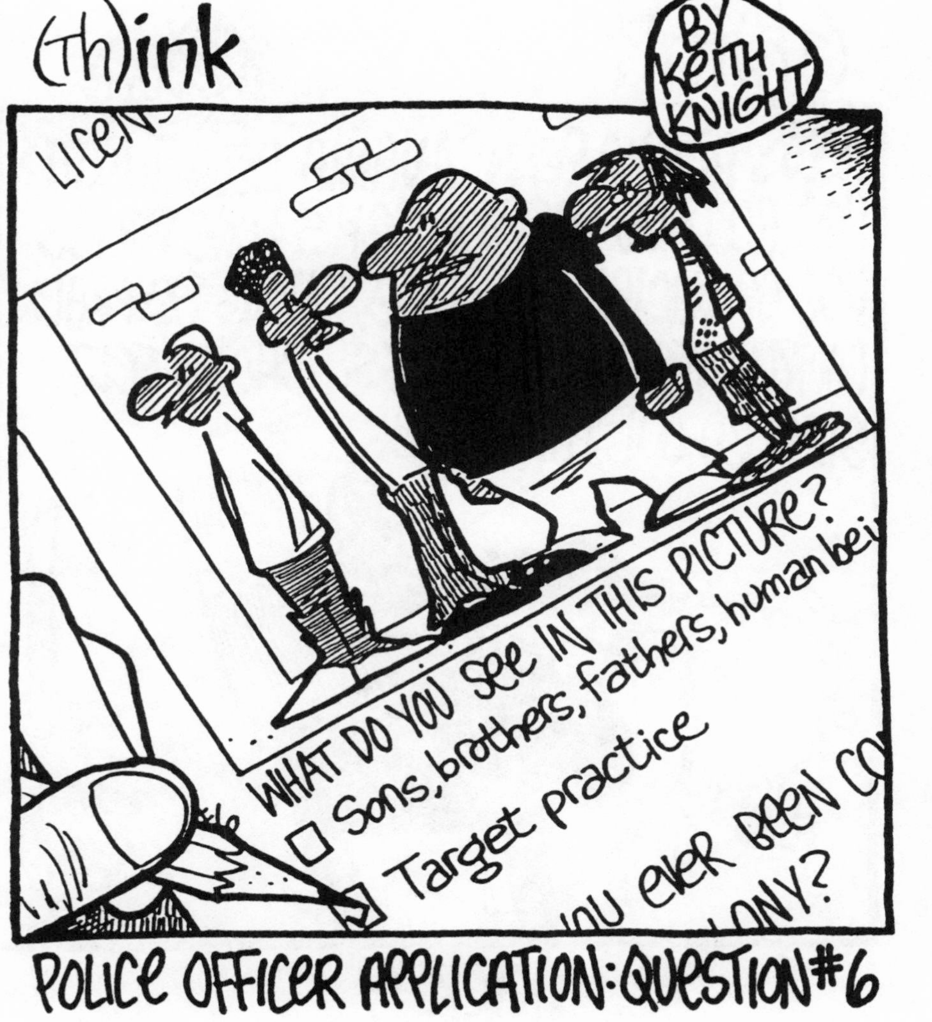
(th)ink
BY KEITH KNIGHT
LICENS
WHAT DO YOU SEE IN THIS PICTURE?
☐ Sons, brothers, fathers, human bei
☑ Target practice
OU EVER BEEN CO
LONY?

POLICE OFFICER APPLICATION: QUESTION #6

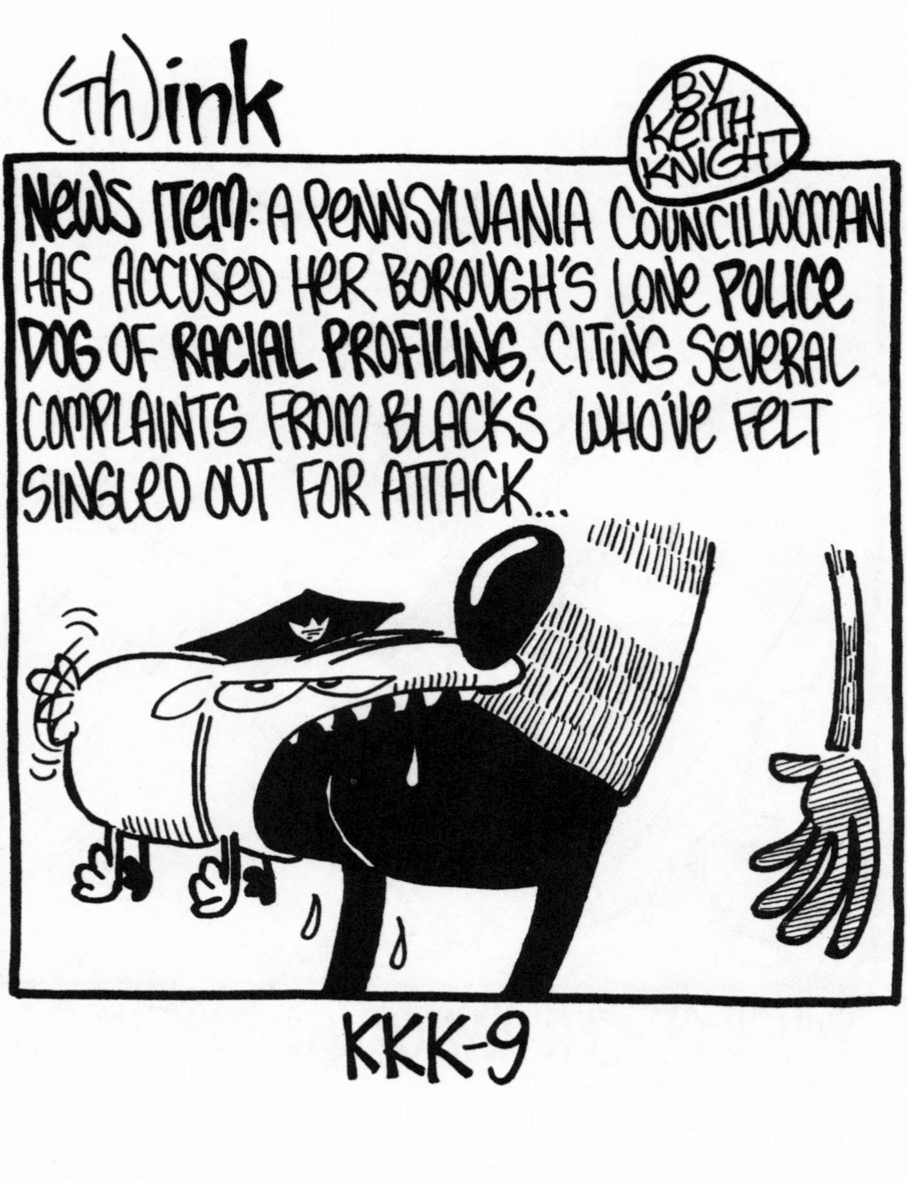
(TH)INK
BY KEITH KNIGHT
NEWS ITEM: A PENNSYLVANIA COUNCILWOMAN HAS ACCUSED HER BOROUGH'S LONE POLICE DOG OF RACIAL PROFILING, CITING SEVERAL COMPLAINTS FROM BLACKS WHO'VE FELT SINGLED OUT FOR ATTACK...
KKK-9

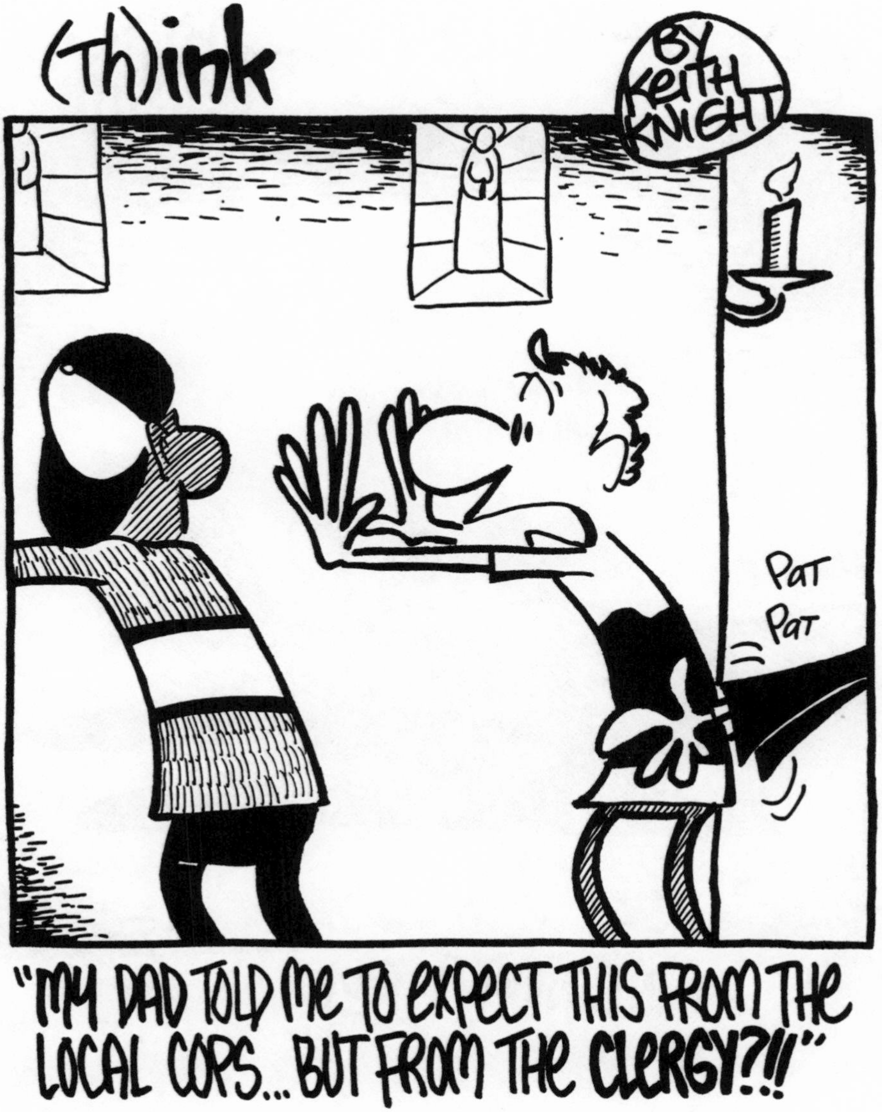
(th)ink
BY KEITH KNIGHT
PAT
PAT

"MY DAD TOLD ME TO EXPECT THIS FROM THE LOCAL COPS... BUT FROM THE CLERGY?!!"

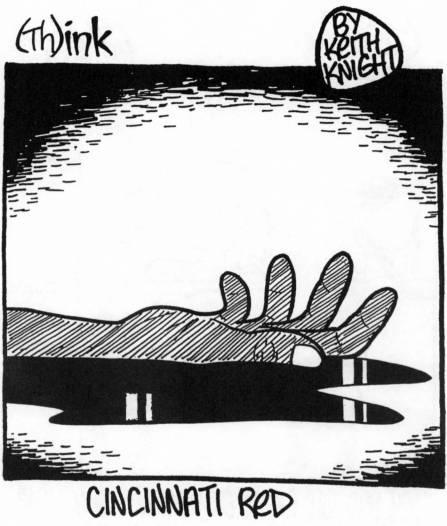

(th)ink

BY KEITH KNIGHT

CINCINNATI RED

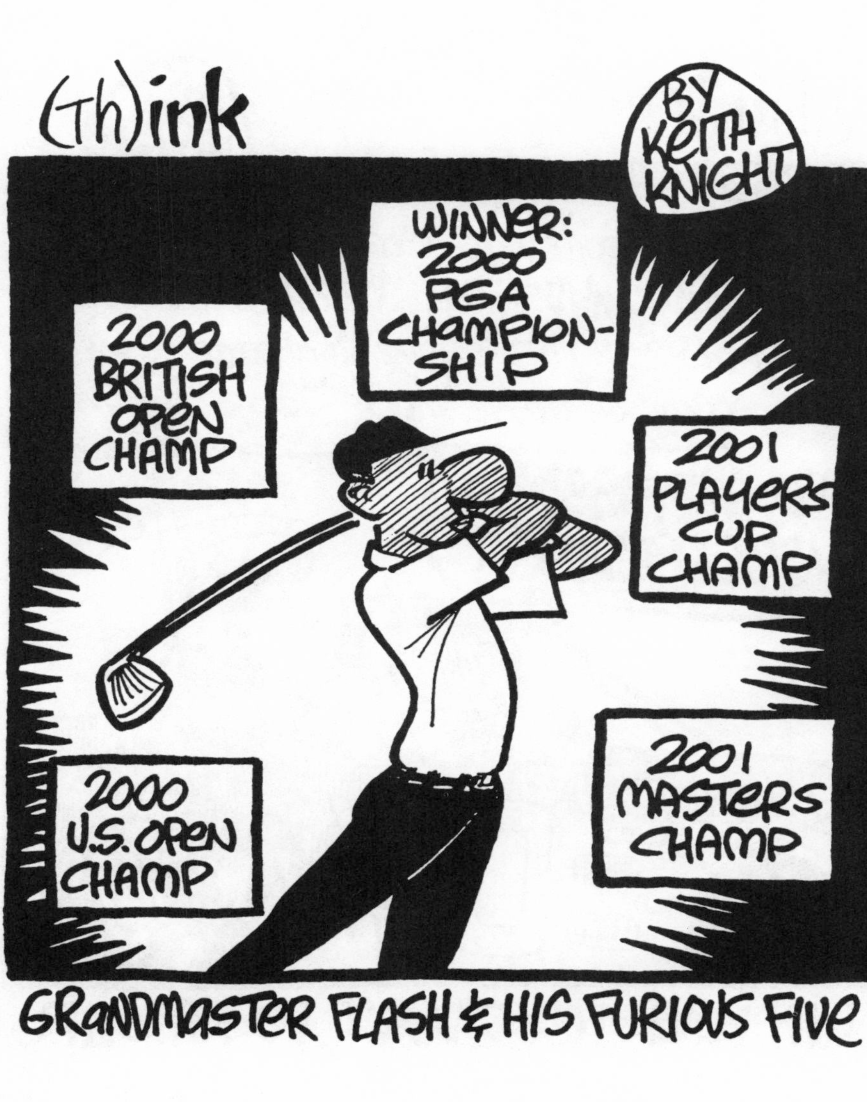
(TH)INK
BY KEITH KNIGHT
WINNER: 2000 PGA CHAMPIONSHIP
2000 BRITISH OPEN CHAMP
2001 PLAYERS CUP CHAMP
2000 U.S. OPEN CHAMP
2001 MASTERS CHAMP
GRANDMASTER FLASH & HIS FURIOUS FIVE

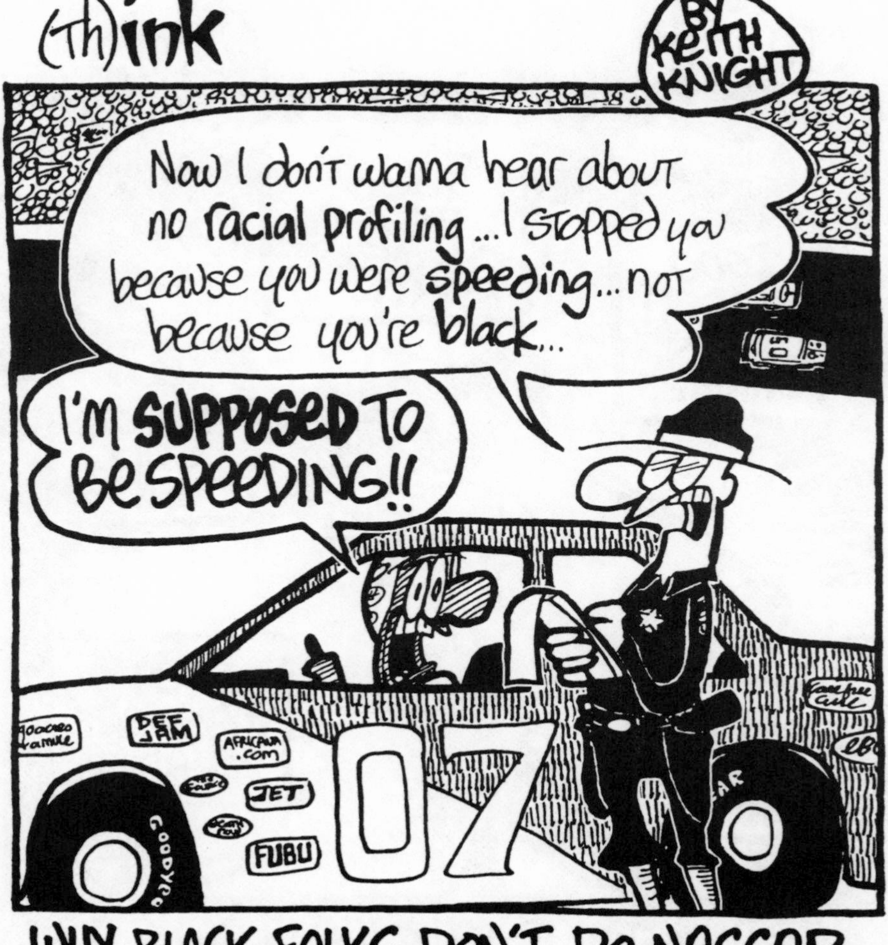
(TH)ink
BY KEITH KNIGHT
Now I don't wanna hear about no racial profiling... I stopped you because you were speeding... not because you're black...
I'm SUPPOSED TO Be SPEEDING!!
DEF JAM
AFRICANA .com
JET
FUBU
07

WHY BLACK FOLKS DON'T DO NASCAR

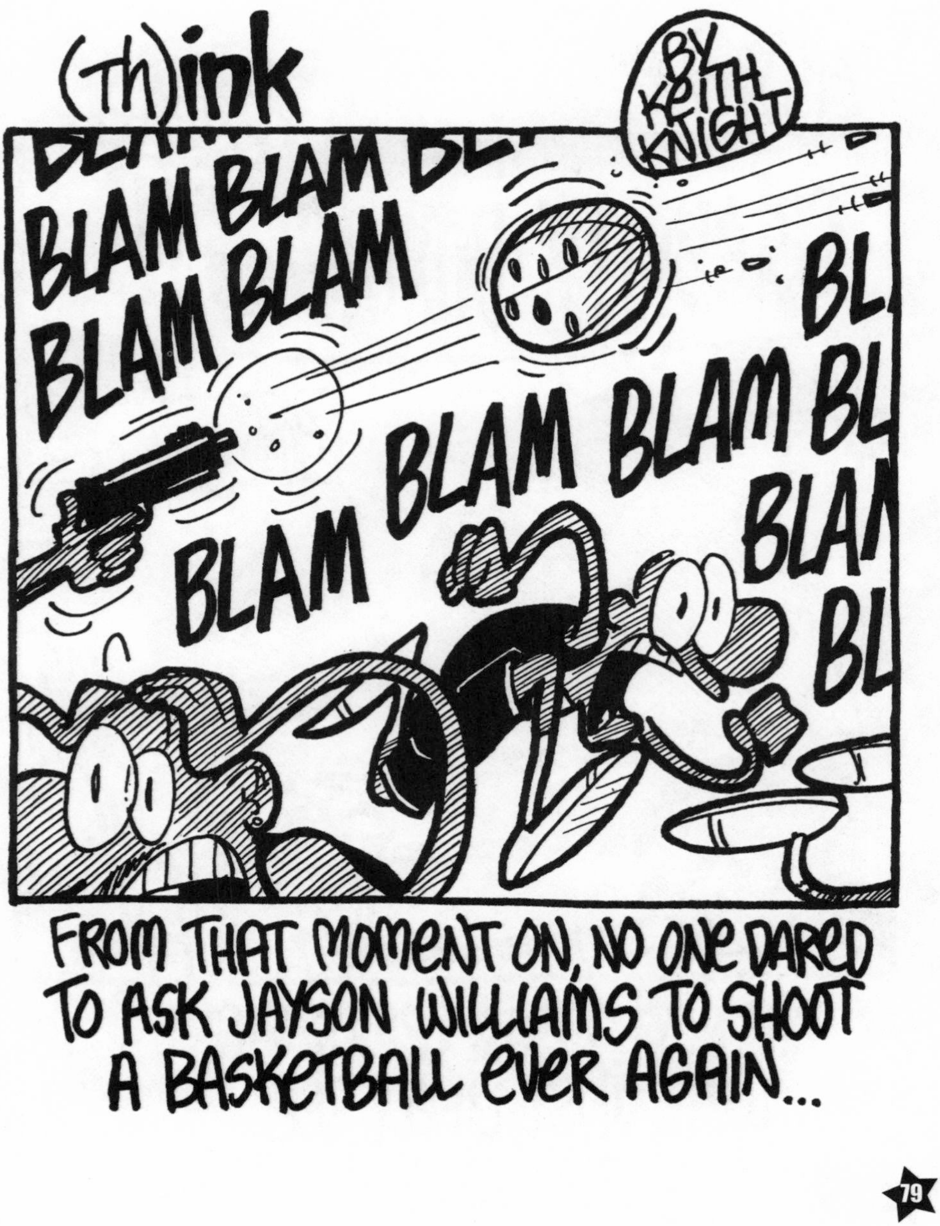
(Th)ink
BY KEITH KNIGHT
BLAM BLAM BLAM
BLAM BLAM
BLAM BLAM BLAM
BLAM

FROM THAT MOMENT ON, NO ONE DARED TO ASK JAYSON WILLIAMS TO SHOOT A BASKETBALL EVER AGAIN...

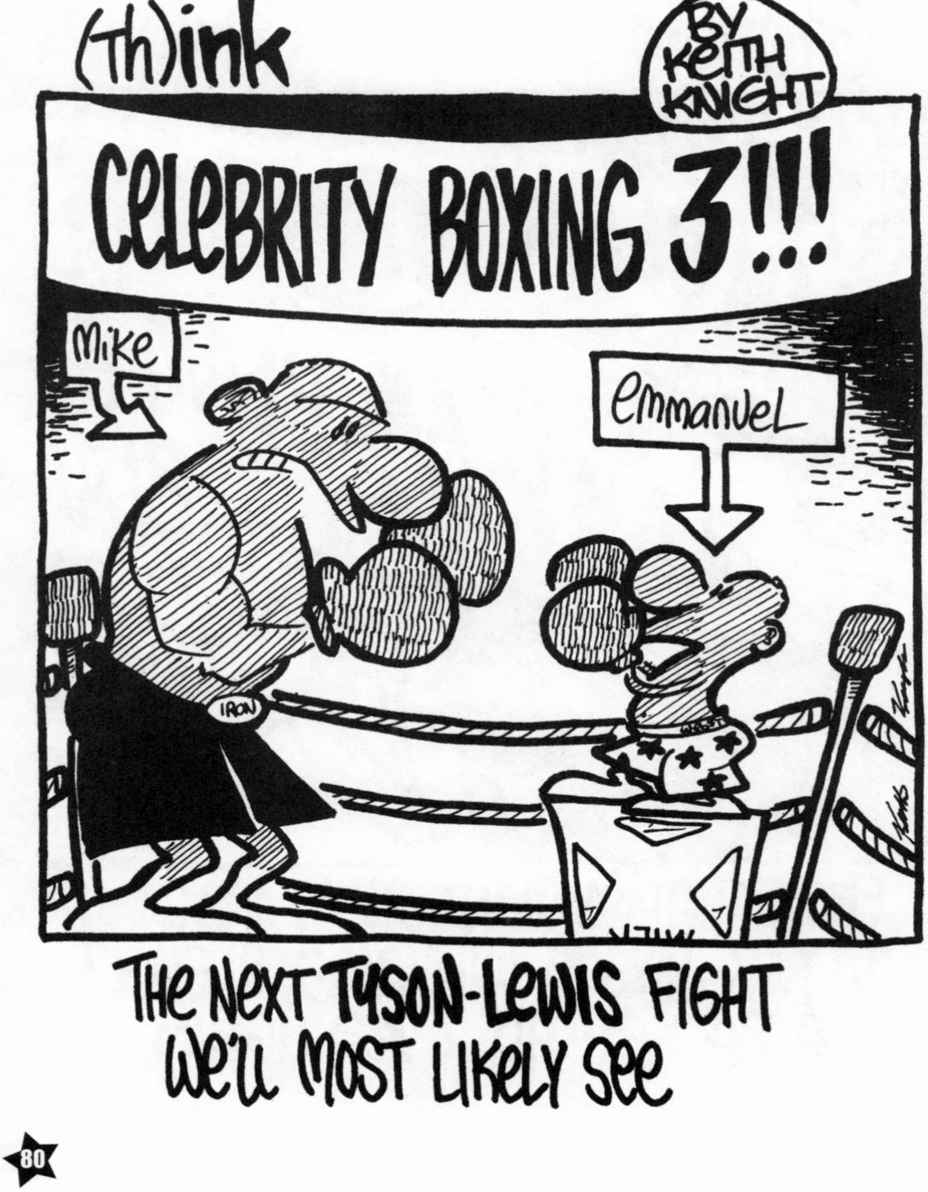
(th)ink
BY KEITH KNIGHT
CELEBRITY BOXING 3!!!...
Mike
Emmanuel
IRON
THE NEXT TYSON-LEWIS FIGHT
WE'LL MOST LIKELY SEE

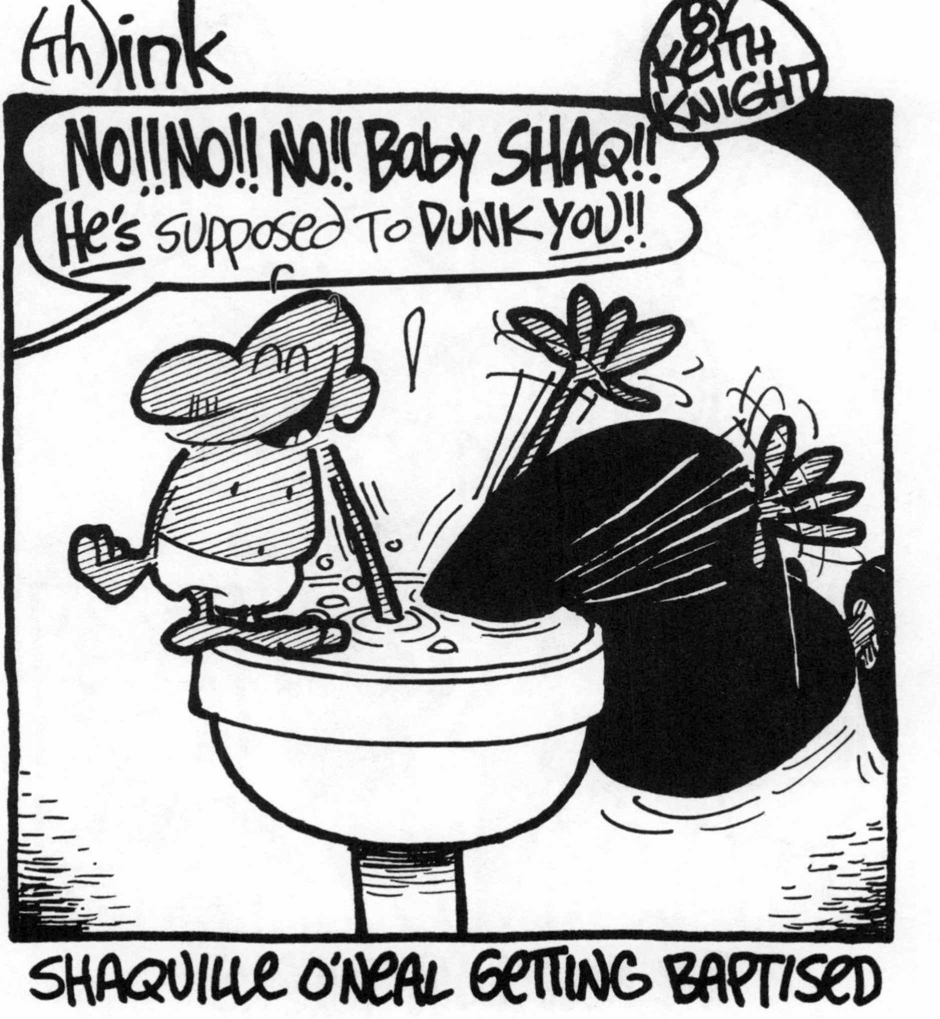
(th)ink
BY KEITH KNIGHT
NO!! NO!! NO!! Baby SHAQ!! He's supposed To DUNK YOU!!

SHAQUILLE O'NEAL GETTING BAPTISED

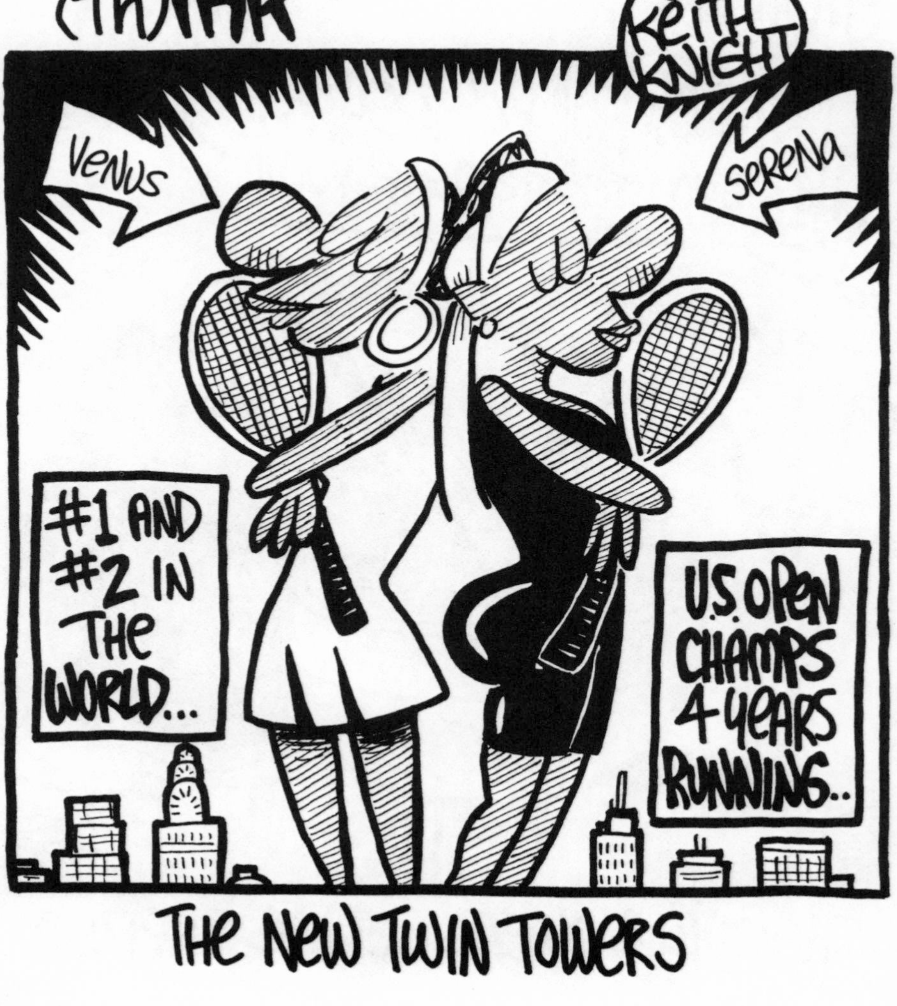
(th)ink
BY KEITH KNIGHT
VENUS
SERENA
#1 AND #2 IN THE WORLD...
U.S. OPEN CHAMPS 4 YEARS RUNNING..
THE NEW TWIN TOWERS

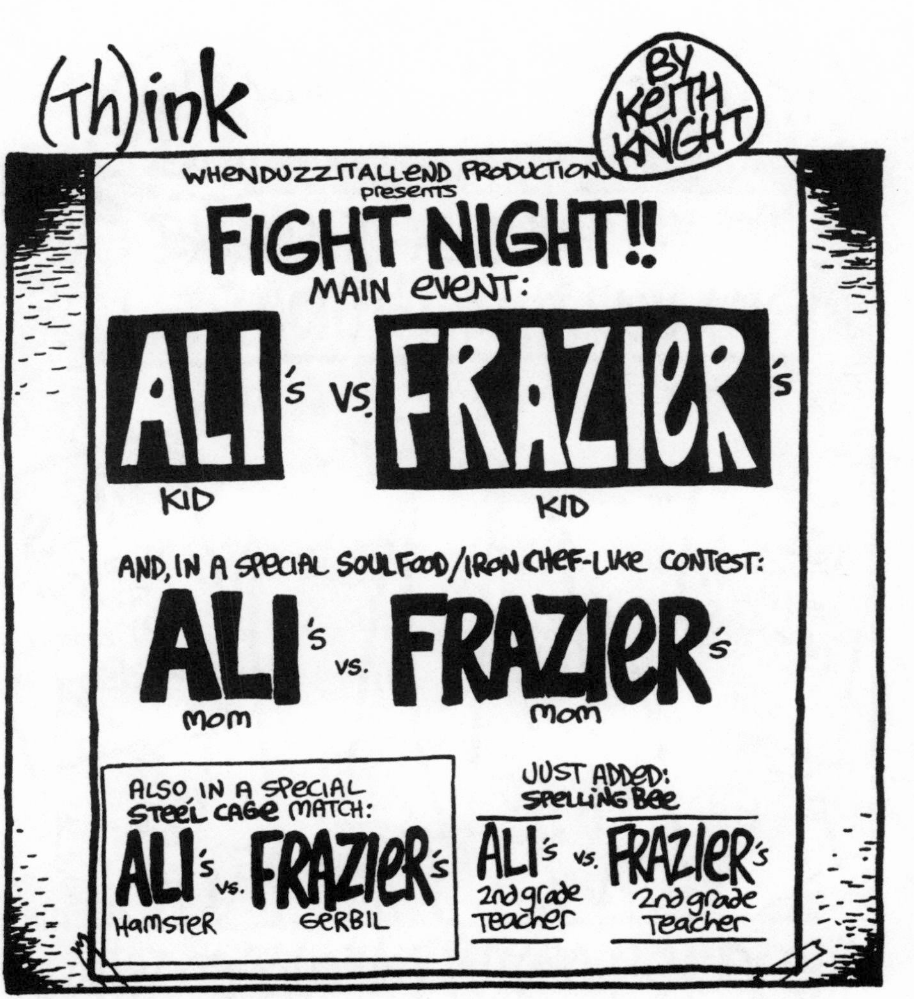
(Th)ink
BY KEITH KNIGHT
WHENDUZZITALLEND PRODUCTIONS presents
FIGHT NIGHT!!
MAIN EVENT:
ALI's KID vs. FRAZIER's KID
AND, IN A SPECIAL SOULFOOD/IRON CHEF-LIKE CONTEST:
ALI's MOM vs. FRAZIER's MOM
ALSO, IN A SPECIAL STEEL CAGE MATCH:
ALI's HAMSTER vs. FRAZIER's GERBIL
JUST ADDED: SPELLING BEE
ALI's 2nd grade Teacher vs. FRAZIER's 2nd grade Teacher

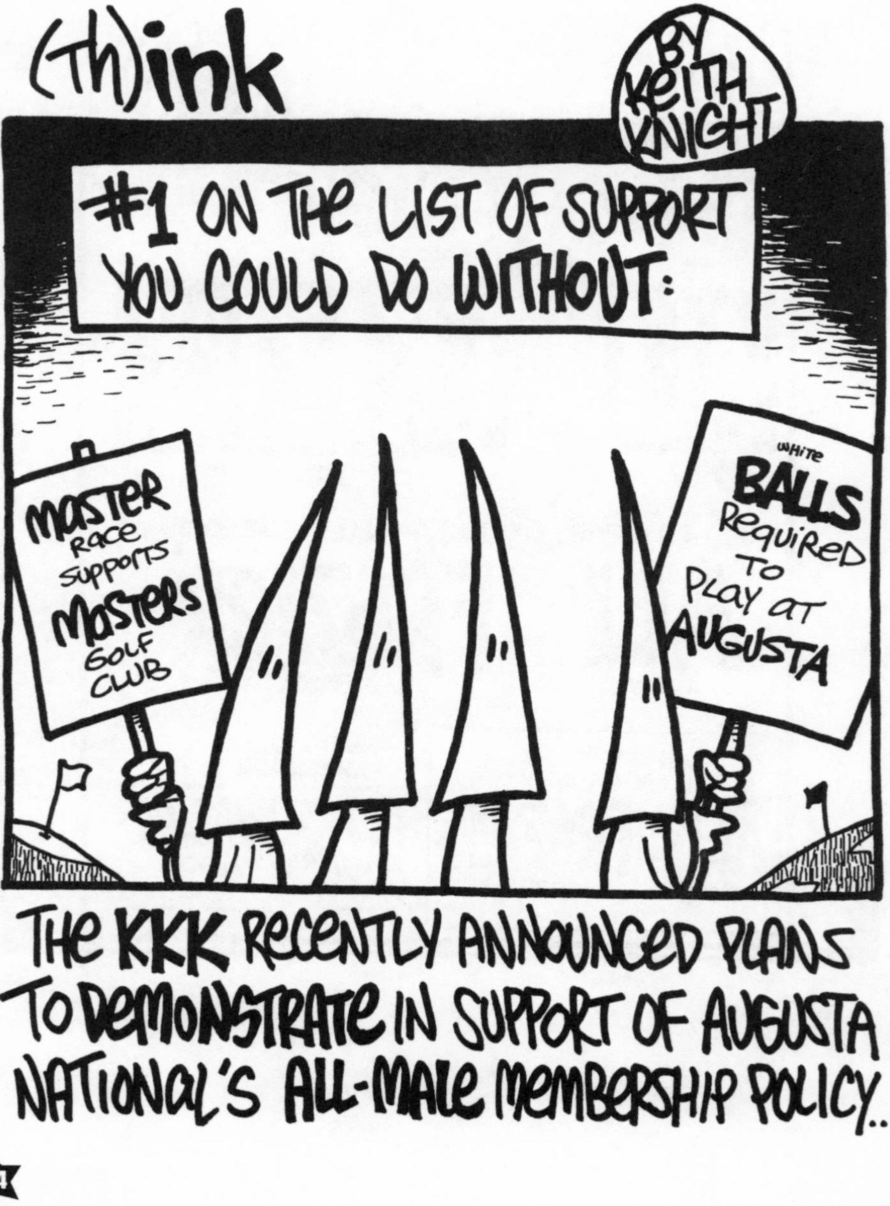
(th)ink
BY KEITH KNIGHT
#1 ON THE LIST OF SUPPORT YOU COULD DO WITHOUT:
MASTER RACE SUPPORTS MASTERS GOLF CLUB
WHITE BALLS REQUIRED TO PLAY AT AUGUSTA
THE KKK RECENTLY ANNOUNCED PLANS TO DEMONSTRATE IN SUPPORT OF AUGUSTA NATIONAL'S ALL-MALE MEMBERSHIP POLICY..

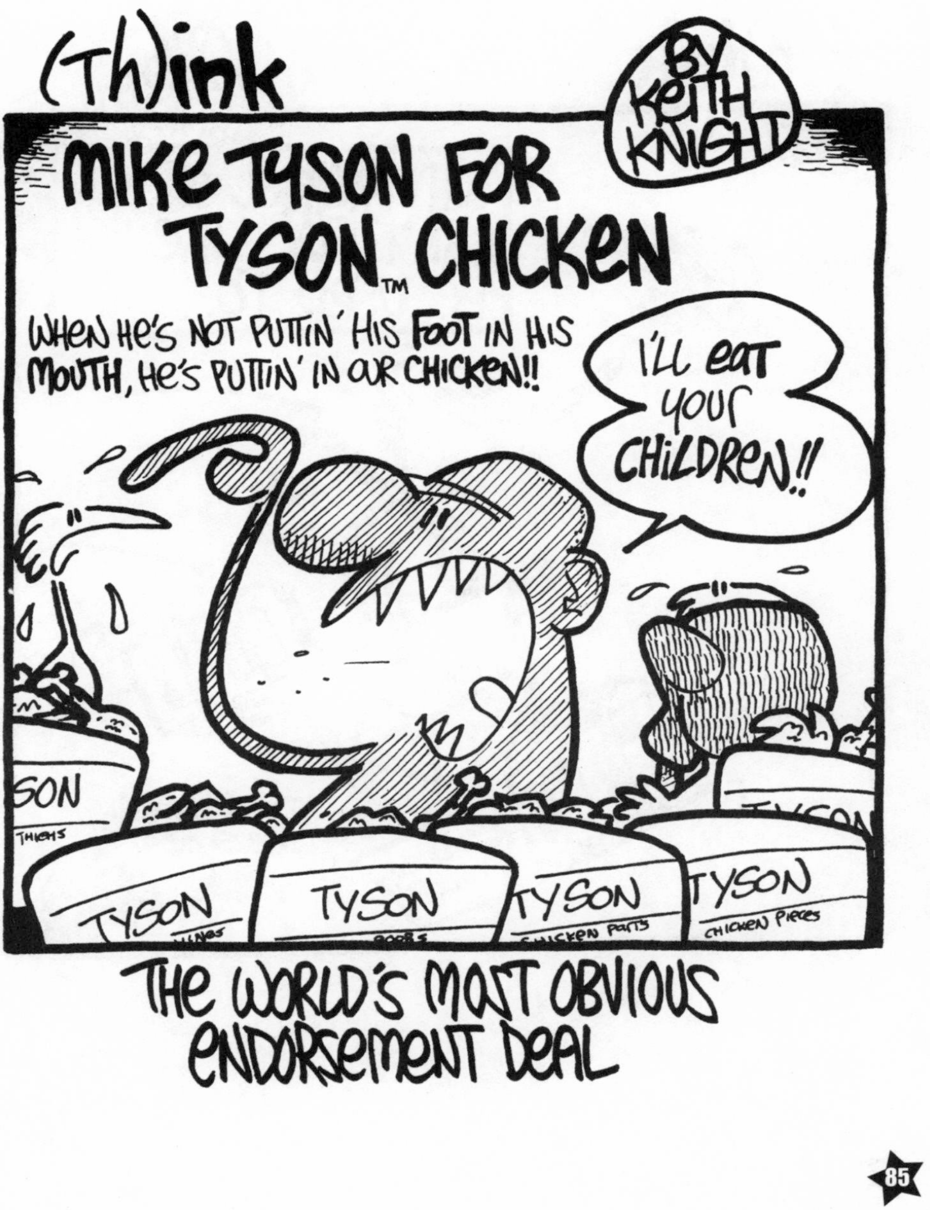
(Th)ink
BY KEITH KNIGHT
MIKE TYSON FOR TYSON™ CHICKEN
WHEN HE'S NOT PUTTIN' HIS FOOT IN HIS MOUTH, HE'S PUTTIN' IN OUR CHICKEN!!
I'LL eat your CHILDREN!!
SON
THIGHS
TYSON
TYSON
TYSON
CHICKEN PARTS
TYSON
CHICKEN PIECES
THE WORLD'S MOST OBVIOUS ENDORSEMENT DEAL

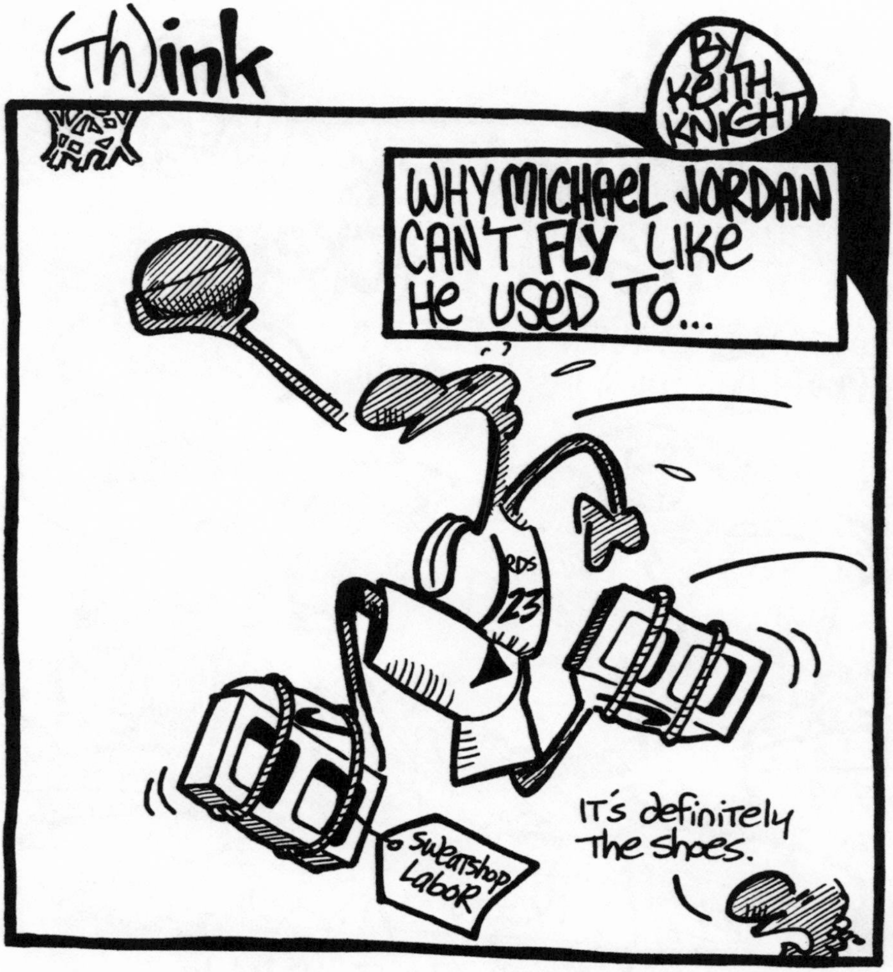
(Th)ink
BY KEITH KNIGHT
WHY MICHAEL JORDAN CAN'T FLY LIKE HE USED TO...
23
Sweatshop Labor
IT's definitely The shoes.

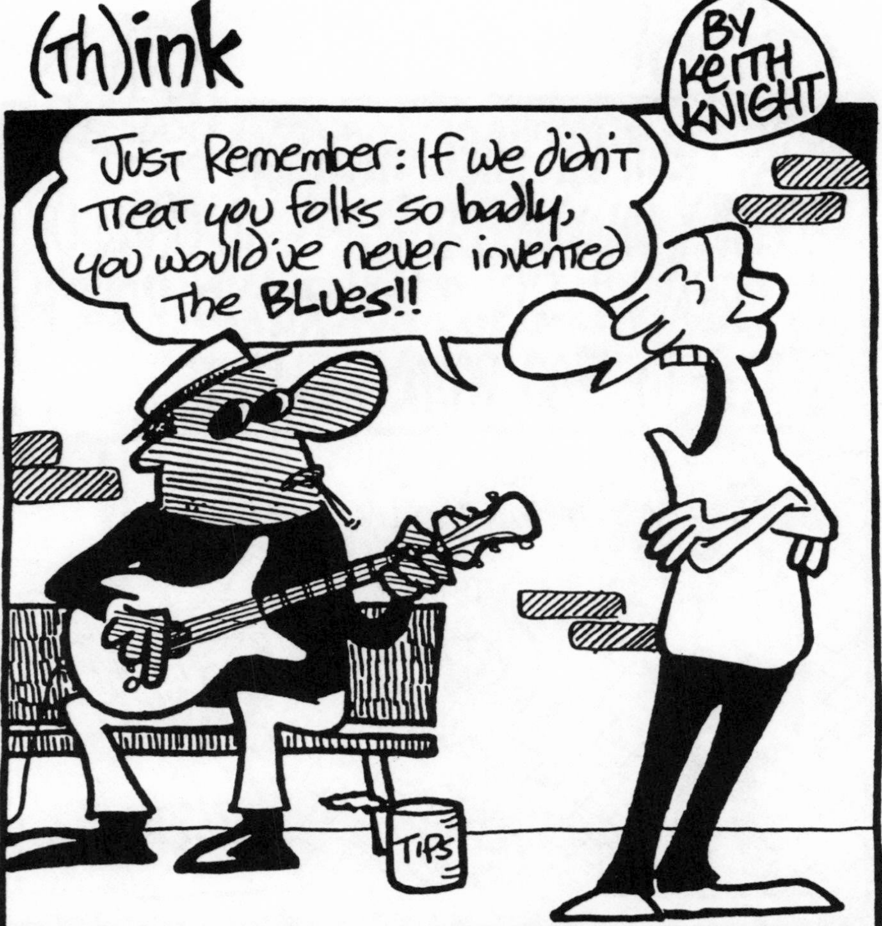
(th)ink
BY KEITH KNIGHT
JUST REMEMBER: IF WE DIDN'T TREAT YOU FOLKS SO BADLY, YOU WOULD'VE NEVER INVENTED THE BLUES!!
TIPS

BIFF ARGUES THE POSITIVES OF RACISM

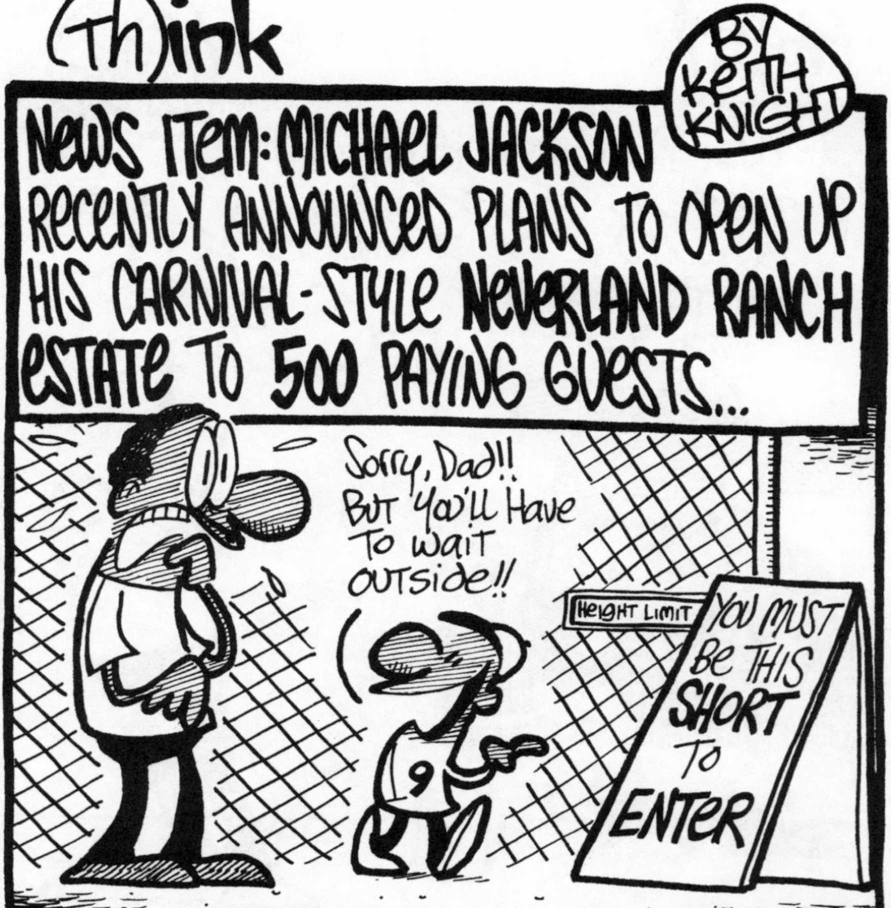
(Th)ink
BY KEITH KNIGHT
NEWS ITEM: MICHAEL JACKSON RECENTLY ANNOUNCED PLANS TO OPEN UP HIS CARNIVAL-STYLE NEVERLAND RANCH ESTATE TO 500 PAYING GUESTS...
Sorry, Dad!! But You'll Have To wait outside!!
HEIGHT LIMIT
YOU MUST BE THIS SHORT TO ENTER

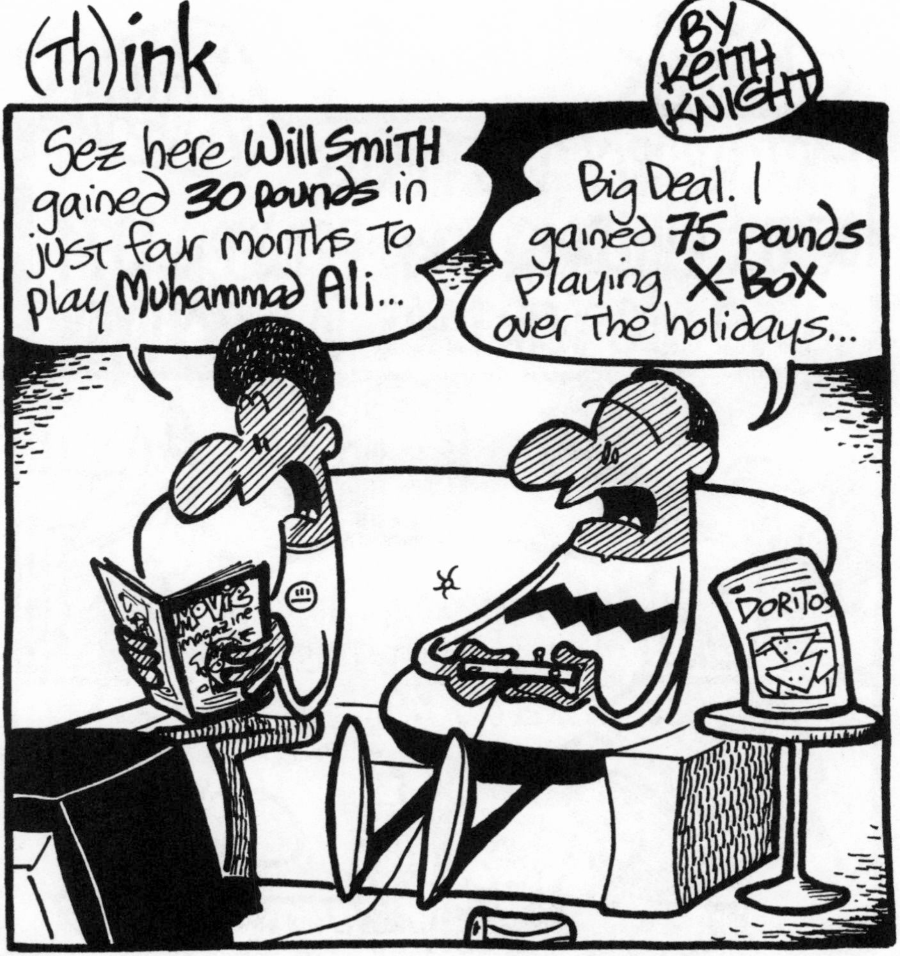
(Th)ink
BY KEITH KNIGHT
Sez here Will Smith gained 30 pounds in just four months to play Muhammad Ali...
Big Deal. I gained 75 pounds playing X-Box over the holidays...
DORITOS

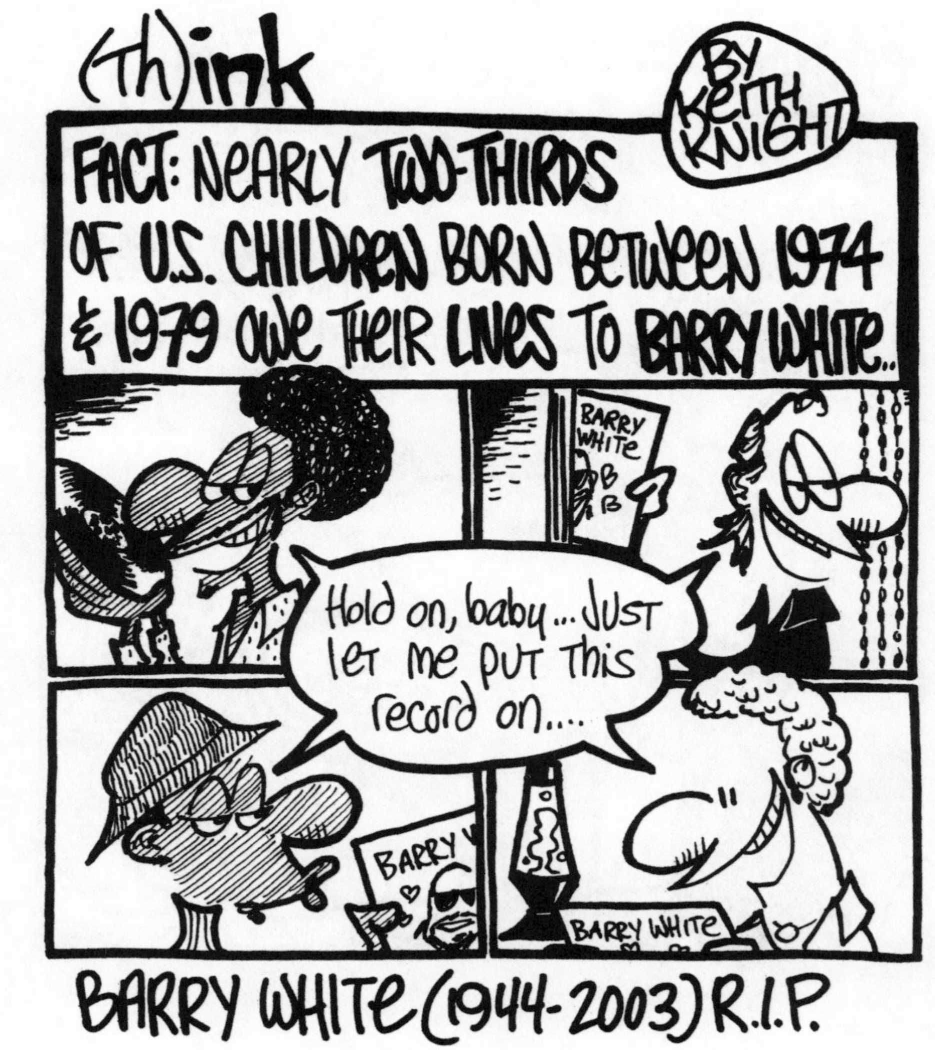
(Th)ink
BY KEITH KNIGHT
FACT: NEARLY TWO-THIRDS OF U.S. CHILDREN BORN BETWEEN 1974 & 1979 OWE THEIR LIVES TO BARRY WHITE..
BARRY WHITE
Hold on, baby... JUST let me put this record on....
BARRY
BARRY WHITE
BARRY WHITE (1944-2003) R.I.P.

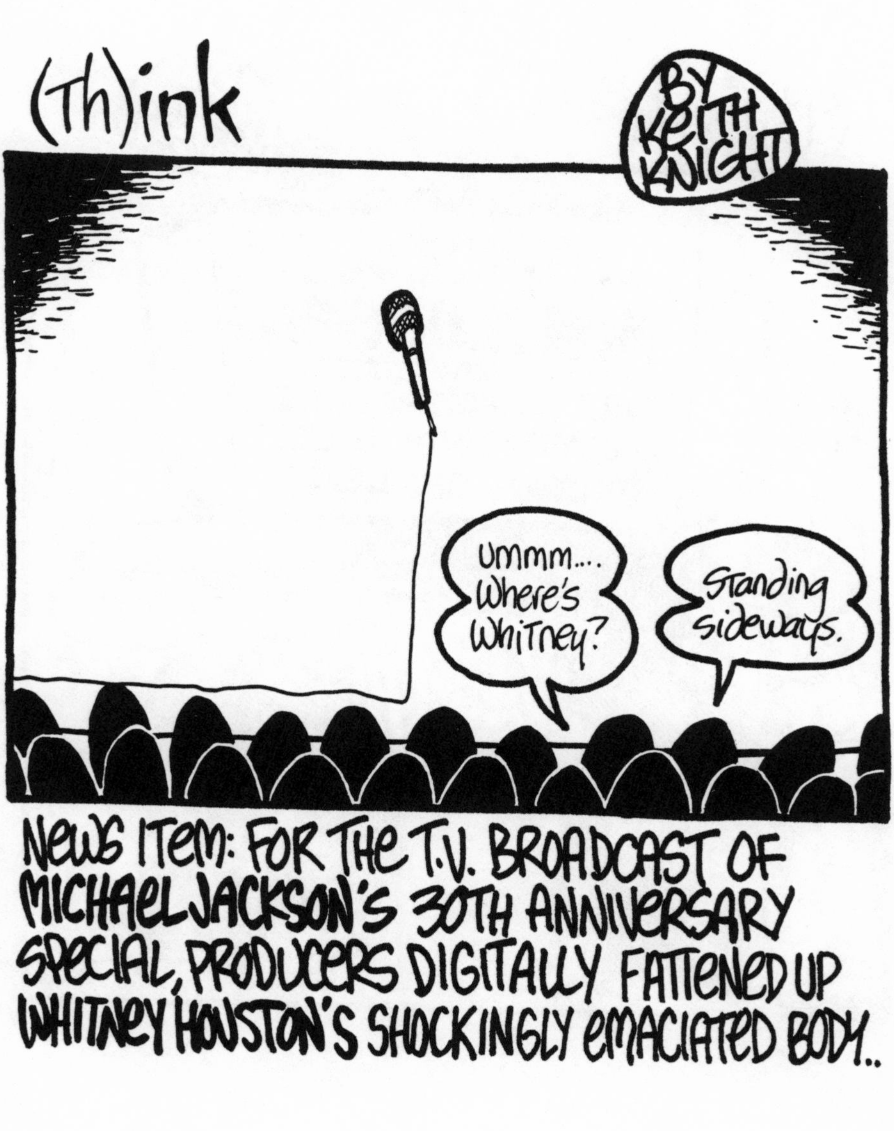
(Th)ink
BY KEITH KNIGHT
Ummm.... Where's Whitney?
Standing sideways.
NEWS ITEM: FOR THE T.V. BROADCAST OF MICHAEL JACKSON'S 30TH ANNIVERSARY SPECIAL, PRODUCERS DIGITALLY FATTENED UP WHITNEY HOUSTON'S SHOCKINGLY EMACIATED BODY..

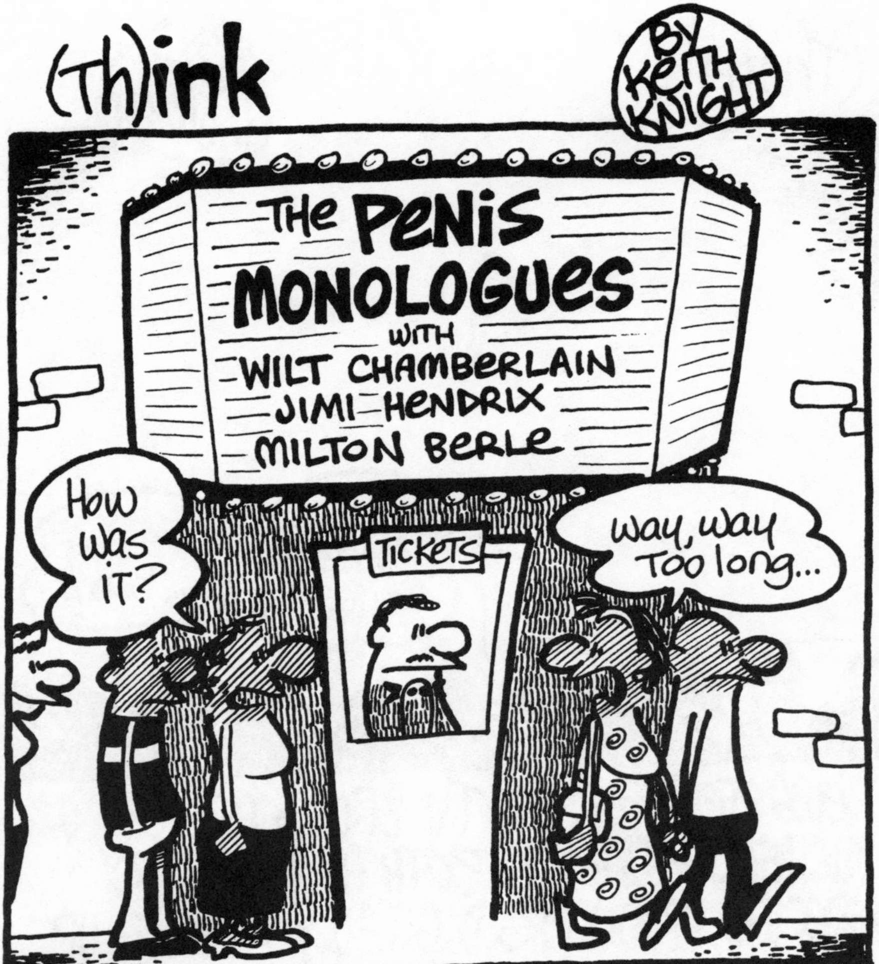
(Th)ink
By Keith Knight
The Penis Monologues with Wilt Chamberlain Jimi Hendrix Milton Berle
Tickets
How was it?
Way, way too long...

(Th)ink

BY KEITH KNIGHT

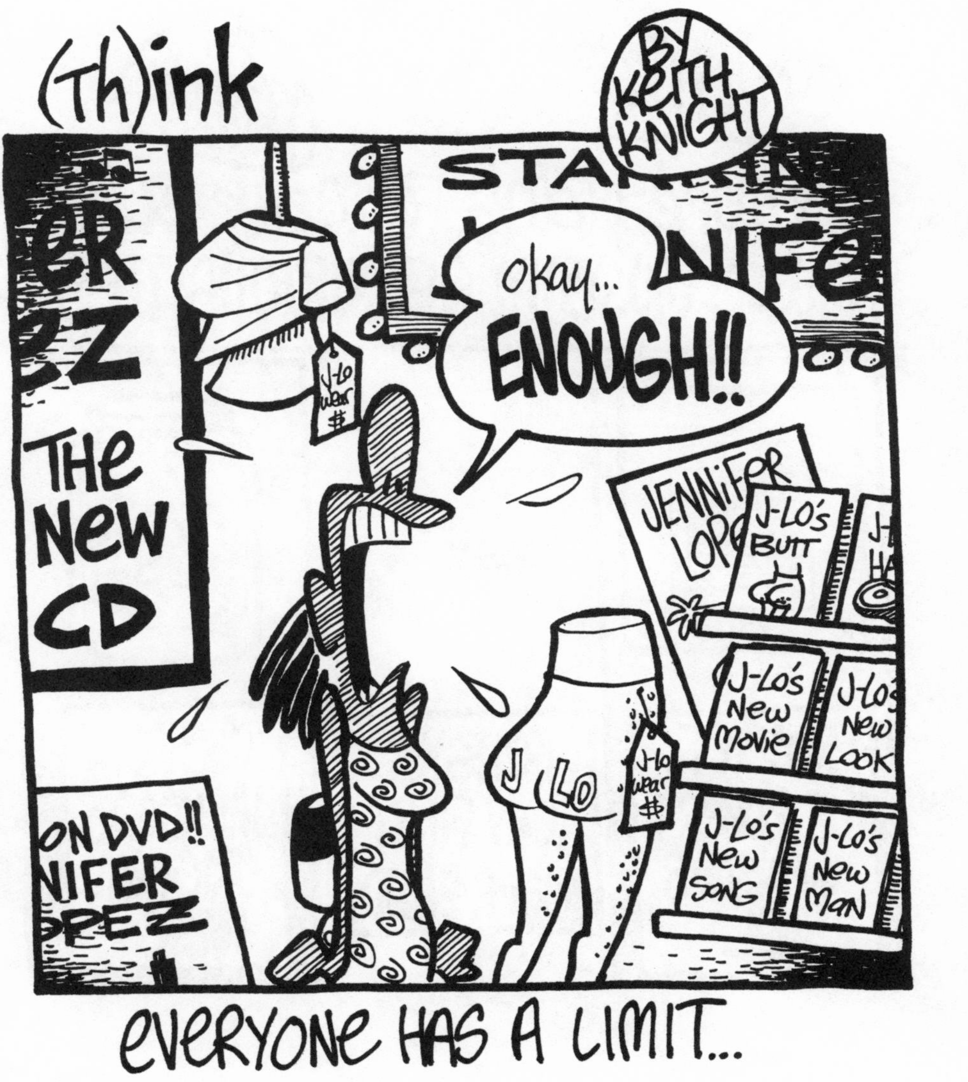

okay... ENOUGH!!
THE New CD
J-Lo wear $
JENNIFER
J-LO's BUTT
J-Lo's New Movie
J-Lo's New Look
J-Lo's New Song
J-Lo's New Man
ON DVD!!
J LO

EVERYONE HAS A LIMIT...

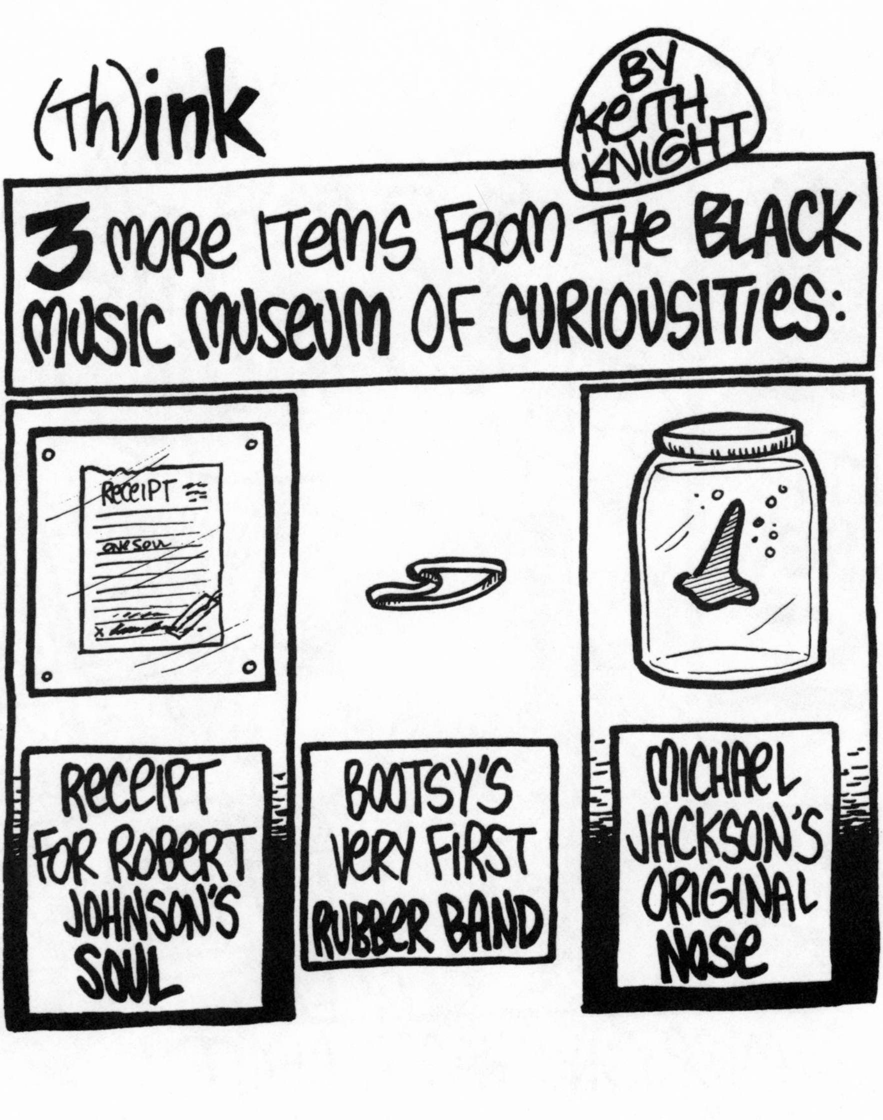

(th)ink
BY KEITH KNIGHT
3 MORE ITEMS FROM THE BLACK MUSIC MUSEUM OF CURIOUSITIES:
RECEIPT
ONE SOUL
RECEIPT FOR ROBERT JOHNSON'S SOUL
BOOTSY'S VERY FIRST RUBBER BAND
MICHAEL JACKSON'S ORIGINAL NOSE

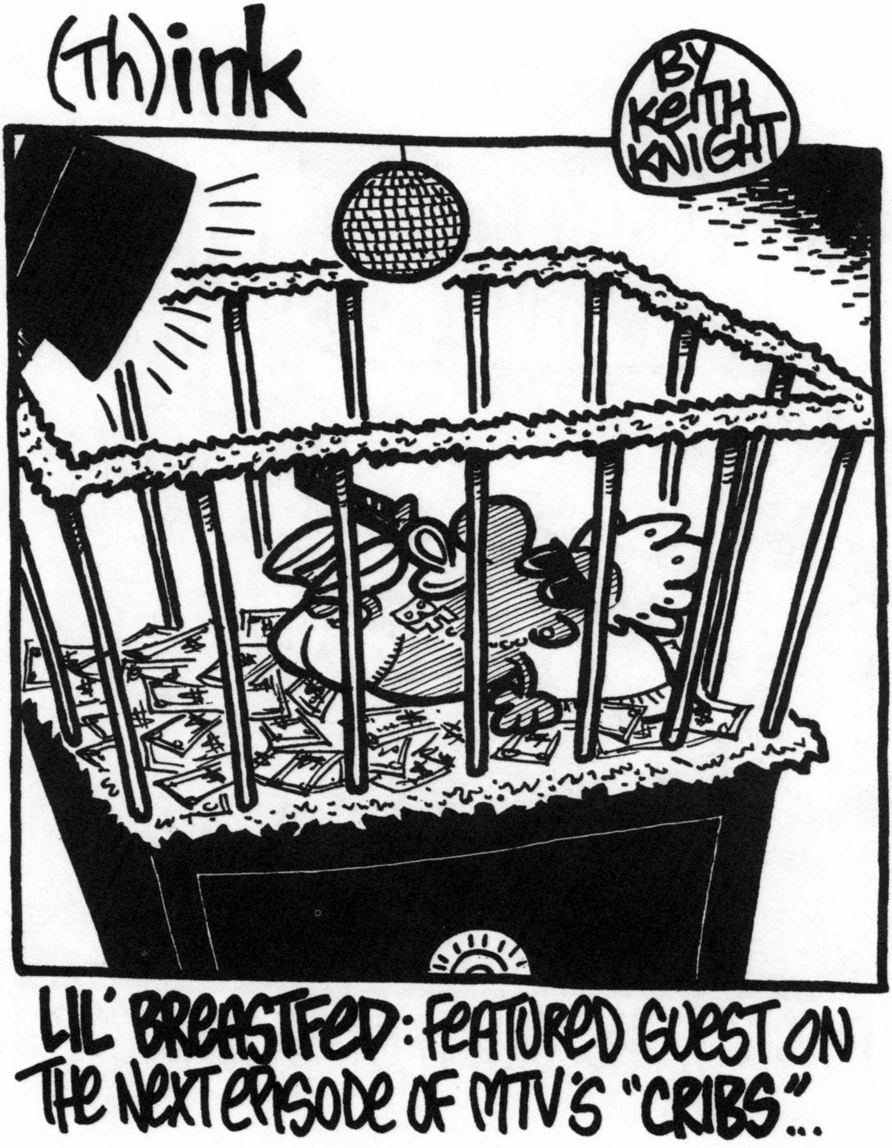
(Th)ink
BY KEITH KNIGHT
LIL' BREASTFED: FEATURED GUEST ON THE NEXT EPISODE OF MTV'S "CRIBS"...

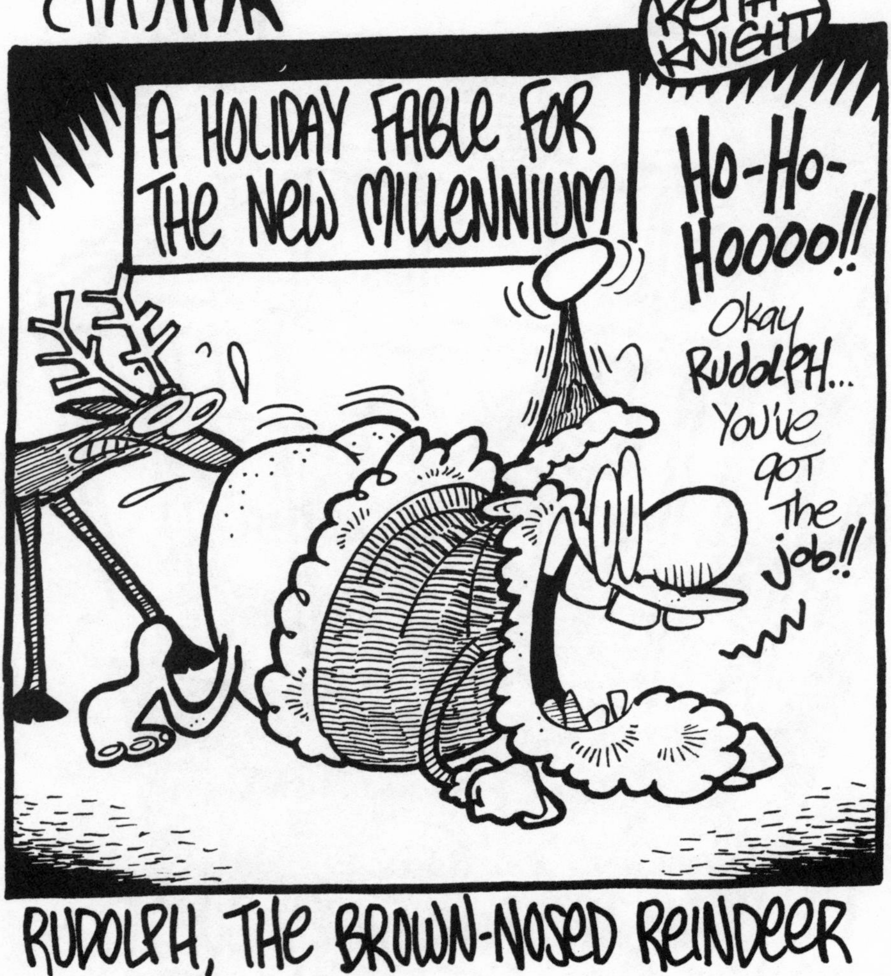
(Th)ink
BY KEITH KNIGHT
A HOLIDAY FABLE FOR THE NEW MILLENNIUM
Ho-Ho-Hoooo!!
Okay Rudolph... You've got the job!!
RUDOLPH, THE BROWN-NOSED REINDEER

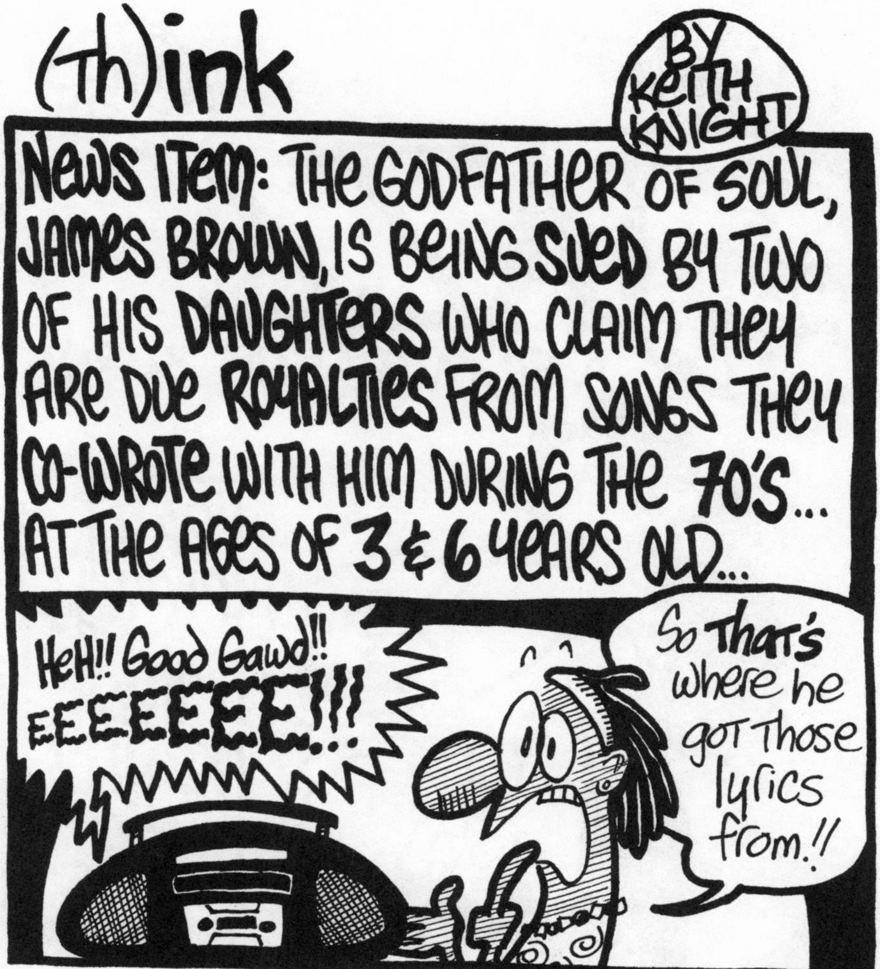
(Th)ink
BY KEITH KNIGHT
NEWS ITEM: THE GODFATHER OF SOUL, JAMES BROWN, IS BEING SUED BY TWO OF HIS DAUGHTERS WHO CLAIM THEY ARE DUE ROYALTIES FROM SONGS THEY CO-WROTE WITH HIM DURING THE 70'S... AT THE AGES OF 3 & 6 YEARS OLD...
HEH!! Good Gawd!! EEEEEEE!!!
So That's where he got Those lyrics from.!!

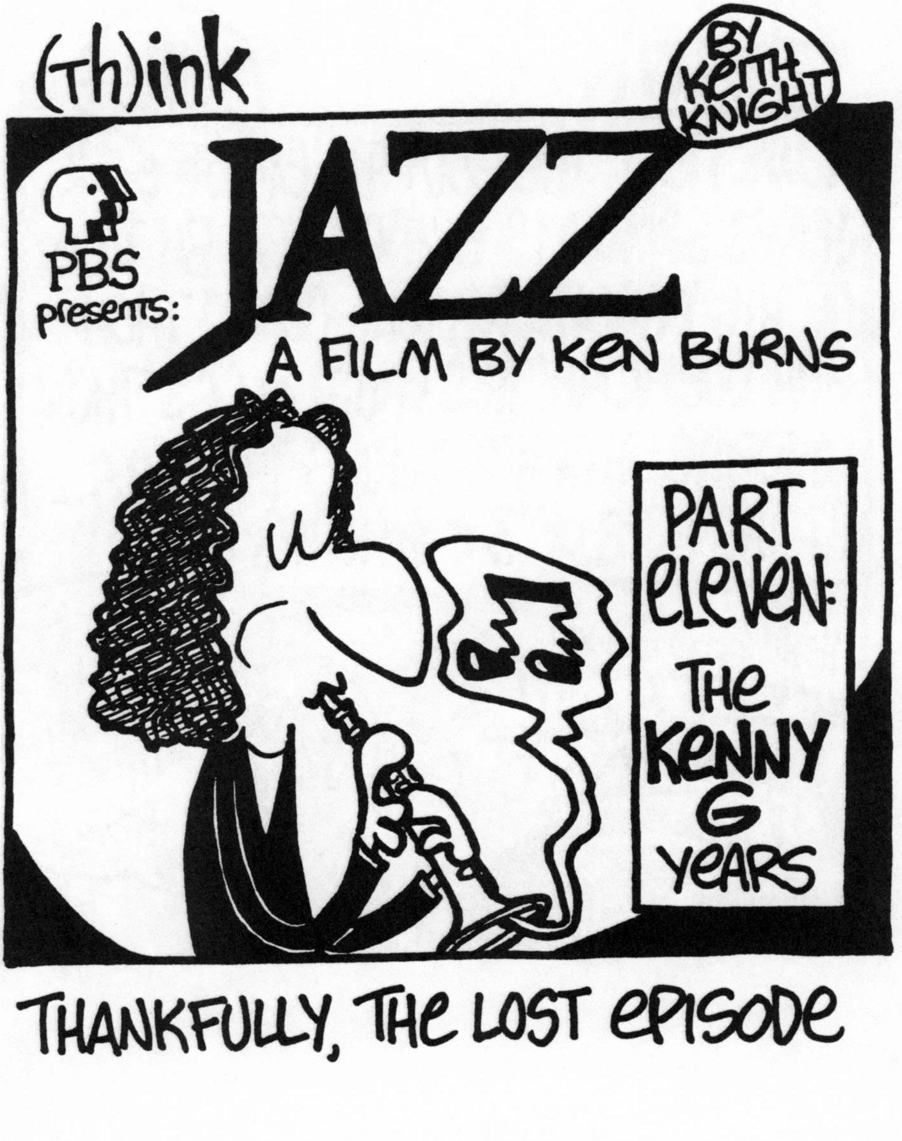
(th)ink
BY KEITH KNIGHT
PBS presents:
JAZZ
A FILM BY KEN BURNS
PART ELEVEN: THE KENNY G YEARS
THANKFULLY, THE LOST EPISODE

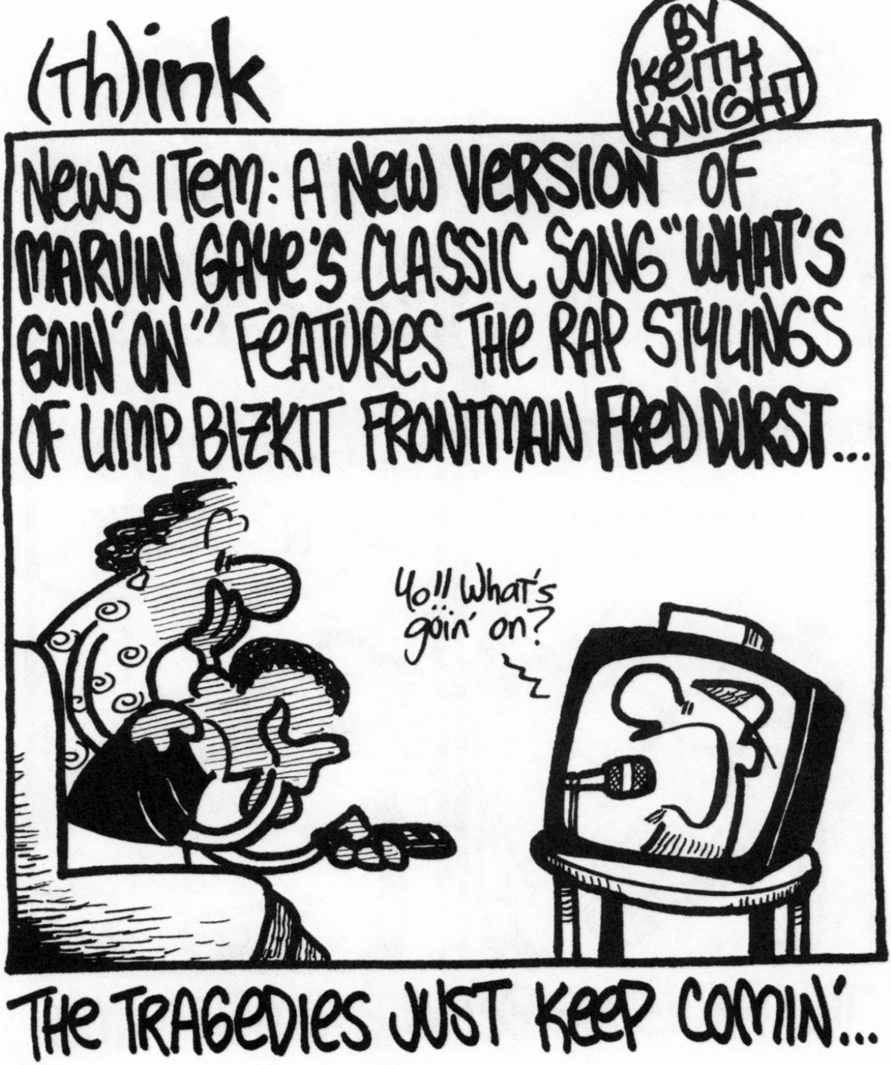
(Th)ink
By Keith Knight
News item: A new version of Marvin Gaye's classic song "What's goin' on" features the rap stylings of Limp Bizkit frontman Fred Durst...
Yo!! What's goin' on?
The tragedies just keep comin'...

(Th)ink
BY KEITH KNIGHT
Yo!! Peep The SELLOUT Tryin' To be WHITE!!
Great!! When We wear BLACKFACE IT'S RACIST, but when you wear WHITE-face, IT'S ART!!
THE PERILS OF BEING A BLACK MIME

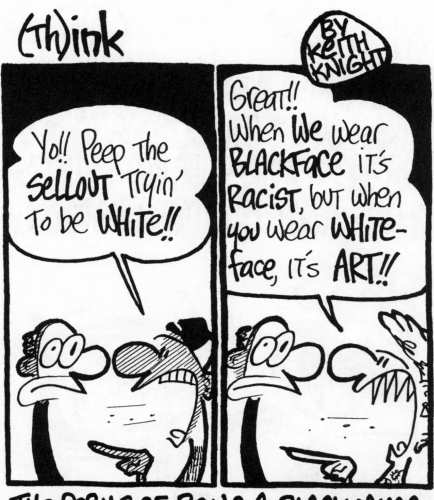

(Th)ink

BY KEITH KNIGHT

NEWS ITEM: QUEEN LATIFAH RECENTLY HAD **BREAST REDUCTION** SURGERY, ALTERING HER **BRA SIZE** FROM A **DOUBLE D** TO A SIZE **C**....

BEFORE

PHEW

AFTER

BRINGIN' DOWN THE BLOUSE

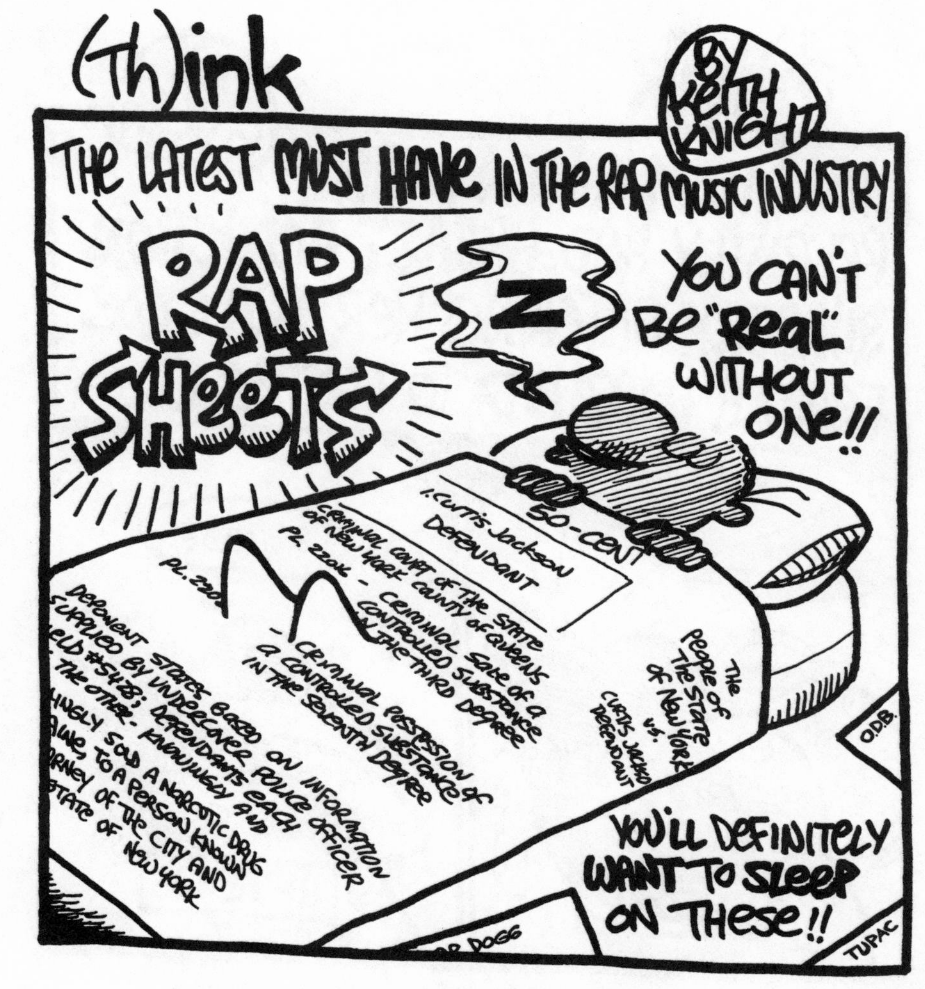

(Th)ink
BY KEITH KNIGHT
THE LATEST MUST HAVE IN THE RAP MUSIC INDUSTRY
RAP SHEETS
Z
YOU CAN'T BE "REAL" WITHOUT ONE!!
50-CENT
1. CURTIS JACKSON DEFENDANT
CRIMINAL COURT OF THE STATE OF NEW YORK COUNTY OF QUEENS
PL. 220.06 - CRIMINAL SALE OF A CONTROLLED SUBSTANCE IN THE THIRD DEGREE
- CRIMINAL POSSESSION OF A CONTROLLED SUBSTANCE IN THE SEVENTH DEGREE
DEPONENT STATES BASED ON INFORMATION SUPPLIED BY UNDERCOVER POLICE OFFICER
THE PEOPLE OF THE STATE OF NEW YORK V.S. CURTIS JACKSON DEFENDANT
O.D.B.
YOU'LL DEFINITELY WANT TO SLEEP ON THESE!!
TUPAC

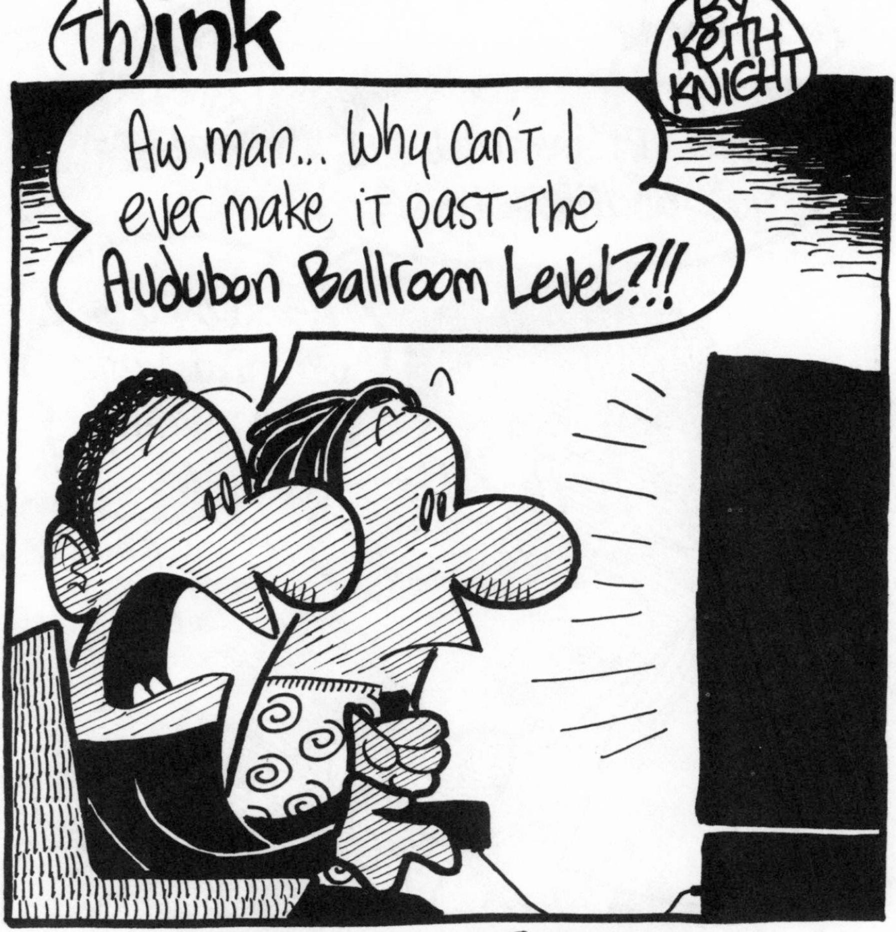
(Th)ink
By Keith Knight
Aw, man... Why can't I ever make it past the Audubon Ballroom Level?!!

MALCOLM X-BOX

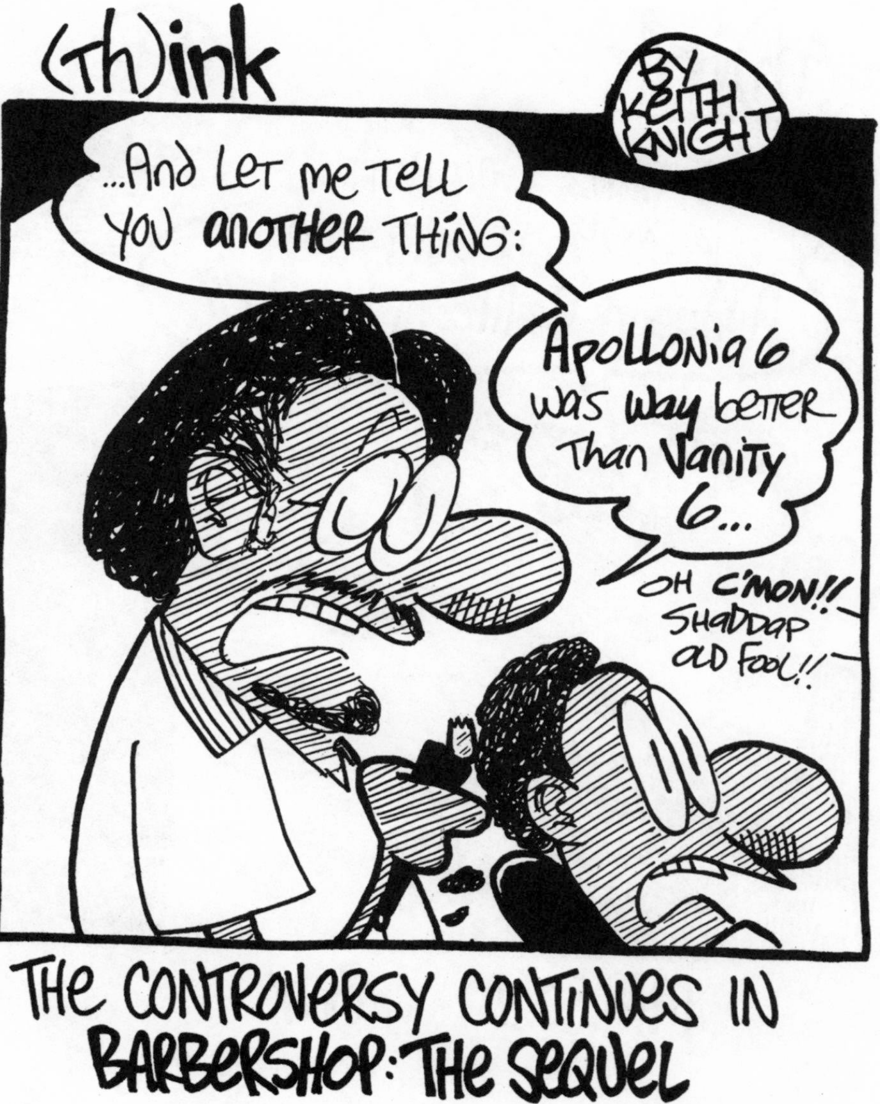
(TH)ink
BY KEITH KNIGHT
...And Let me Tell you another THiNG:
Apollonia 6 was way better Than Vanity 6...
OH C'MON!! SHADDAP OLD FOOL!!

THE CONTROVERSY CONTINUES IN BARBERSHOP: THE SEQUEL

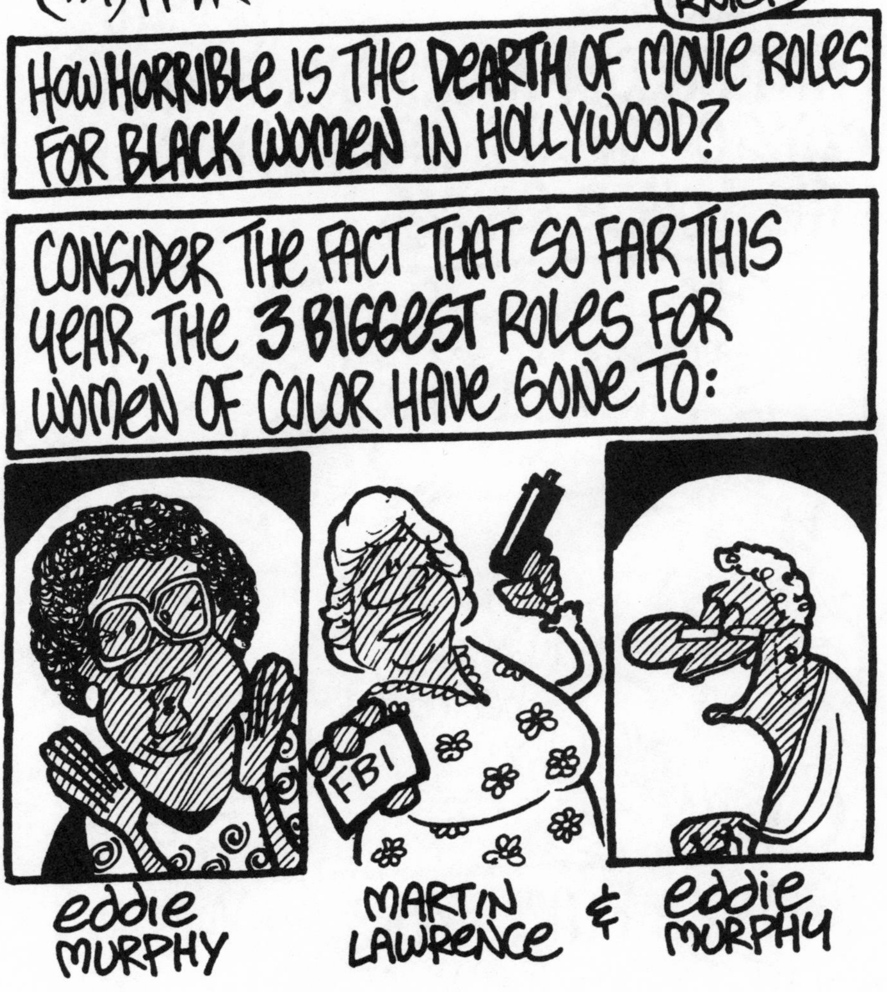
(TH)INK
BY KEITH KNIGHT
HOW HORRIBLE IS THE DEARTH OF MOVIE ROLES FOR BLACK WOMEN IN HOLLYWOOD?
CONSIDER THE FACT THAT SO FAR THIS YEAR, THE 3 BIGGEST ROLES FOR WOMEN OF COLOR HAVE GONE TO:
FBI
EDDIE MURPHY
MARTIN LAWRENCE
&
EDDIE MURPHY

(Th)ink

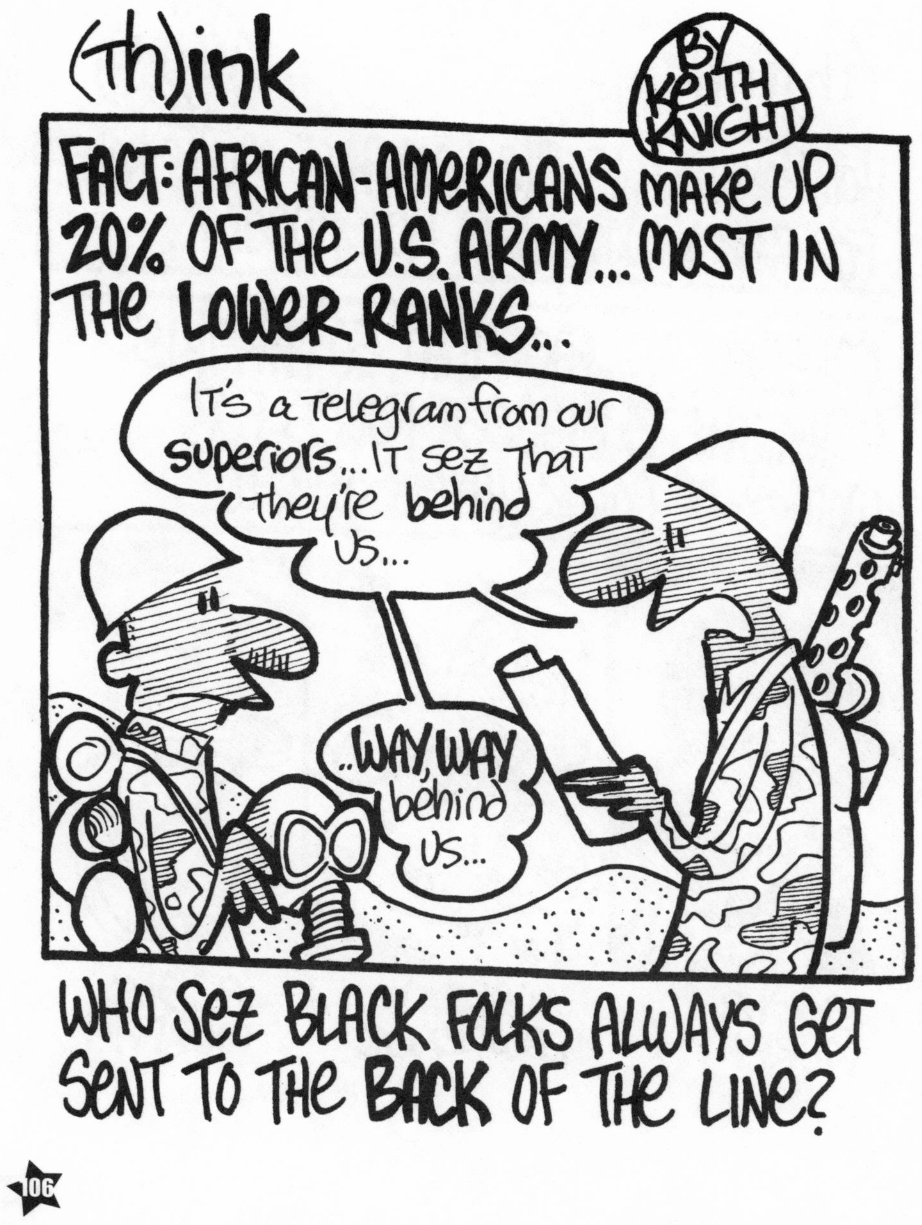
By Keith Knight
FACT: AFRICAN-AMERICANS MAKE UP 20% OF THE U.S. ARMY... MOST IN THE LOWER RANKS...
IT'S A TELEGRAM FROM OUR SUPERIORS... IT SEZ THAT THEY'RE BEHIND US...
...WAY, WAY BEHIND US...

WHO SEZ BLACK FOLKS ALWAYS GET SENT TO THE BACK OF THE LINE?

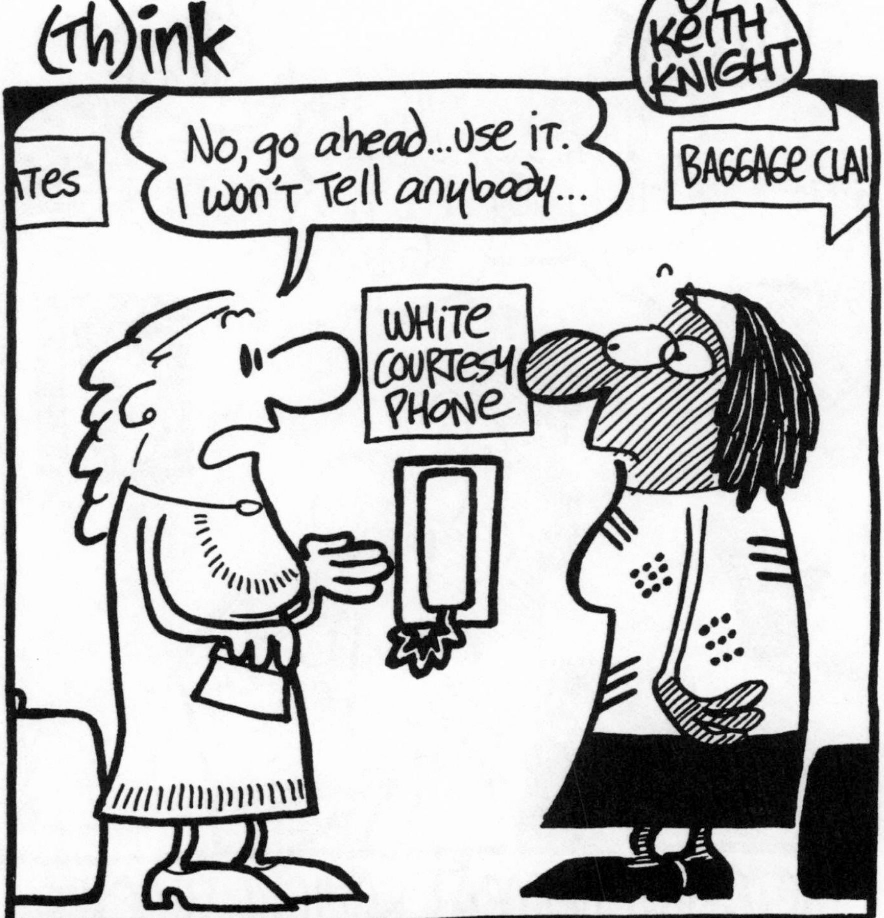
(Th)ink
By Keith Knight
ATES
No, go ahead...use it.
I won't tell anybody...
BAGGAGE CLAI
WHITE COURTESY PHONE

People unclear of the concept

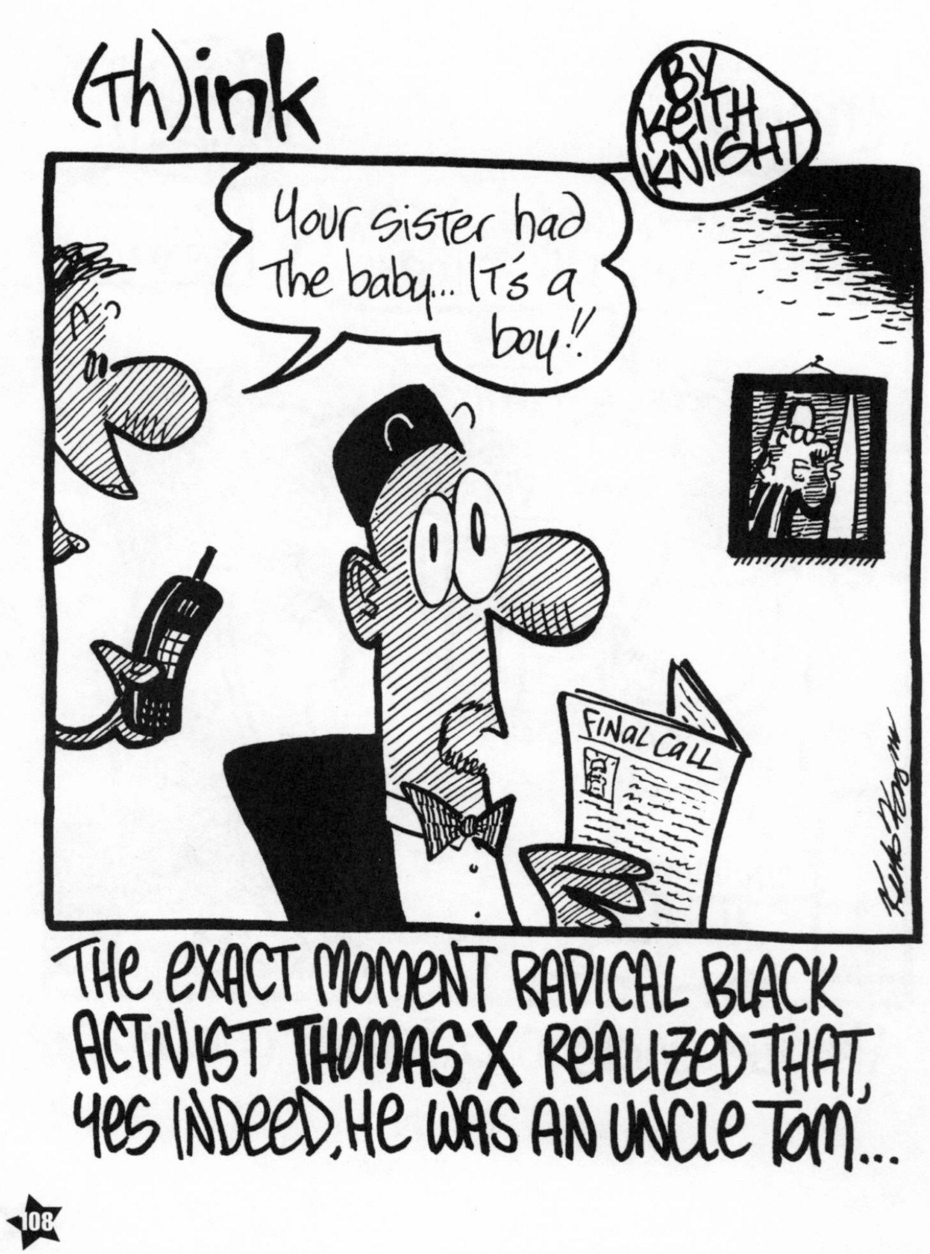
(Th)ink
By Keith Knight
Your sister had The baby... It's a boy!!
FINAL CALL

THE EXACT MOMENT RADICAL BLACK ACTIVIST THOMAS X REALIZED THAT, YES INDEED, HE WAS AN UNCLE TOM...

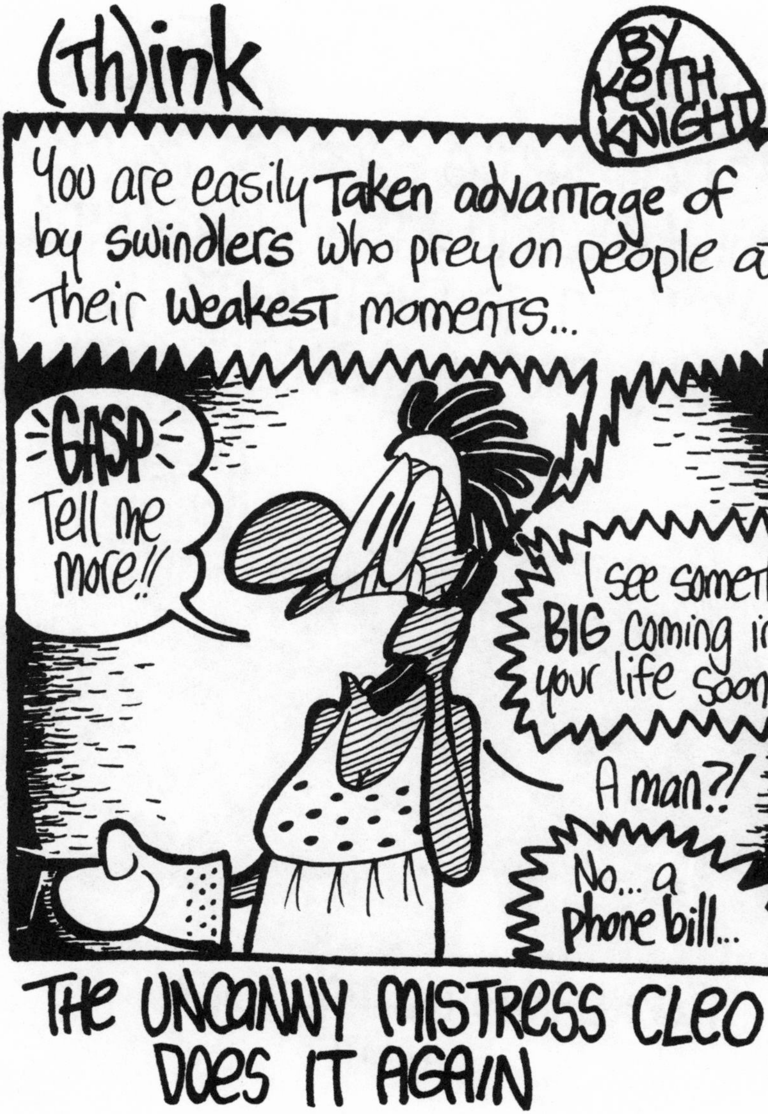
(Th)ink
BY KEITH KNIGHT
You are easily Taken advantage of by swindlers who prey on people at Their weakest moments...
GASP Tell me more!!
I see something BIG coming into your life soon...
A man?!
No... a phone bill...
THE UNCANNY MISTRESS CLEO DOES IT AGAIN

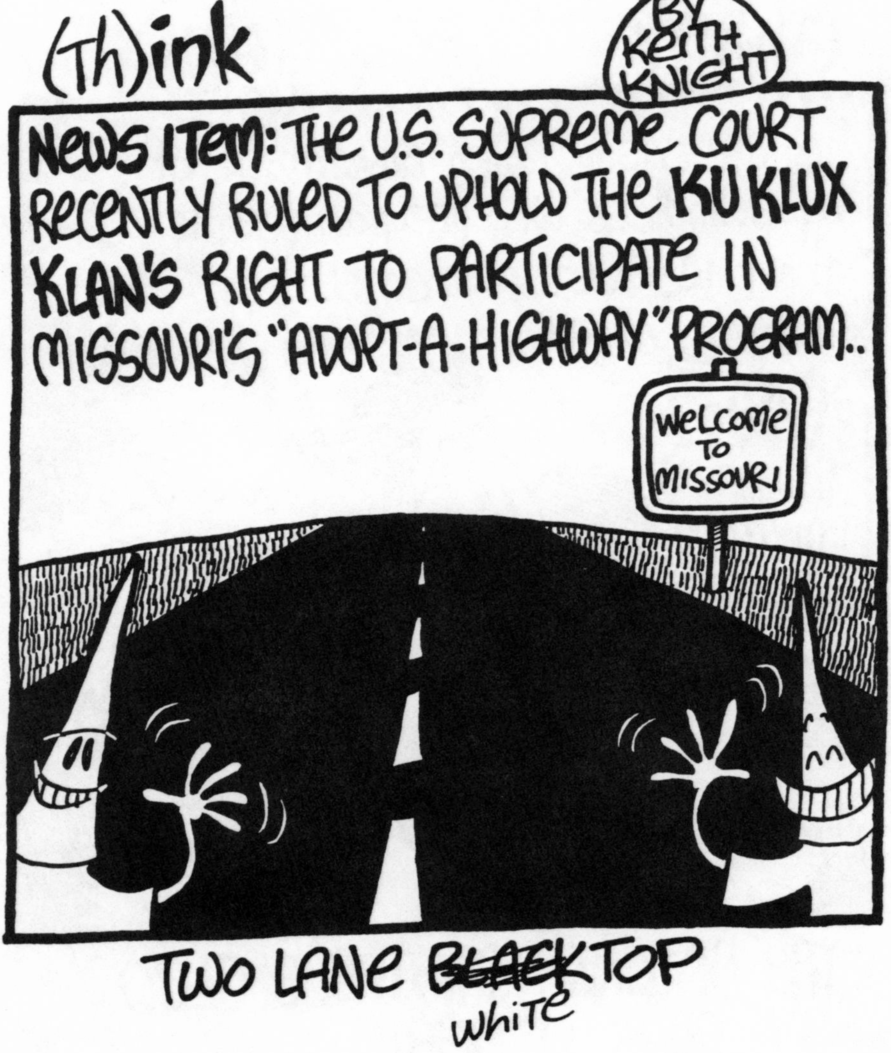
(Th)ink
BY KEITH KNIGHT
NEWS ITEM: THE U.S. SUPREME COURT RECENTLY RULED TO UPHOLD THE KU KLUX KLAN'S RIGHT TO PARTICIPATE IN MISSOURI'S "ADOPT-A-HIGHWAY" PROGRAM..
WELCOME TO MISSOURI
TWO LANE ~~BLACK~~ TOP
white

(th)ink

BY KEITH KNIGHT

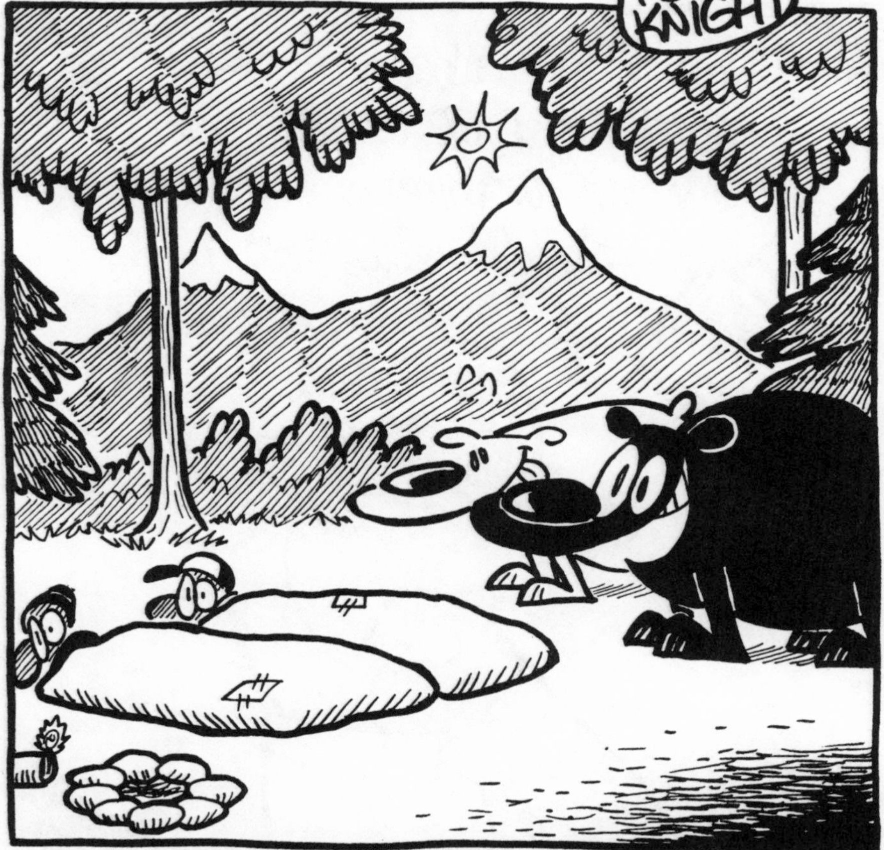

"OOO...LOOK, CEDRIC!!...BURRITOS!!"

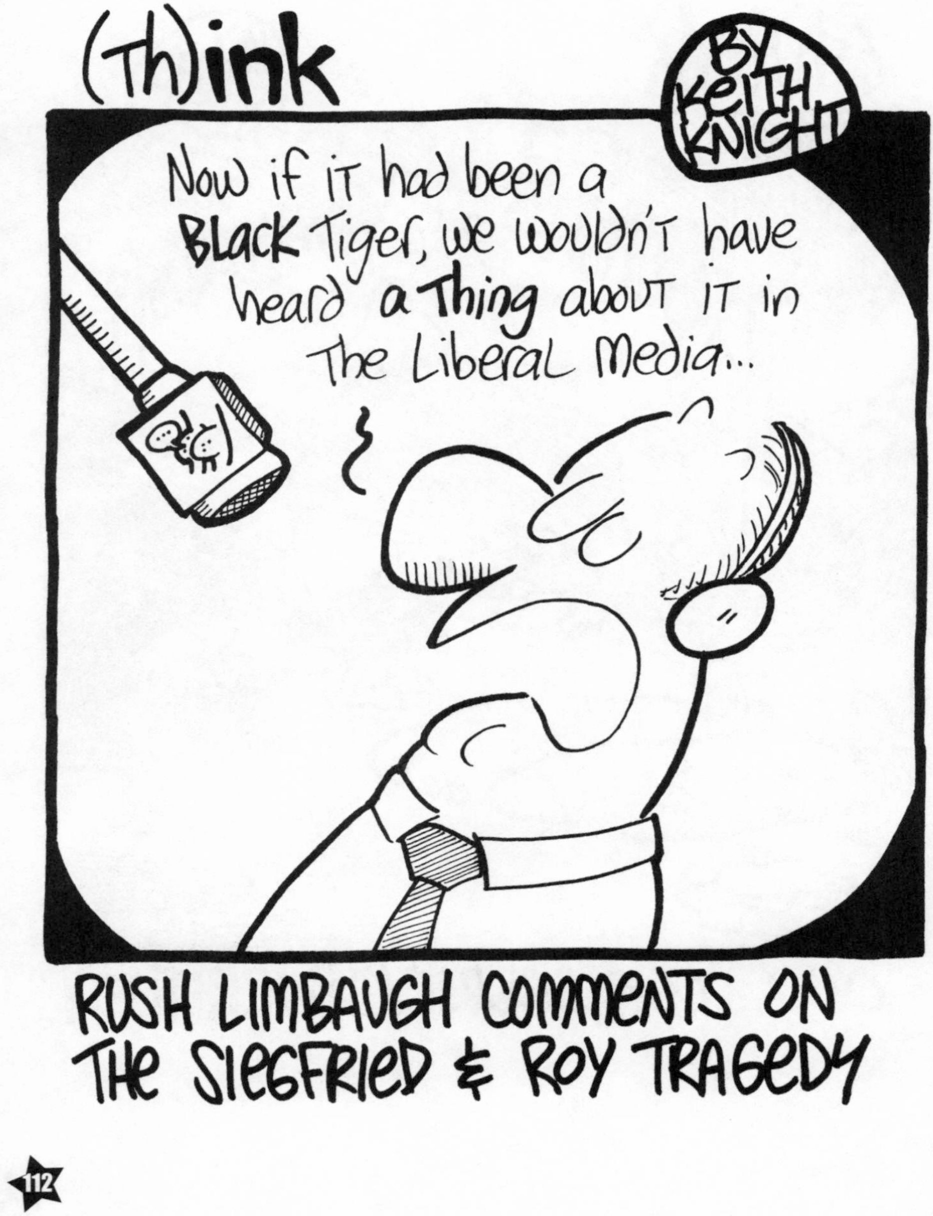
(Th)ink
By Keith Knight
Now if it had been a BLACK Tiger, we wouldn't have heard a Thing about it in The Liberal Media...

RUSH LIMBAUGH COMMENTS ON THE SIEGFRIED & ROY TRAGEDY

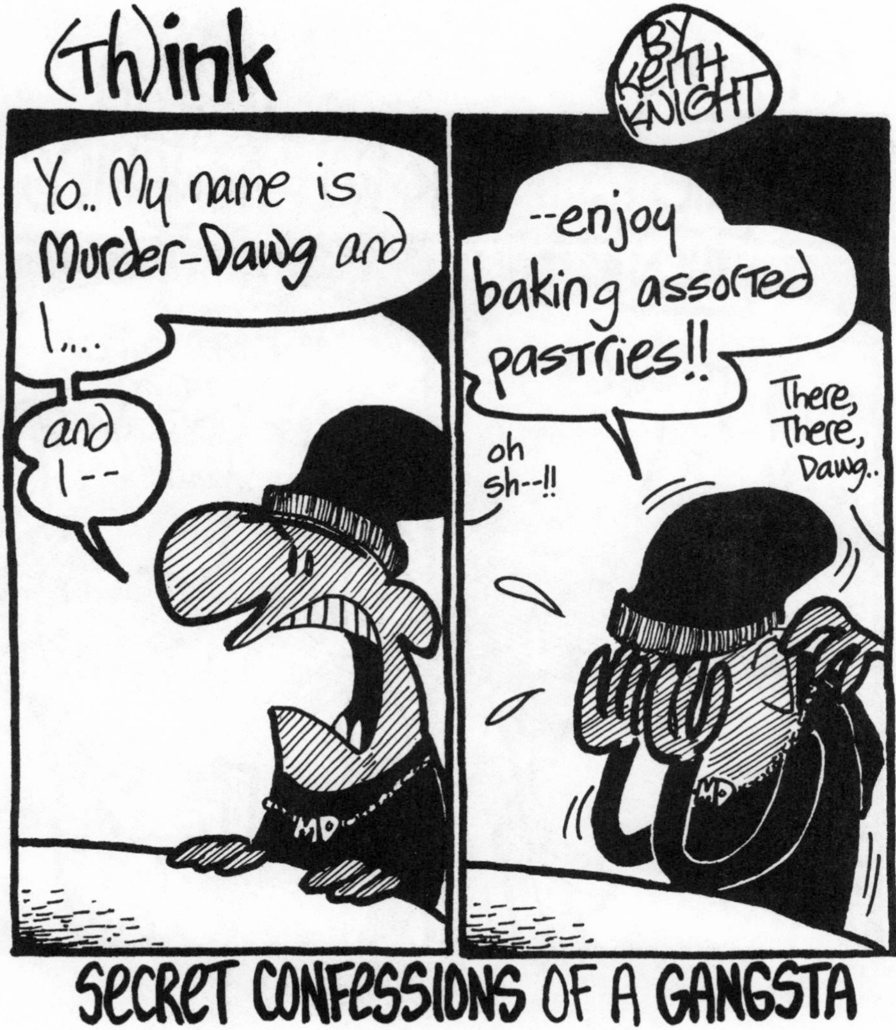
(Th)ink
BY KEITH KNIGHT
Yo.. My name is Murder-Dawg and I....
and I--
--enjoy baking assorted pastries!!
oh sh--!!
There, There, Dawg..
MD
MD
SECRET CONFESSIONS OF A GANGSTA

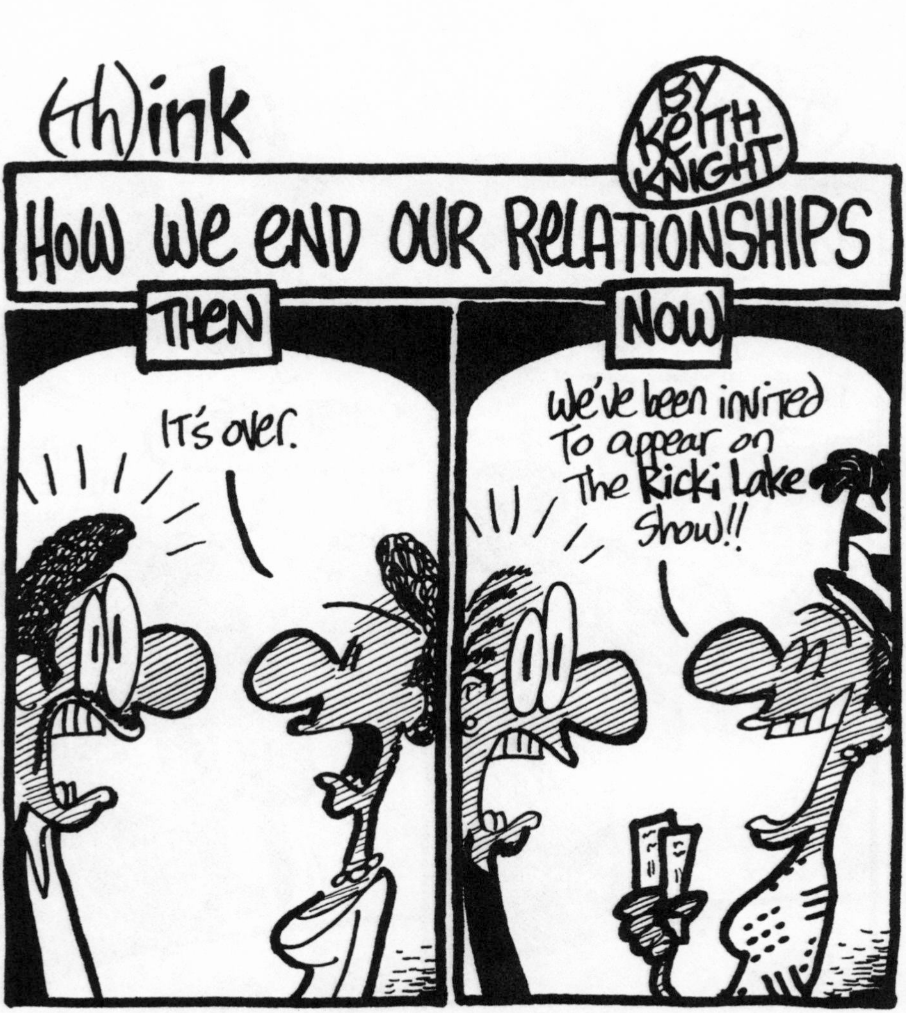
(th)ink
BY KEITH KNIGHT
HOW WE END OUR RELATIONSHIPS
THEN
IT'S over.
NOW
We've been invited To appear on The Ricki Lake Show!!

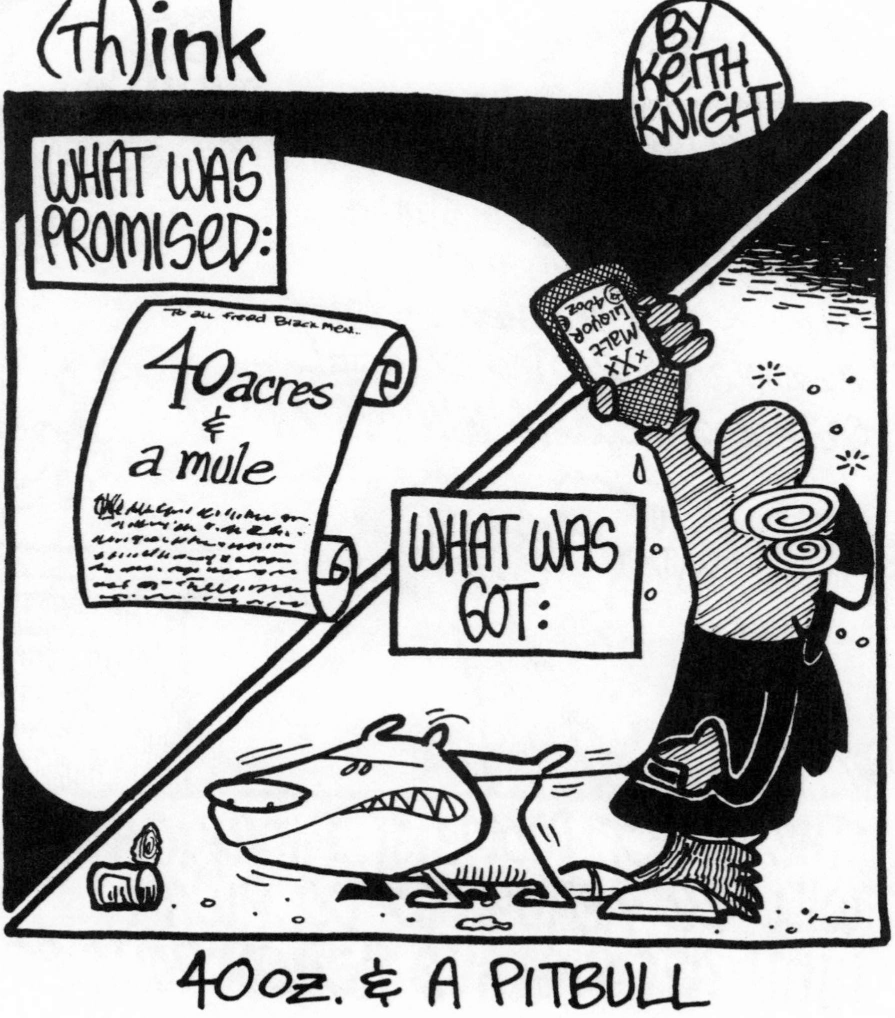
(Th)ink
BY KEITH KNIGHT
WHAT WAS PROMISED:
To all freed Black Men..
40 acres & a mule
WHAT WAS GOT:
XX Malt Liquor 40oz
40oz. & A PITBULL

(th)ink

BY KEITH KNIGHT

What?!! He's getting in and staying **LONGER** even though He did **LESS** than me?!! This is just another **BLATANT** example of **QUOTAS** & **RACIAL** preference!! **EQUAL WHITES NOW!!**

U.S. CRIM COURT
JUDGE GRA

THE EXACT MOMENT AMERICA WILL BE READY TO DO AWAY WITH **AFFIRMATIVE ACTION** POLICIES..

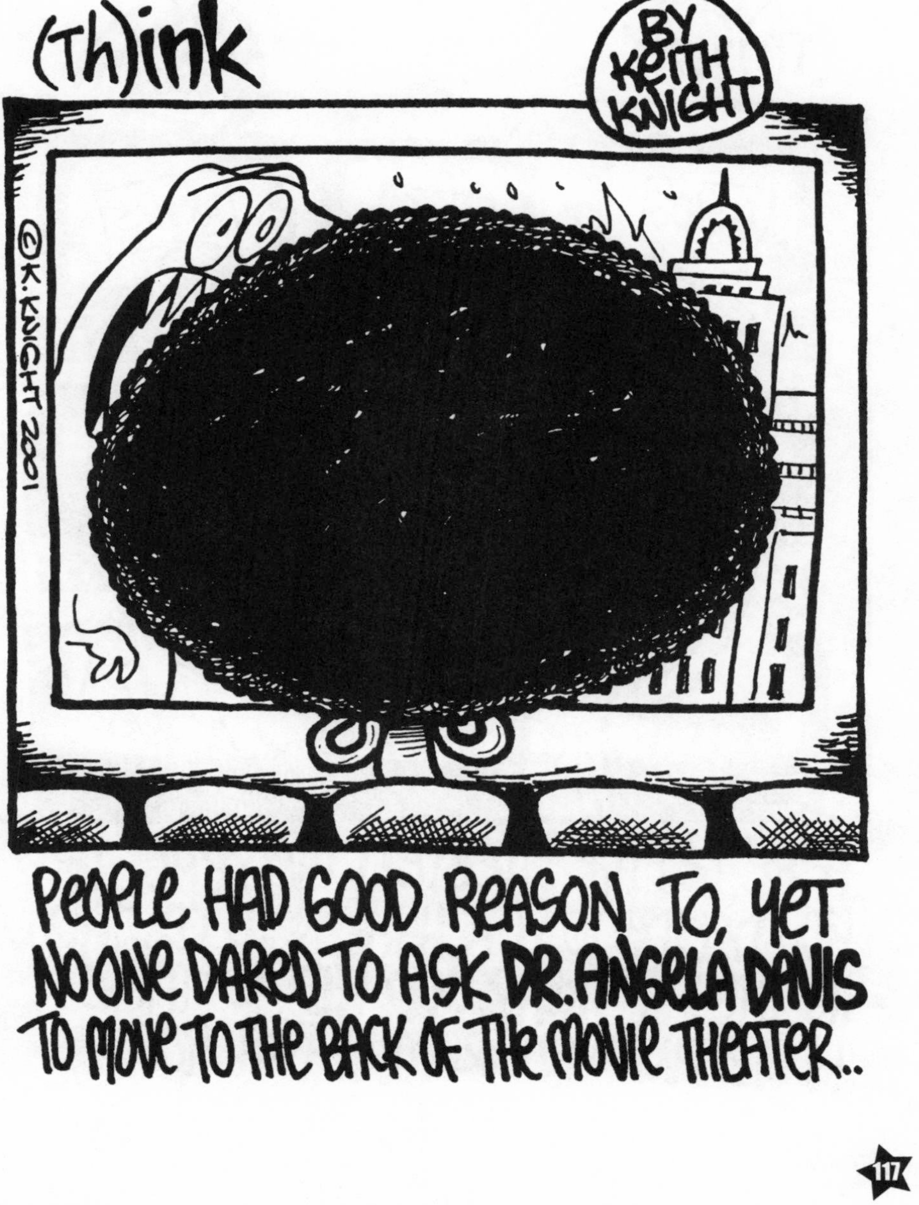
(Th)ink
BY KEITH KNIGHT
© K. KNIGHT 2001

PEOPLE HAD GOOD REASON TO, YET NO ONE DARED TO ASK DR. ANGELA DAVIS TO MOVE TO THE BACK OF THE MOVIE THEATER...

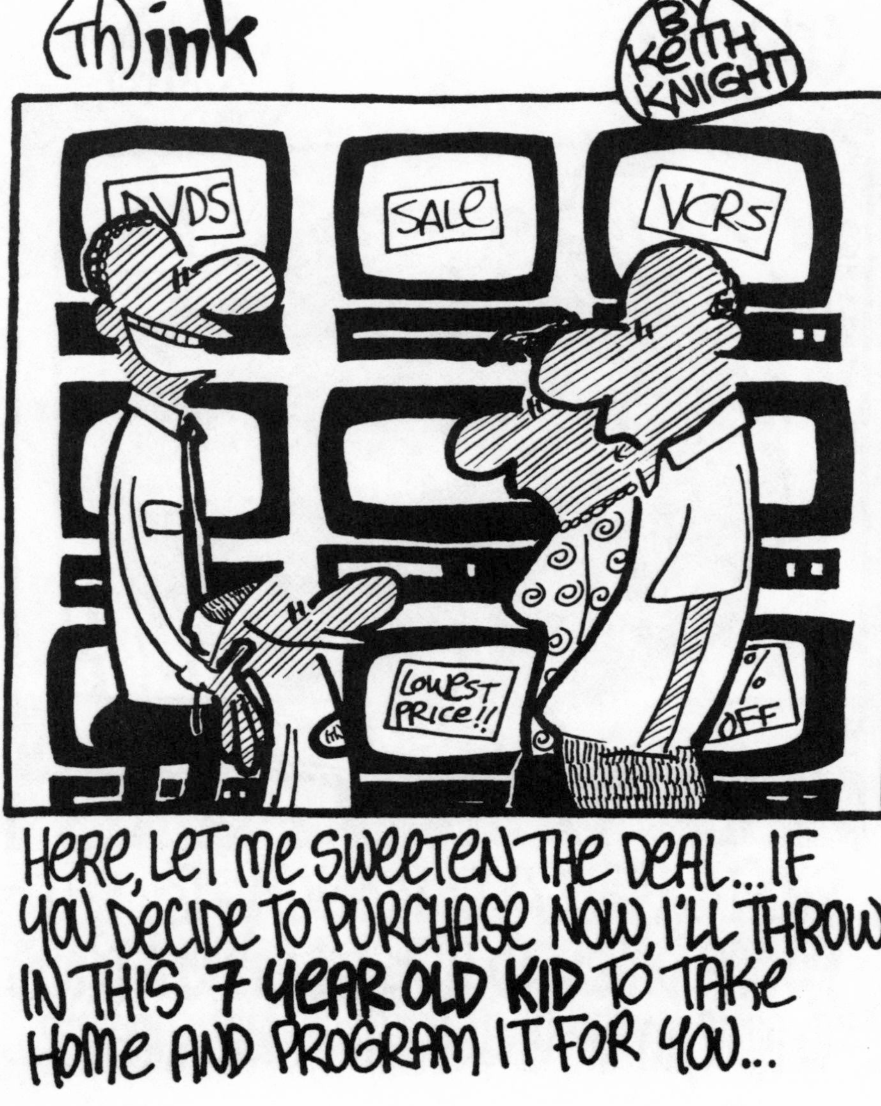
(TH)ink
BY KEITH KNIGHT
DVDS
SALE
VCRS
LOWEST PRICE!!
% OFF
HERE, LET ME SWEETEN THE DEAL... IF YOU DECIDE TO PURCHASE NOW, I'LL THROW IN THIS 7 YEAR OLD KID TO TAKE HOME AND PROGRAM IT FOR YOU...

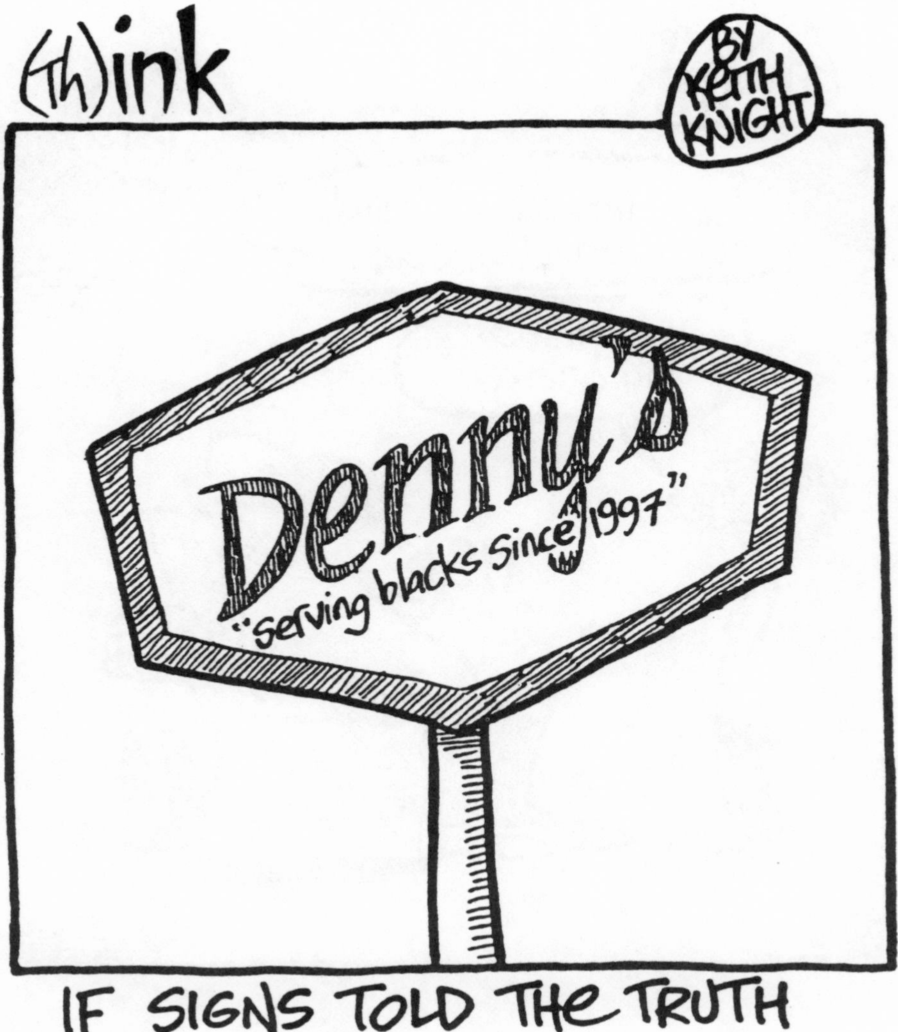
(th)ink
BY KEITH KNIGHT
Denny's
"serving blacks since 1997"
IF SIGNS TOLD THE TRUTH

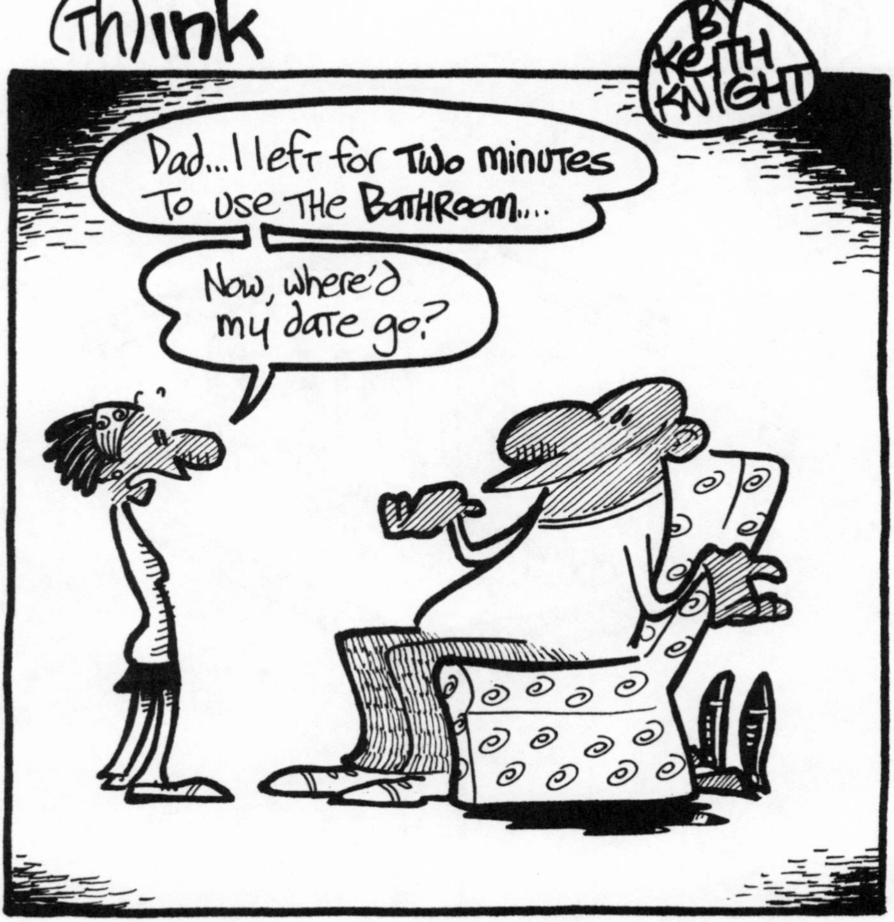
(th)ink
BY KEITH KNIGHT
Dad...I left for TWO MINUTES To use THE BATHROOM....
Now, where'd my date go?

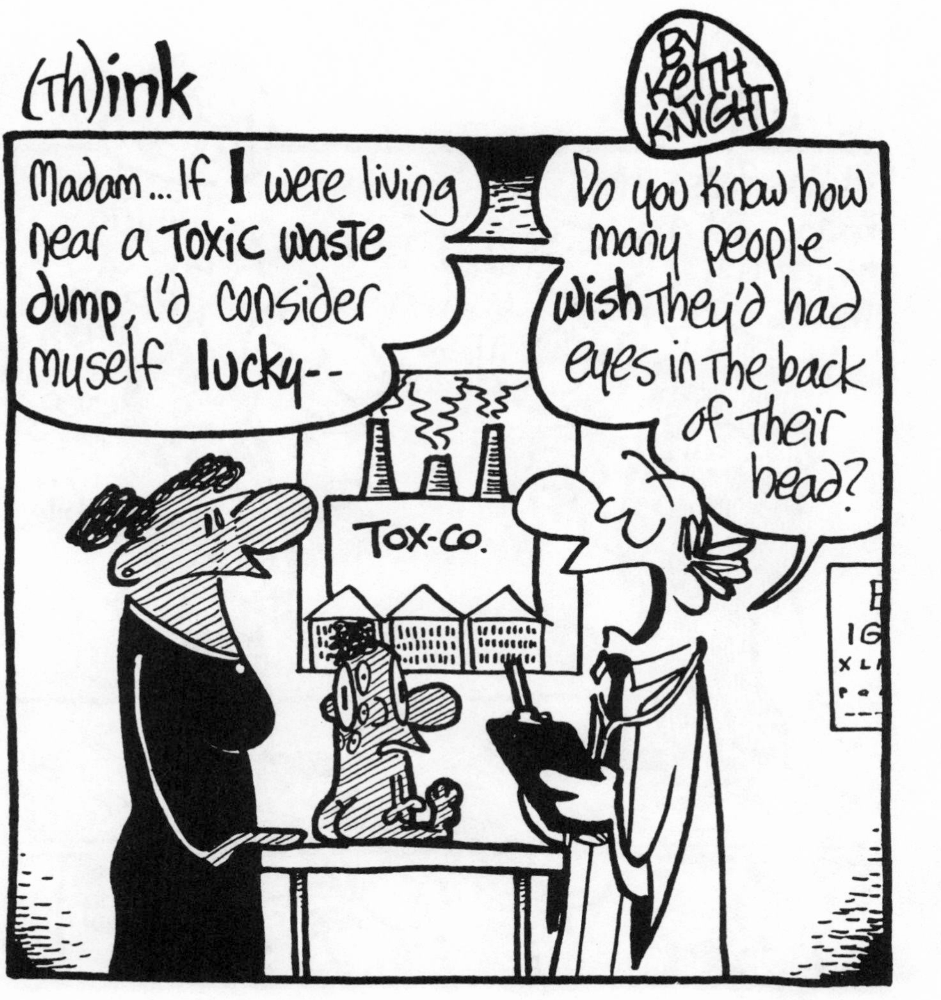
(TH)ink
BY KEITH KNIGHT
Madam... If I were living near a TOXIC WASTE dump, I'd consider myself lucky--
Do you know how many people wish they'd had eyes in the back of their head?
TOX-CO.

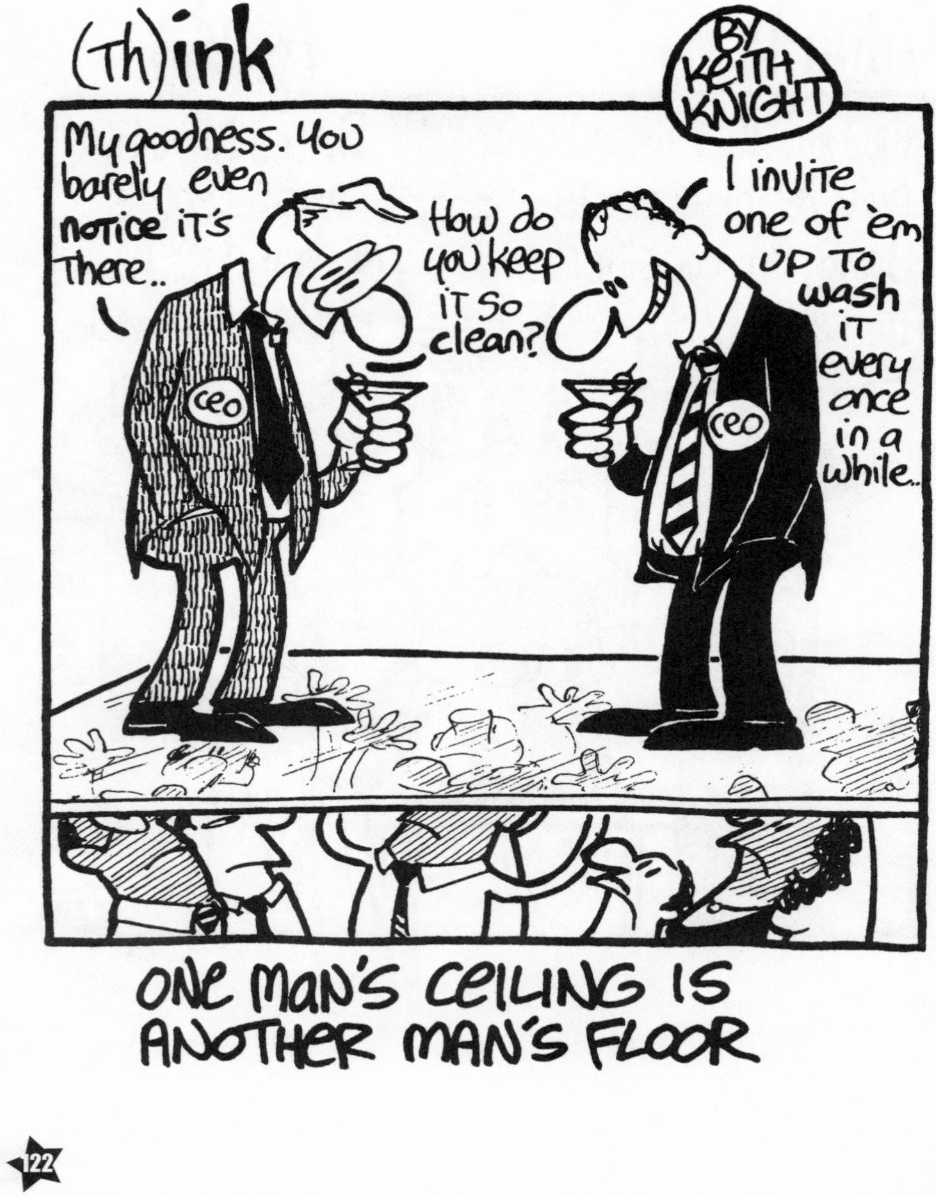
(Th)ink
By Keith Knight
My goodness. You barely even notice it's there...
How do you keep it so clean?
I invite one of 'em up to wash it every once in a while...
CEO
CEO

ONE MAN'S CEILING IS ANOTHER MAN'S FLOOR

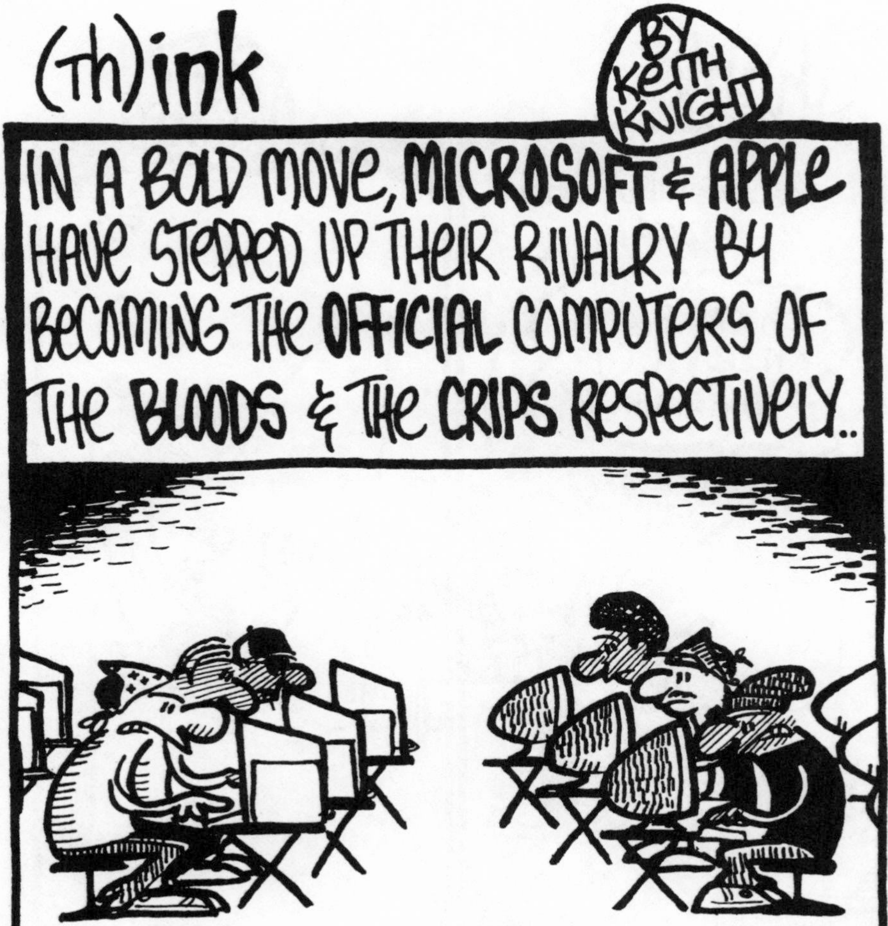
(th)ink
BY KEITH KNIGHT
IN A BOLD MOVE, MICROSOFT & APPLE HAVE STEPPED UP THEIR RIVALRY BY BECOMING THE OFFICIAL COMPUTERS OF THE BLOODS & THE CRIPS RESPECTIVELY..

(th)ink different

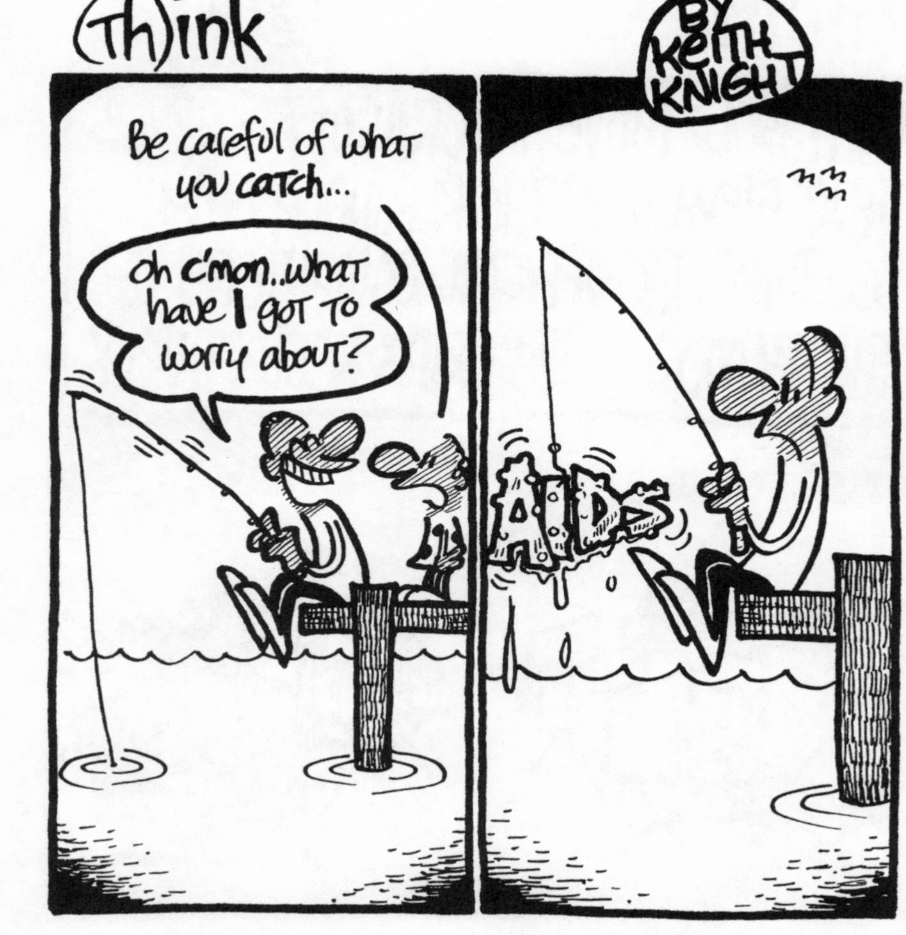
(Th)ink
BY KEITH KNIGHT
Be careful of what you catch...
Oh c'mon..what have I got to worry about?
AIDS

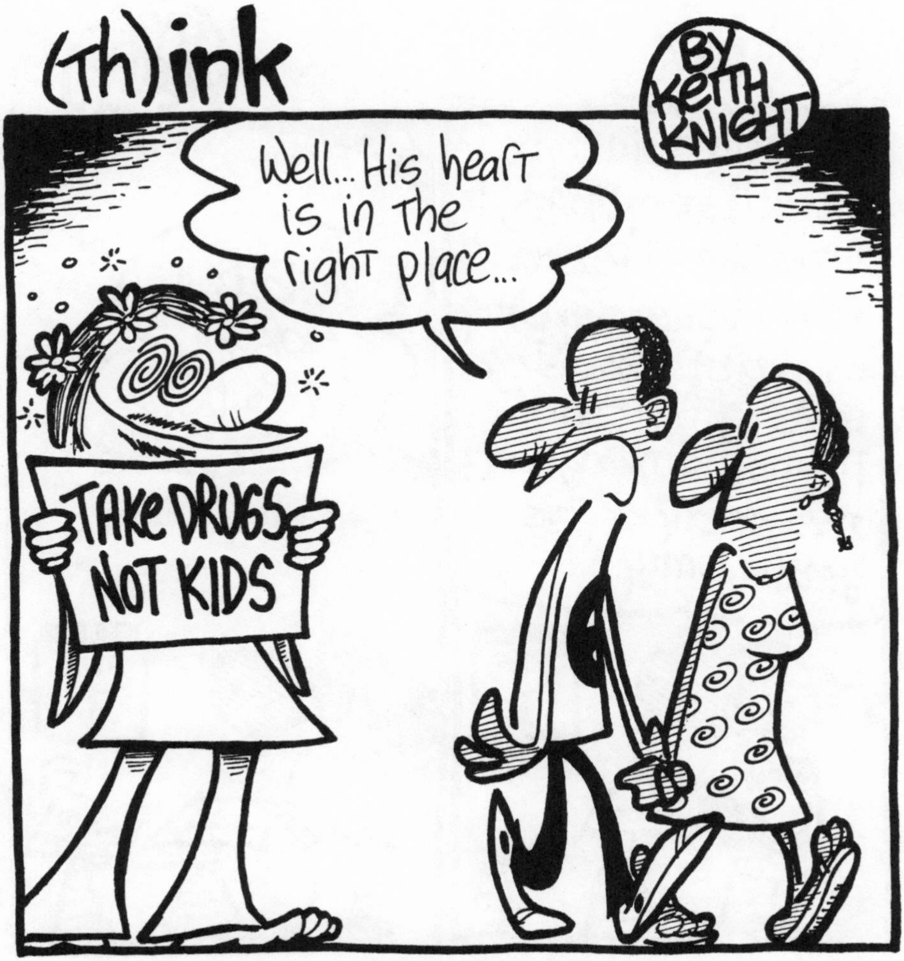
(Th)ink
BY KEITH KNIGHT
Well... His heart is in the right place...
TAKE DRUGS NOT KIDS

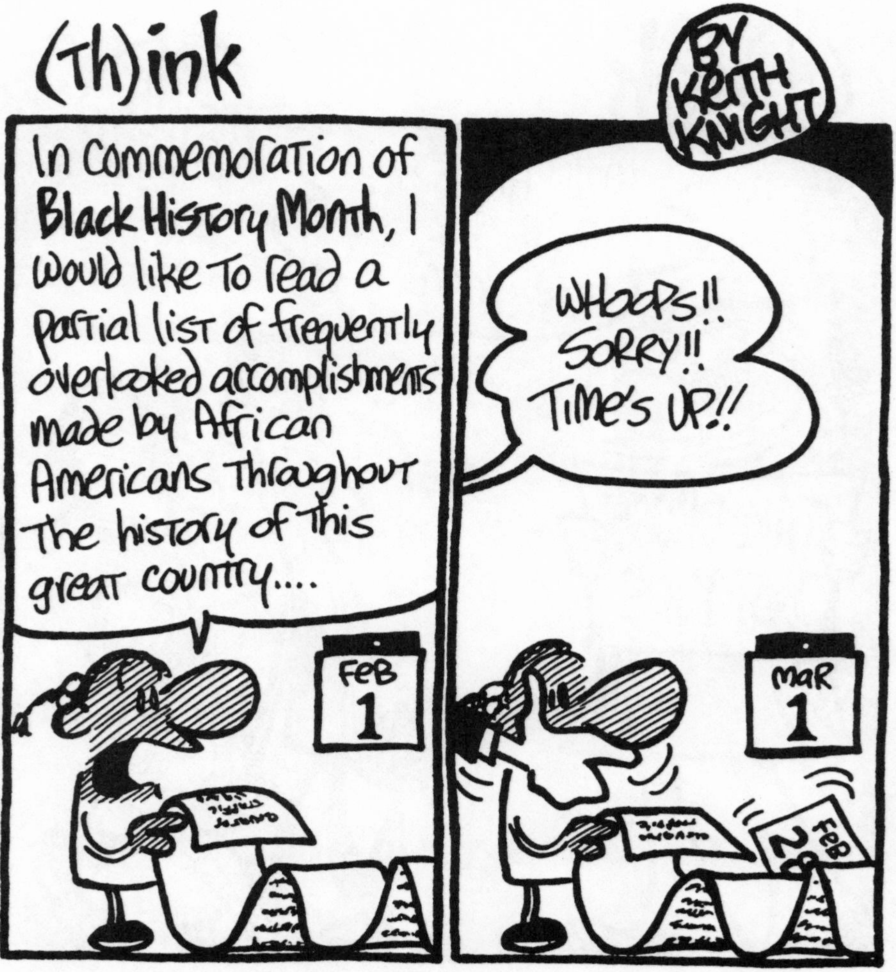
(Th)ink
BY KEITH KNIGHT
In commemoration of Black History Month, I would like to read a partial list of frequently overlooked accomplishments made by African Americans throughout the history of this great country....
FEB 1
WHOOPS!! SORRY!! TIME'S UP!!
MAR 1
FEB 2

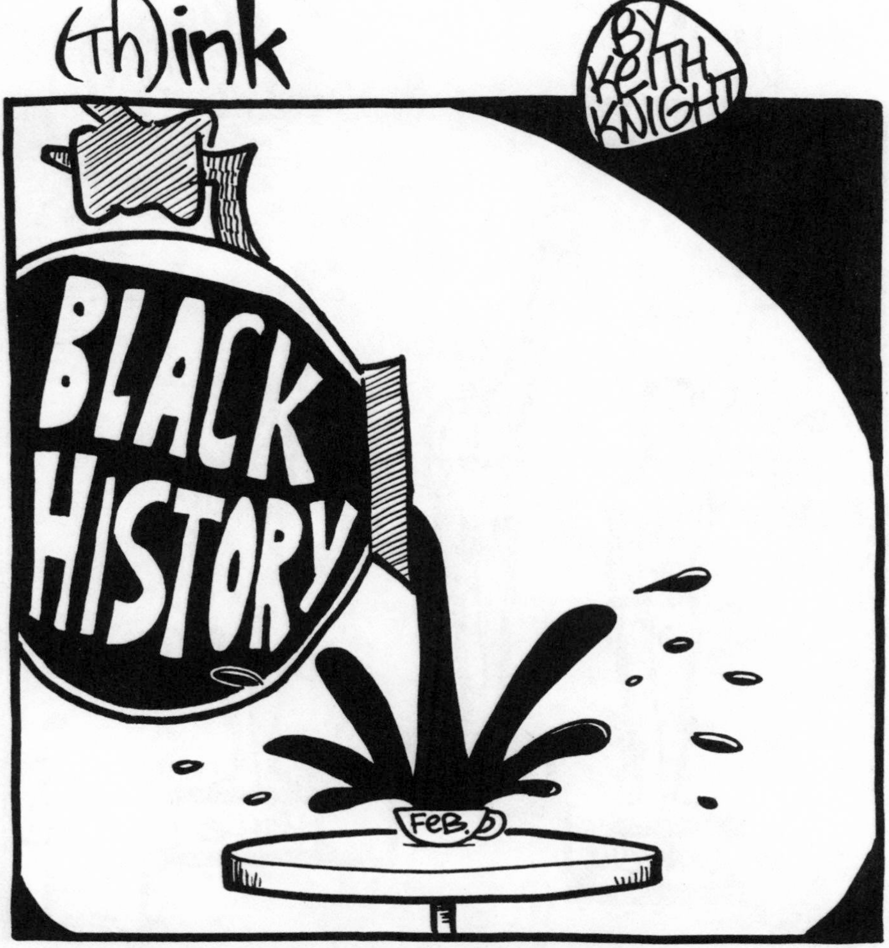
(th)ink
BY KEITH KNIGHT
BLACK HISTORY
FEB.

THY CUP RUNNETH OVER

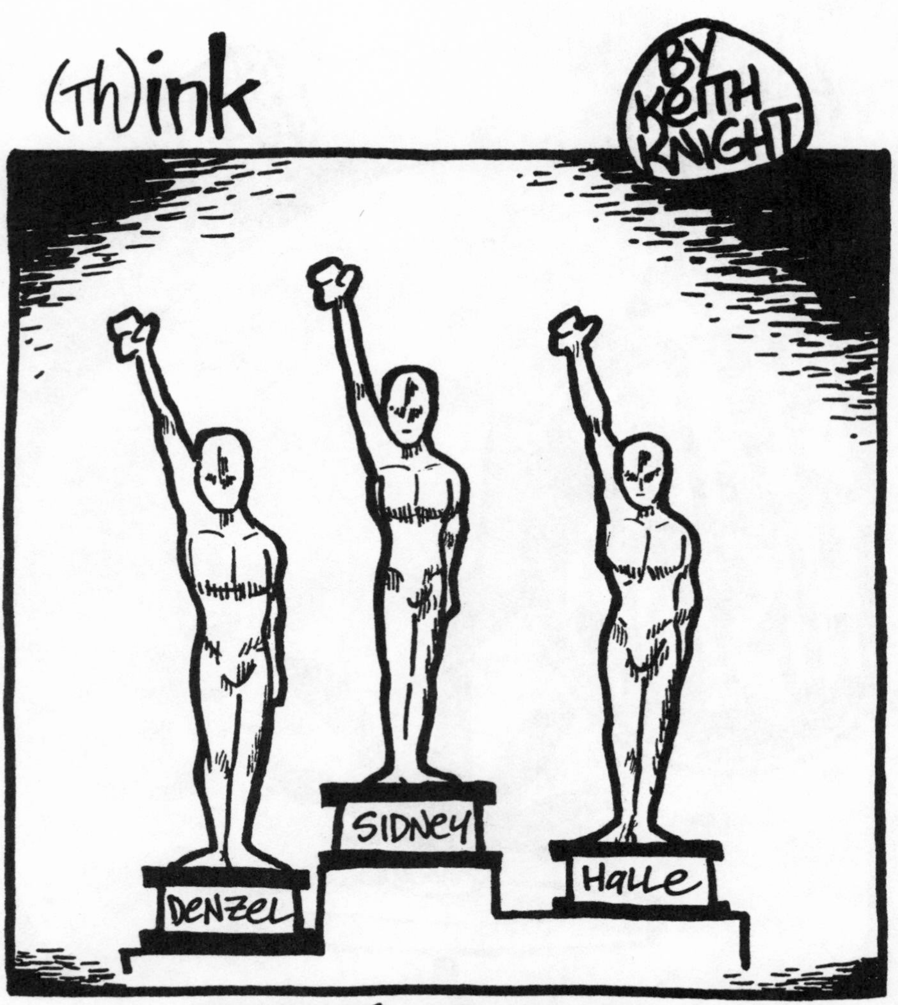
(TH)INK
BY KEITH KNIGHT
DENZEL
SIDNEY
HALLE

FADE TO BLACK

RED, WHITE, BLACK & BLUE
A (th)ink ANTHOLOGY

Dave!!
cheers!!

ote!!

RED, WHITE,

CARTOONS BY KEITH KNIGHT

Manic D Press
San Francisco